ALSO BY CHRIS BULL

PERFECT ENEMIES
The Religious Right, the Gay Movement, and the Politics of the 1990s
(Coauthor, with John Gallagher)

THE ACCIDENTAL ACTIVIST

A PERSONAL AND POLITICAL MEMOIR

CANDACE GINGRICH

WITH CHRIS BULL

A TOUCHSTONE BOOK

PUBLISHED BY SIMON & SCHUSTER

TOUCHSTONE
Rockefeller Center
1230 Avenue of the Americas
New York, NY 10020

First Touchstone Edition 1997

TOUCHSTONE and colophon are registered trademarks of Simon & Schuster Inc.

DESIGNED BY ERICH HOBBING

Manufactured in the United States of America

1   3   5   7   9   10   8   6   4   2

Library of Congress Cataloging-in-Publication Data is available.

ISBN 0-684-82462-0
0-684-83655-6 (Pbk.)

To my family,
for their love and support—
and to activists everywhere,
whose work is too often overlooked

CONTENTS

CONTENTS

AUTHOR'S NOTE

Some of the names of the gay people in this book have been changed to protect them from the discrimination they might face were they identified.

INTRODUCTION

There is no such thing as a problem without a gift for
you in its hand.

—RICHARD BACH,
Illusions

I could not believe my ears. As I nervously approached the podium at the Gay and Lesbian Alliance Against Defamation awards dinner in March 1995, I suddenly realized that the more than sixteen hundred people in attendance were on their feet, giving me a thunderous ovation. Recovering my composure, I mumbled into the microphone, "I don't understand why you are applauding me; I should be applauding you. You are the ones who have earned recognition, working in the trenches for years. I was just born into it."

The crowd laughed, and I relaxed a bit as I delivered my speech, in what was one of my first public appearances. But the fear remained. What had I done to deserve the recognition, even adulation, I had received since coming out with great fanfare as the lesbian little sister of House Speaker Newt Gingrich? I was not the only one asking the questions. Some reporters, not to mention the ubiquitous antigay activists, were asking essentially the same thing. Was I jealous of the fame and power my big brother had achieved? Was I being used as part of a liberal plot to bring him down? I knew that writing this book would only exacerbate the difficult questions about my motives. After all, I can hardly plead neutrality.

It didn't take me long, however, to overcome the reservations—my own at least. I quickly realized that I was striking a chord with people, and not just because of my surname. To my surprise, my family situa-

to resonate with all kinds of people because I could be
...yke little sister. Not only that, I turned out to be pretty
good at telling my own story and advocating gay rights. Growing up a
Gingrich meant that I had some practice making my point.

In the spring of '95, after I began a fifty-one-city tour for the
Human Rights Campaign Fund (the country's largest gay and lesbian
political organization, which shortly thereafter dropped "Fund" from
its name), I realized I had a way with the press and with audiences. At
my first appearance in Seattle, I sweated and stumbled through a short
speech. After that debacle, however, it was pretty much smooth sailing.
I felt at ease in front of audiences, no matter how large or small. I
enjoyed meeting people across the country, all with different stories to
tell. I don't know if I inherited the same genes that make Newt such a
phenomenally successful politician, but I feel I have an important contribution to make to American politics in general and to gay politics in
particular. Some people say that I was pushed into gay activism. But I
wasn't pushed. I jumped—headfirst. At age twenty-eight, I had found
my calling, at long last.

At the GLAAD dinner, Robin Abcarian, a *Los Angeles Times* columnist to whom I presented an award, said that Newt's elevation to
Speaker answered the prayers of "columnists of the humanitarian per-
suasion." "Dear God," she had repeated to herself before the Republican victory, "please give us a way to put a face on the conservative
menace now sweeping the country like a plague." Not only did God
give her Newt, Robin said, "she gave Newt a gay sister." (The lesbian
comic Lynda Montgomery told audiences that "learning Newt had a
lesbian sister was like finding out that Dan Quayle had a brother in
MENSA," the society of certified geniuses.)

I was happy to fill the role of liberal counterbalance to Newt's conservative excesses, but I didn't just want to be a warm body blocking
my relative's so-called revolution, like a lesbian Patti Davis. Nor did I
see myself as that Chinese student heroically standing in the tank's
path at Tiananmen Square. I wanted to use the opportunity to become
a top-notch advocate in my own right. Suddenly, a whole new world
was opening up in front of my eyes. What others would call courage
just felt like being myself and doing what needed to be done. Courage,
it seems, is a word usually applied in retrospect.

This was my chance to make a difference. I had quietly watched for
all of my adult life while Newt had been crusading for conservative

causes. Now it was my turn. My brother's celebrity (or should I say notoriety?) offered me a platform from which to raise a strong, distinctive voice for gay and lesbian rights. There have been many talented gay and lesbian leaders over the years—Barney Frank, the Democratic whip in the House from Massachusetts; Urvashi Vaid, the former director of the National Gay and Lesbian Task Force; Del Martin and Phyllis Lyons, a couple instrumental in the formation of the modern gay rights movement; and my boss at the Human Rights Campaign, Elizabeth Birch, to name just a few. But these trailblazers have never had a soapbox anywhere near as prominent as Newt's. Maybe, with some hard work and a little good luck, I could contribute to correcting that disparity.

Of course, I was also aware of a deeper criticism. Some said that I was feeding directly into an obsession with celebrity politics at the expense of substantive debates. From *Ms.* magazine to the *Wall Street Journal*, reporters were having a field day pitting me against my famous brother and watching the two of us squirm. Even though I tried my best to steer journalists to a more pertinent discussion of antigay discrimination in America and the political agenda of the Human Rights Campaign, many, under pressure from editors for juicier copy, could not resist circling back to the family drama. While that angle can be productive—gay politics is more about family than about sex—it risks glossing over some pretty profound questions about American society and how it treats its sexual minorities.

I can't pretend that all my motives in gay activism were altruistic. At the GLAAD dinner, for instance, I had the privilege of meeting pop singer Melissa Etheridge and her girlfriend, Julie Cypher. I had been a fan since 1988, when a friend in college turned me on to her music. She came up to me and said, "I thought you were taller than you are," which was funny, because at just over five foot one, she's only about a quarter of an inch taller than I am. (I've been described in the press as everything from "elfin" to "ninety pounds sopping wet." I like to think of myself as petite.) I also met Roseanne, who, in a quip characteristic of her gift at reversals, said, "Don't worry, honey, I've got a weird brother, too."

In November 1995, I traveled to Los Angeles at the invitation of a producer to appear on an episode of the hit sitcom *Friends.* I got paid union scale to play a minister who performs a commitment ceremony for the lesbian couple on the show. (Despite boycotts from two TV stations, the show had the highest ratings that week, with an estimated 37 million Americans tuning in.) Meeting politically progressive celebrities, traveling, and having a say are all opportunities I would probably not have had if I had stayed in my hometown of Harrisburg working for United Parcel Service for the rest of my life—and if Newt hadn't assumed the Speakership.

At the GLAAD dinner, Los Angeles writer Andy Friedman prepared a brief speech for me. One of his jokes went, "Newt asked me to apologize for not being here. But he did give me his AmEx card. Dinner's on Newt!" In the speech Andy dubbed me the "accidental activist," which has since found its way onto the cover of this book. I'm fond of the term because it indicates that anyone, sometimes involuntarily, can become a protagonist in social change. Being gay gives many a special motivation to become active, but all people have something in their lives that might prompt more vigorous participation. I don't want to give the impression that political engagement is simply a big accident. As I've become more involved over the last two years, the term reminded me that the most successful social movements are anything but accidental.

In general Americans tend to be reactionary. Most people, gay or straight, don't become activists until something alarming happens to them. But Americans concerned about fairness can't afford to sit around and wait for good things to happen or for some benign outside force—as in *Star Wars*, one of Newt's favorite science fiction movies— to reach down and organize us. No one is going to hand us our rights, particularly in Newt's Congress. We can even learn from the opposition: despite their belief in divine justice, the religious right's leaders didn't just sit around and wait for power to be bestowed upon them. They worked hard, employed savvy organizing strategies (and a heavy dose of verbal gay-bashing), and grabbed that power.

And I'm not just talking about gay issues. If I could achieve one thing with this book, it would be to encourage Americans to become activists on whatever cause is dear to them, whether it be a woman's right to control her reproductive choices, rescuing our streets from the scourges of guns and drugs, or reversing the decline of our cultural institutions due to a lack of funding for the arts. Every program the Republicans have targeted for cuts offers a chance for community-minded Americans to band together. If we're smart about it, the Contract with America may turn out to be one of the best organizing tools since the Great Depression. But no one is going to create change for us. I like to think of liberalism as a sleeping giant; it just needs to be roused.

What follows is the story of how and why I became an activist and some tips for how you can do the same. In the process, I hope to shed some light on the gay movement and the role of antigay activism in Newt's self-proclaimed Republican "revolution." Like filmmaker Michael Moore in *Roger & Me,* the funny chronicle of Moore's search for General Motors chairman Roger Smith, I've set out to discover the "real" Newt, the Newt I knew growing up as a kid. The Newt who believed in justice and equality for all and accepted me for who I am without question.

Most importantly, it's the story of *family*—the Gingrich family and its peculiar dynamics that produced two often-clashing activists, how we became who we are, and what might bring us together again. Whether the subject is my staunchly Republican parents, sister and Christian Coalition member Susan, pro-choice niece Kathy, or gay cousin Darell, the Gingrich family has usually managed to place love and respect for one another's humanity over ideology. Now it's time for Newt to join the fold. Mom, doing her best Rodney King "can't we all just get along" imitation, likes to tell me, "If we could just get you and Newt to sit down in a room together, we could work it all out." In the pressure cooker of American politics, I hope Mom's old-fashioned wisdom is not simply naïveté.

In my often awkward attempt to transform myself from an accidental activist to an effective political agent, I'm certainly going to do my best to make Mom's wish come true. I'm sure Newt will, too. He's doing what he felt called to do. With regard to me, I think Andy Friedman put it best in a letter to me after the GLAAD dinner: "Despite what I wrote, it's no accident. You're obviously meant to be doing what you're doing." On that count, I hope Newt agrees.

PART ONE

GROWING UP
GINGRICH

CHAPTER ONE

THE METAMORPHOSIS

What a long, strange trip it's been.
—GRATEFUL DEAD,
"Truckin'"

Now I know how Gregor Samsa felt. As I awoke on a chilly fall day, November 9, 1994, I knew that it was not I, but my own government, that had become a monstrous vermin akin to the one from Kafka's imagination. I could literally feel it nipping at my heels, even from my home in small-town Harrisburg, Pennsylvania, over a hundred miles away from the U.S. capital. For the first time in my twenty-eight years, mean-spirited, right-wing Republicans controlled Congress, making the old, moderate "Rockefeller" Republicans, whom my brother so often assailed, look like ancient relics. Unlike most people who pay only passing attention to the pendulum swings of American politics, I knew the election had changed my life forever.

That's because the Republican takeover had propelled my half brother, Newt, to the pinnacle of American politics, and because I'm a lesbian, a member of a community against which Brother Newt, as I knew him growing up, had campaigned vigorously, even viciously. As the newly elected Speaker of the House, Newt's power now rivaled even that of President Clinton, who was reaching new lows in public opinion polls and who, pathetically, was soon insisting on his own relevance. Political insiders were already whispering about a Gingrich presidential bid in 1996. However enticing the prospects of family visits to the White House, this suggestion sent chills up my spine.

Most people would have been proud that a sibling had achieved a lifetime goal and become the most talked-about person in the nation.

And I was proud. I loved and admired Newt for his relentless hard work, courage, and leadership—values our parents instilled in us both. While I disagreed with many of its principles, Newt's Contract with America was a stroke of pure political genius, at least until the election. Although Newt's powerful multimillion-dollar political arm, GOPAC, would eventually fall under investigation by the House Ethics Committee, it undoubtedly helped get dozens of Republicans elected. He'd succeeded where his Democratic counterparts had largely failed: creating a compelling vision for America's future and setting up the machinery to make it happen. Though a liberal Democrat and a die-hard Clinton supporter, I wasn't necessarily opposed to every aspect of Newt's platform. I could see that the federal government had become bloated and unresponsive, that welfare needed revamping, and that the country's values needed strengthening. It was in the solutions to the problems that we parted company.

In the respect of achieving his aims for power through dogged orchestration, I realized he might even become his generation's Richard Daley, Chicago's autocratic Democratic mayor of three decades ago whose political machine ruled the city for a quarter century. On a national level, he might end up the Republican Sam Rayburn, the legendary Democratic Speaker responsible for passage of the New Deal, reigning over the House twice as long as his predecessors.

Still, for all my admiration, I was—and remain—deeply troubled. As a lesbian, I feared that Newt was leading a conservative dominance of American politics that would prove extremely dangerous for my gay and lesbian brothers and sisters and very difficult to dethrone. Though I'd never been much of an activist myself, I felt indebted to the thousands of pioneering gay and lesbian activists who had come before me, many of whom risked everything so that a younger generation could live a little less besieged by violence and discrimination. In just a few years, I fretted, the Republicans threatened to roll back what it took these freedom fighters well over three decades to achieve.

While Newt had never gone so far, some of his more extreme supporters on the religious right had publicly called homosexuals perverts, child molesters, and even serial killers. The Reverend Lou Sheldon, who maintains close ties to Newt as head of the Traditional Values Coalition, has called gays and lesbians "the most pernicious evil today." Frank Cremeans, the Ohio Republican who received GOPAC support for his '94 campaign for the House, claimed that homosexuality was responsible for the decline of the ancient Roman and Greek empires, a claim so ludicrous it would be funny if he were not serious. (Believe it or not, he's now sitting in Congress.)

In an atmosphere such as this, it's no surprise that gays and lesbians have become among the most frequent victims of hate-inspired violence—or that Newt's Congress has taken no action to combat it. Never had I heard Newt publicly condemn outlandish statements like Cremeans's or the gay-bashing epidemic to which remarks like this lend implicit encouragement. On several occasions Newt has come awfully close to condoning them. Shortly before his party's 1994 election triumphs, he suggested in an interview published in the *Washington Blade,* a gay newspaper, that gays and lesbians were at least partly responsible for the decline of the nuclear family, an utterly groundless charge that gives comfort to the ranks of disturbed souls who might enforce the words of politicians and religious leaders with brute force.

No single issue highlights the plight of gay Americans quite as clearly as violence. As gays have become more visible, so has the backlash. According to the New York City Gay and Lesbian Anti-Violence Project, violent attacks on gays increased more than 100 percent from 1992 to 1994. But when it comes to antigay crimes, get-tough-on-crime conservatives find it in their hearts to pardon the perpetrators. Time and again, Newt and some of his conservative allies have fought tooth and nail to exclude homosexuals from legislation increasing penalties for assaults based on the real or perceived sexual orientation of the victims. It leaves the impression that antigay crimes are somehow less serious than, for instance, those based on race or religion. It makes it easy for people to think, "Well, maybe they deserved it," the ultimate exercise in blaming the victim.

Texas is a hot spot for antigay rhetoric—and murder. In 1994 alone, at least eight gay men were butchered by gay-bashers. In January 1996, Fred Mangione was stabbed thirty-five times by two young punks who admitted setting out that evening in Katy, Texas, to "hurt a fag." Mangione's lover of sixteen years, Ken Stern, held him in his arms as he bled to death. If Newt's sidekick Dick Armey, the House majority leader, who hails from Texas, really wanted to clean up the state's moral climate, he would start with these cold-blooded thugs by making it abundantly clear that attacking gay people is legally and morally unacceptable. (Instead, his contribution to the gay rights debate has been to deride his gay House colleague as "Barney Fag.")

Contrary to the stereotype promulgated by the right wing of lonely gay men cruising the streets in search of sex, Mangione and Stern were tax paying, contributing members of their local community who hung out mostly with heterosexual friends. The couple also displayed "family values" in a real, rather than rhetorical, fashion. They lived with and cared for their elderly, widowed moms. It makes me wonder how Newt's Republican colleagues would respond if I were beaten up by gay-bashers. At least I don't have to worry about how Newt would react. I know he and the rest of the family would be by my side in a flash.

Growing up in small-town Dauphin, Pennsylvania, I lived nestled in the shadows of the Appalachian Mountains. As a child, the slopes on the horizon represented safety and strength. As a teenager, I ran and hiked with my friends on a myriad of mountain trails. That peaceful vision was shattered forever in 1989. Claudia Brenner and Rebecca Wight were shot while camping on the northeastern side of the mountains. Brandishing a shotgun along the trail, a young loner named Stephen Ray Carr stalked the women for hours. Brenner, seriously wounded, survived the attack to crawl miles along the trail looking for help. When she returned, Wight was dead. Invoking what has become known as the homosexual-panic defense, Carr testified in court that he opened fire on the women because they "put on a show" for Carr and "teased him." (Carr was sentenced to life in prison.)

For Republicans, even the smallest steps forward in criminalizing antigay violence have seemed wrenching—and fraught with infighting. Six months before the Kafkaesque 1992 National Republican Convention in Houston, when the two Pats—Buchanan and Robertson—declared cultural war on their fellow citizens, Robert Mosbacher, chairman of Bush's reelection campaign, agreed to meet with several gay leaders, including Urvashi Vaid of the National Gay and Lesbian Task Force. The meeting came two years after a controversial invitation from administration officials to gay activists to attend the signing of the 1989 Hate Crimes Statistics Act, a bill that improved federal reporting mechanisms for hate crimes. Arranged with White House approval, the meeting was largely a courtesy by Mosbacher to his daughter Dee, who is a lesbian. A decent sort, Mosbacher expressed sympathy for victims of antigay violence but made no promises to address the problem.

How did Newt react to this benign, mostly symbolic, move by a Republican official to show concern for a serious problem? He joined with eight conservative members of Congress, including the rabidly antigay southern-California Republican William Dannemeyer, in urging the president to cut any contact with gay activists and "re-establish yourself as a protector of traditional family values." Since when does merely discussing with gay activists how we might decrease the numbers of antigay attacks somehow conflict with "traditional family values"? Even in the midst of the country's culture wars, it seems to me that one value on which Americans should be able to unite is that antigay violence is a national disgrace. Does Newt really mean to suggest that "traditional values" include the widespread acceptance of violence against gays and lesbians?

On the issue of gay rights, there seemed to be two Newts. When our mother, Kathleen, told him nearly a decade ago that I was a lesbian, he displayed great sensitivity, assuring both of us that it did not change the way he felt about me. I used to take my then girlfriend, Ann, to family gatherings on the holidays, and Newt always treated her and our relationship with the utmost respect. Around me at least, Newt seems to have a live-and-let-live attitude about sexuality and relationships. Yet in currying the favor of his right-wing allies, he has resorted to the most gratuitous antigay insults.

Take the 103rd Congress. Out of five votes on issues involving gays, AIDS, or abortion, Newt sided with gays only on the Ryan White Act, the AIDS bill that provides federal funding for areas particularly hard hit by the epidemic. He voted to reject President Clinton's compromise on the gays-in-the-military issue; to prohibit the use of federal funds for public schools that use pro-gay curricula; to discharge service members who test HIV-positive; and to overturn a District of Columbia bill that allows unmarried couples to register as domestic partners. On abortion rights, another issue near and dear to my heart, he voted to prohibit federal funds for abortion except in the case of rape, incest, or when the life of the mother is in danger. In fact, looking over Newt's voting record since the Human Rights Campaign began keeping track in 1988, I failed to locate a single pro-gay vote he's cast. He didn't even vote for gays by mistake. I just can't begin to fathom how my own brother could not find it in his heart to support gays' positions even once.

Despite his alliance with the Christian right, Newt could hardly claim to have perfect "family values," that elusive appellation religious conservatives like the Reverend Lou Sheldon use to condemn anyone who dares to disagree with them or who happens to live within a different family structure. Hearing Republicans invoke the term, I think it's become an excuse to attack candidates personally rather than to confront the ugly realities of legislating one narrow version of morality. (To be fair, some of Newt's critics have been guilty of the same transgressions, albeit with a different rallying cry.)

To hear Newt carry on sometimes, you'd think he was the paragon of virtue and his opponents, especially liberal supporters of gays and lesbians, the epitome of vice. His political supporters are, as he put it once, "normal Americans," while everyone else is somehow not. Politics and morality, however, are rarely so black-and-white. Raised in a single-parent household for the first few years of his life, Newt went through a messy divorce in which he famously asked his wife, Jackie, to discuss signing divorce papers while she was in the hospital recuperating from cancer surgery. As he himself has admitted, Newt's marriage to his second wife, Marianne, has been a struggle as well. To be honest, I would not want my own personal life, which has had its share of ups and downs, held to an impossibly high standard. "To err is human," as the poet Alexander Pope said. But if Newt's going to preach moral standards, he'd better adhere to them himself or risk ending up like the buffoonish Gene Hackman character in *The Birdcage,* whose hypocrisy ends up on broad display.

But back in Harrisburg, I had little awareness until well after the 1994 election of the political intrigue surrounding my brother and gay issues. Long before, I had adopted a "hear no evil, speak no evil" attitude toward politics and had instituted my own version of the military's "don't ask, don't tell" policy as regards my sexual orientation. This personal and political blackout left me ignorant and complacent in my second-class status. I told myself that I just wanted to be like everyone else. Working by day for my sister Roberta, who heads up the Family and Consumer Sciences division of the state Department of Education, and by night for UPS, it was easy to pretend that I was.

Despite the long hours of two jobs, I was leading a relatively comfortable existence. I hung out with my friends and family, played rugby matches on weekends, frequented the local women's bar, and went to the movies. In short, I lived like a happy young dyke a few years out of college. But in the aftermath of the election, as I went about my life in Harrisburg, I knew I had to do *something.* I used to laugh away the joke of a female friend of mine who goes by the name Bob that I was the Democratic Party's secret weapon. "Now," I thought, "it might be time to bring out the heavy artillery."

All along, it wasn't just my own confusion and complacency that were inhibiting my announcement to the world of who I was. Up to that point, I hadn't felt comfortable asserting myself because I was afraid of how my family might react to the disclosure. Although no one ever said, "Don't come out because you will hurt your brother's career," no one needed to. I was complicit in my family's wish to keep my sexual orientation from public view. Who was I to challenge Newt's politics? In the back of my mind, I presumed my family would be pretty pissed off. If I rode at the head of the gay pride parade or wrote letters to the editor or chained myself to the White House fence, they wouldn't appreciate it in the least. And it wasn't just Newt I was protecting.

I was wary that Dad would be subjected to razzing down at the firehouse bar and the American Legion post, where he hung out with the guys, and that Mom would face irate customers at Boscov's, the Camp Hill department store where she worked special events. (For the last two Presidents' Days, she's dressed up as Martha Washington to hand out coupons. And I thought I was the only one in the family that did drag!) Despite my family's eccentricities, they might react by rejecting me, a possibility that always lurked just below the surface.

The fear of such repercussions is exactly what stifles lots of potential gay activism. In my travels across the country, I've heard countless stories where siblings or parents have warned gay people in their families not to come out publicly for fear that grandparents or some other relative in precarious health would be unable to handle the truth. In some cases, gays blamed themselves and their own eventual honesty for the death of relatives. But, as I soon discovered, frankness isn't fatal, and silence, which offers no surefire protection, eats at the soul.

In the end, my coming out publicly turned out to be no big deal at all. Though Dad did make a halfhearted attempt to cancel my interview on the *Eye to Eye with Connie Chung* special in January 1995, no one in my family was hurt by my revelation, and that includes Newt, who used it as an opportunity to tout his "love the sinner, hate the sin" line. The guys at the firehouse treated Dad like always, and Mom got far more grief about her infamous Hillary Clinton "bitch" comment to Connie Chung than about my sexuality. In fact, Mom said that after my coming out, strangers would come up and tell her, "Oh, you must be Newt *and* Candace's mother," rather than the usual references to Newt alone. In one fell swoop, Mom doubled her pride.

Indeed, when it came to coming out publicly, I was already pretty well prepared in private. For several years I had been out of the closet to my family, friends, and coworkers, so at least people could not say they were caught off guard. Those difficult conversations had already taken place. Coming to terms with my sexuality had never been a struggle. In fact, my experience was quite different from that of a lot of people who face both external and internal opposition to coming out. As a result, I had the inner confidence it took to stand up for myself and face down my critics.

Newt might have been collecting one of those lucrative congressional pensions before another gay relative of one of the Republican leaders felt ready to speak out. By then it would be too late to limit the damages they could inflict on gay and lesbian Americans. I know of many, many children of antigay activists, including some of the most prominent in the country, who remain in the closet. Some will eventually come out; some will go to their graves with their secret. By the time I came out in late 1994, Dee Mosbacher, daughter of Bush administration treasurer Robert, and Ty Ross, the grandson of former senator Barry Goldwater, among others, had already blazed trails for me. As I soon discovered, I wasn't even the only gay Gingrich. With the growing national interest in Newt, I always suspected someone would uncover my secret. It would happen sooner or later, maybe even before I had the chance to come out publicly of my own accord.

As it happened, it was sooner. Just days after the November 8 election, reporters descended on Harrisburg by the dozens to interview the family about Newt. It didn't take long for one smart young journalist to figure out my story. Mom was flipping through some old family photos with Associated Press reporter Jill Lawrence, who had been assigned to profile the new Speaker. Coming across one of my high school pictures, in which I have long flowing hair and wear a frilly blouse, Mom told Jill that it was the most recent shot she had displayed of me because she didn't like my college photos. Mom then whipped out my college pictures, which show me with a butch little crew cut. Jill remembers thinking that I looked like a man or, in my case, a boy. When Mom left the room, Jill, sensing something amiss, turned to my sister Susan and asked if her sister was a lesbian. In characteristic Gingrich fashion, Susan sarcastically responded, "Which sister?"

The cat, so to speak, was out of the bag. I was on my way to unforeseen fame. Later in the day, I met Jill for drinks at Angelino's, a Harrisburg pizza parlor. Jill says that she knew her hunch was correct as soon as she saw me drive up in my Tracker, which was adorned as usual with my gay rainbow flag, rugby sticker, and Grateful Dead skull-and-roses decal. I was still sporting a modified crew cut (which today looks as if someone placed a cereal bowl on my head and cut around it) and my ever-present striped rugby shirt. After a long, friendly discussion in which we both danced around the topic, Jill came right out and asked me, explaining that Mom had practically "outed" me to her. That's when I told her the truth. As Jill can attest, even though I had steeled myself to coming out, when it came right down to it, I was still apprehensive. I could see the end of my comfortable, small-town existence flashing before my eyes.

Several days later, the *New York Times* picked up Jill's story (without crediting her) in a long, page one profile of Newt. I was off to the races, or at least the daises, in what soon became a cross-country speaking tour for the Human Rights Campaign, the national lobby group that seeks equal rights for gays and lesbians. At the time, however, I had no idea just how rocky—and exhilarating—my leg of the road to equality would be.

CHAPTER TWO

LIFELINES

City of accidents, your true map
is the tangling of all our lifelines.

—ADRIENNE RICH,
"Blue Ghazals,"
The Will to Change

The journey began on a brisk winter night in 1941, when Kathleen Daugherty walked from her home to the skating rink in Royalton, Pennsylvania, a middle-class town downriver from Harrisburg. It was like every Royalton night: local teens would meet for flirting, fighting, or plain old fun. But unbeknownst to Kathleen, who went by the name Kitty, that particular night would forever change not only the course of her life, but that of the country. Kitty met Newton C. McPherson Jr., a dashing young auto mechanic who took an immediate fancy to her. Before long, the tumultuous relationship would produce little Newton Leroy McPherson, the future Speaker of the House.

In those days, women were supposed to hitch up with the right guy as soon as he came along. The idea of postponing marriage to pursue a career was reserved for Greenwich Village bohemians. Kitty, who would one day produce me as well, reluctantly agreed when Newton asked her to marry him not long after they began dating. She liked him well enough. Yet at the same time she knew something was missing. Love, for starters. After all, she was only seventeen, had never graduated from high school, and had barely ventured beyond the outskirts of the town. She longed to see the world. And she had an uneasy feeling that Newton's charm masked a violent streak. After they had begun dating, Newt became possessive, threatening any man who happened to come across her path.

Shortly before the wedding, Kitty pleaded with her mother to call it off. But the wedding announcement had already been mailed to the local newspaper. (Talk about form over substance!) From the beginning, Kitty had felt pressured into an early marriage by her mother, Ethel, who had lost her husband in a tragic car accident when Kitty was in her early teens. Ethel and her husband, Leroy, had a fairy-tale marriage. A train conductor, Leroy would stop the train in the middle of its route, dash to the one-room schoolhouse where Ethel taught, and give her a kiss. Ethel wanted her darling Kitty to experience the same happiness.

Newton would turn Ethel's dream into a nightmare. Not long after the wedding, Newton's violent underside surfaced. He had taken to staying out late, boozing with his friends at the local tavern, and sleeping through the start of work the next day. As Mom tells it, one day when she tried to rouse him for work at the nearby Hershey Chocolate factory, he struck her in the face. After Newton's father intervened with a stern admonition never to use force again, Newton enlisted and shipped out for the European theater of World War II, returning to face the divorce papers Kitty had prepared in his absence.

Not long after her husband's departure, Kitty discovered that she was pregnant. She gave birth to Newt on June 17, 1943, at Harrisburg Hospital. Kitty considered little Newtie her compensation for the ugliness of the marriage, which had lasted less than three months. She cherished him. As an adult, Newt has said many times that his mother's nurturing alone gave him the strength to climb great mountains.

After ridding herself of the louse Newt McPherson, Kitty found her situation vastly improved. Though still a time of limited opportunities for women, the war did offer some the chance to work Rosie-the-riveter jobs in factories. While Mom toiled at the plant during the day, Ethel, with help from the McPherson family, looked after little Newt. The tight-knit extended family, all of whom doted on the boisterous child, made for an idyllic boyhood. The combination of the incomes from Mom's factory job, Grandma's teaching salary, and the McPhersons' generosity made for a stable, middle-class existence. The resourcefulness that Mom displayed in those days may help explain Newt's well-known antipathy for the "welfare state" and why he has so comfortably adopted the religious right's "family values" agenda, though I wish it gave him more sympathy for different family settings. In interviews, Newt has acknowledged that he's spent much of his adulthood coming to grips with the fact that he has two fathers.

The family did not remain unconventional for long. Kitty remained a single mother only until 1945, when she met Robert Gingrich, a young Army enlistee, this time at a roller-skating rink. (Robert pronounced his name Gin*rick;* most Americans mispronounce it Gin*rich.*) Next to the violent Newt McPherson, young Robert's gentleness and quiet intelligence shone. Before long, Kitty became Kathleen Gingrich. The two rented a tiny apartment in Hummelstown, just miles from Royalton. Robert was studying biology at Gettysburg College because a hernia forced him to stay away from combat duty until the tail end of the war.

Robert had a checkered family past himself. His unwed teenage mother had abandoned him as an infant on the doorstep of a family with nine children, who took him in and gave him a warm and loving home. As a result, Robert wanted to make sure that little Newt would always have a solid family. Officially adopting the boy, he gave him the Gingrich surname. On May 5, 1948, Kathleen gave birth to Susan. The couple's second child, Roberta, was born March 30, 1950. By then Robert was serving in Korea as an Army captain. His career would take the family on an intercontinental hopscotch that would last until 1974. Among the stops were Army bases in Germany and France, where Newt and his younger sisters learned to appreciate European civilization and toured many of the continent's great cities. Only at the end of this odyssey—sixteen years after Roberta—on June 2, 1966, was I born in Baltimore to Kitty and Robert, who was then stationed at Fort Holliberd, an Army base that has since been closed. From then on, our moves were limited to the United States and Panama.

As in any family, no matter how loving, inevitable tensions bubbled below the surface tranquillity. Much has been made of Newt's relationship to his adopted father. In their short biography, *Newt Gingrich: Speaker to America,* Judith Warner and Max Berley contend that Newt has spent much of his life trying to win Robert's approval through an obsessive emphasis on achievement. It's true that the first time Kitty brought Robert home to meet little Newt, who was two, Newt responded with a swift kick to his adopted father's shins.

According to the biographers, that first exchange set the tone for the father-son relationship. Robert was disappointed that Newt was an awkward athlete who spent much of his youth reading, rather than engaging in more "masculine" pursuits of the sort Dad advocated. As a dedicated and disciplined military man, Robert was also said to be disappointed that Newt avoided the draft by taking a 4-F for his poor eyesight. "I think Robert considered him a sissy," Warner and Berley quote a friend of Newt's as saying. The authors claim the animosity between the two was such that, during Newt's historic inauguration ceremony on the House floor, Dad refused to stand and applaud with the rest of the adoring audience. I know for a fact that's not the case because I was there. We did stand for the first couple of ovations, but it started to get tiresome so we sat. Dad certainly didn't mean any disrespect. If he was so cold to Newt, why does he spend so much time talking about him and have so many mementos of his political milestones displayed prominently throughout the house? In fact, I've heard Robert and Newt speak of each other only in admiring, albeit a bit stilted, terms.

Dad certainly contributed to Newt's intellectual and political development. Noticing that Newt was already a voracious reader at a young age, Dad bought him the *Encyclopedia Americana,* which Newt practically memorized. Though Dad can be reserved to the point of aloofness, he instilled in each of us the need to speak up loudly for what we believe. As early as age ten, Newt was already a budding politician. An animal lover, he launched a campaign, which included a stop at the mayor's office and an article in a local paper, for a publicly funded zoo in Harrisburg. Warner and Berley quote a newspaper editor exclaiming of Newt, "A few minutes' conversation with Newton leaves an awed adult with a flying start toward an inferiority complex." (I can relate to the editor's bemusement. At that age, I was too busy skipping class and playing softball to pay any attention to politics.)

In 1960, when Robert moved the family to Baltimore, Newt stayed in Columbus, Georgia, where Dad had been stationed at Fort Benning for six years. Newt, who established himself as an academic and political star at Baker High School, left his heart in Georgia, literally. He had fallen in love with his high school geometry teacher, Jackie Battley, who was twenty-five. Jackie was a strict Southern Baptist in everything but, as Warner and Berley point out, her "taste in younger men." In Newt's senior year, the two began surreptitiously dating. After Newt's graduation, Jackie accepted a teaching job in Atlanta, where Newt attended Emory University on an academic scholarship to study history and politics. He joined the school Young Republicans and leapt headfirst into Georgia politics.

Newt and Jackie were married not long after Newt turned nineteen. Less than a year later the couple had the first of two children, Kathleen, named after Mom; Jackie Sue would come along two years later. Dad, to say the least, did not approve. Having given up his own dream of becoming a physician to support his family on an officer's salary, he felt Newt was marrying before he had the chance to establish his career. The family boycotted the wedding, driving a stake between Newt and Dad that would be removed with the birth of Kathy one year later. Softening at the sight of the infant, Dad quickly took a strong liking to Jackie.

The household in which I was raised was not the one in which Newt grew up. I was certainly aware that Dad had a hard side. At times he could be a stern and unforgiving disciplinarian. Even Susan admits she was terrified at times of her father. As a young girl, I remember knowing that his word was the law. He was probably harder on the head-strong Newt, especially since he was a boy. But like many hot-tempered young military men, Robert mellowed over the years, and I have been the beneficiary of the sweetness that came with the mellowing. Robert was just about the best father a little girl could have. He would play with me in a teasing way that made me feel loved and protected. He'd kneel down on the floor, tickling and roughhousing with me. He more than anyone else is the source of my sarcastic sense of humor, something that has rescued me from numerous debacles, both personal and profes-sional. Nothing like an acid word to fend off the homophobes!

Dad never imposed his wishes on me. As my friends and family can attest, I've always pretty much done my own thing. Maybe I was the athlete he wished Newt had been, but he certainly never objected when I preferred to play with the boys, dress up in boys' clothes at a very young age, or years later, bring my girlfriend home to live with him and Mom. He even looked the other way when I cut off all the hair on the Barbie dolls I'd inherited from Roberta. If he didn't object to these eccentricities of mine, it's hard to see him giving Newt a hard time just because he was something of a nerd.

There's been lots of confusion over my relationship to Newt. People have a tendency to see in it what they want. The gay press uncritically plays up my blood tie to Newt. "Newt's lesbian little-sister speaks out," declared the cover of the March 7, 1995, edition of *The Advocate*, the national gay and lesbian magazine. Critics of my work, meanwhile, underline the fact that I'm actually only his half sister and that we grew up more than a generation apart. Susan says that she becomes angry whenever she sees people diminishing our family bond with Newt. "We're as much a family as any other family," she says.

For most of my life, as Newt pursued his career, first in academe and then politics, we would see each other primarily during the Thanksgiving and Christmas holidays, when he would come up to our house for visits with Jackie and their daughters and later with Marianne, his second wife. Back in the days of expensive airfare, I remember how hard it was for us to find the money to fly down to Georgia to see him. As his responsibilities increased in Congress, Newt made the trip home less often. I knew Newt through those visits and from Mom's constant fussing over his career. We were distant enough from each other when I was a kid that Mom took to reminding me exactly who he was by referring to him as "Brother Newt."

Our relationship was remote enough that when I was twelve, Newt, who was always very generous with me, sent me pink leg warmers as a Christmas present. Though I realize it's the thought that counts, I had to laugh because by then I was the biggest tomboy in the world. No self-respecting tomboy would be caught dead in leg warmers, especially pink ones. They were for girls who were trying hard to impress the boys, something that scarcely interested me even then. When the family did see Newt, we spent most of our time chatting about the weather, what it's like down in Georgia, and the usual family gossip. We were all acutely aware that he got enough political talk the rest of the year.

Even then, my feelings toward Newt's amazing political ascendancy were more complicated than Mom's. I have to admit that at times I felt jealous and even a little resentful of the attention she lavished on him. For as long as I can remember, Mom kept an overflowing scrapbook of press clips detailing his many accomplishments. Over time, one scrapbook became multiple scrapbooks. When I'm asked if she keeps one for me, I say Mom doesn't have the time. She's too busy keeping up with the avalanche of Newt articles. She was fiercely proud of him, and in her eyes he could do no wrong. The substance of his politics was far less important to her than the sheer prominence of it. I could not help but share some of that adulation, especially when I was young and impressionable. But as I developed views of my own, I realized I had to keep some of them to myself. Don't get me wrong, she was a wonderful mother for me, too, displaying the same kind of fierce pride in everything I did. She conscientiously avoided favoring one of us over the other.

But how does one compete with a rising star in Congress, an emerging political legend? Mostly, I didn't try to. I desensitized myself to Newt's political career, doing my own thing instead, which was mostly playing sports and, later, partying. At a young age, evaluating and criticizing, no matter how gently, the content of what he was saying would have constituted a kind of family heresy. Ignoring Newt's politics wasn't so hard to do until he became a media phenomenon in the early 1990s. Until then, despite the strong base he was building, he was just another obscure conservative from the South.

Across the geographical and generational divides of our lives, Newt and I were bonded by family and military life—a bond we would tacitly acknowledge each time we saw each other. For all four of us Gingrich kids, each new Army base was a trial by fire, and surviving it gave us a strength we would all draw upon repeatedly as we grew older and the demands of the world grew more severe.

CHAPTER THREE

WAYWARD GIRL

One is not born, but rather becomes a woman.

—SIMONE DE BEAUVOIR,
The Second Sex

A rebel is made, not born. Shortly after we settled in Indiana, Pennsylvania, I staged my first official protest against the prevailing social order. I was all of three, but it was the first of what I'm sure my family would agree were frequent acts of creative disobedience.

Like the good Lutherans they are, Mom and Dad invited the local minister and his wife over to the house one night for dinner. At the table, the minister's wife sweetly leaned over and asked me, "Where do you go to school, little girl?"

Having learned my father's joking name for my preschool, I replied, "Miss Clements's School for Wayward Girls."

A stunned silence fell over the table as my sisters barely suppressed their laughter. I remember the poor minister's teeth practically falling to the floor. I'm sure he and his wife must have wondered where the heck a three-year-old could come up with a line like that. The answer was, in a word, Dad. As part of his perpetual teasing, he would feed me sassy comments about Mrs. Clements's school. At other times he would jokingly inform me that my name was "Mudd," referring to the doctor who a century before had tended to the broken leg of Lincoln assassin John Wilkes Booth. "Candace Jeanne Mudd," he would say, his straight face betraying just a hint of a smile. In the case of our offended dinner guests, Dad could hardly be sore with me since he was the source of the joke in the first place.

The "wayward girl" remark certainly wasn't the last time the irreverent sense of humor I picked up from Dad got me into a pickle. But when a child moves six times before her eighth birthday, she stands back far enough from new acquaintances to see the comic flaws in them. As an Army brat, just like my half brother, I discovered that you either allow other people to dictate your life or assert yourself and make new friends. Humor, I learned, takes the edge off the aggressiveness you need to thrive in this survival-of-the-fittest world. Moving from town to town, I grew accustomed to taking the battle to other people, rather than waiting for them to come to me. On the political level, these are precisely the skills that made Newt a famous politician. As a gay activist, I've begun to draw upon them, as well.

The Gingrich world tour began early. I was born in Baltimore in 1966, but we didn't stay long. Just months after my birth, Dad re-upped for Vietnam, where he served in an advisory capacity. I can hardly blame him for leaving home. After raising Newt and then Susan and Roberta, he may have changed enough diapers for one lifetime. I'm sure Mom missed him terribly, but at least she had Susan and Roberta to keep her company. And Mom still saw and spoke to Newt, who was studying for his Ph.D. in history at Tulane University in New Orleans. Before long, Dad was back from Vietnam, upset by the carnage he had seen there and ready to resume life in the States.

Our next stop was Indiana, Pennsylvania, home to Indiana University of Pennsylvania and Miss Clements's School. The school's 12,500 students made up the majority of the lively little town, which was dotted with old oak trees, ivy-covered brick buildings, and sprawling lawns. The main drag, Philadelphia Street, featured fading department stores and beer pubs catering to students. My fondest memory of that period was going with Mom and Dad to Oak Grove, a commons at the center of campus, to feed the squirrels, who would eat bread crumbs from my hands. That was an era before drunken college students had driven into them a well-founded fear of bodily harm.

Like the layout of the town, our family life revolved around the campus. Dad, who had already earned a degree in biology, taught Reserve Officers' Training Corps classes and worked toward his master's degree in counseling. My sister Roberta studied at the university for her teaching degree in home economics. The daughter of a professor and the sister of a student, I was fortunate enough to be admitted to the university-run nursery school, one of the best in the state. Years later, drawn by my childhood memories of the town, I attended college there.

Walking across campus with my college friends, I could point to the playground, announcing proudly that I had frolicked there as a little kid.

Our years in Indiana brought my first political memories, though I would not draw lessons from them until many years later. I vividly recall the angry antiwar protesters who organized a massive demonstration at the building that housed the ROTC program and in which Dad had his office. The squat red-brick building was adorned with the obligatory Stars and Stripes and World War II–era cannon. Dad served as the faculty adviser to Tau Kappa Epsilon, one of the school's fraternities. Out of loyalty to Dad, the frat boys formed a human wall around the building to protect him and the ROTC offices from the protesters. The antiwar activists were by no means violent, and Dad's safety was never in doubt, but as it was the height of the antiwar movement in 1970, tensions were running so high that even a four-year-old couldn't help but notice them. Today, I'm sure, my sympathy would be with the protesters, but at the time the family was simply relieved that people were sticking up for Dad. I had nightmares of Dad's being taken hostage.

The protest was the family's first brush with the New Left of the 1960s, which would later help account for our divergent politics. Newt encountered the counterculture at Tulane, where he was studying for his Ph.D. in history. Though still the consummate nerd with pencils sticking out of his shirt pocket and horn-rimmed glasses, he hung out with an eclectic group of friends, listening to Jefferson Airplane and the Beatles' *White Album*. He's even admitted to smoking pot then. (He inhaled!) Still, Newt was no wild-eyed radical. Baptized a Lutheran, Newt converted to Jackie's more conservative Southern Baptist church. The wild sexual-liberationist mores of New Orleans's French Quarter portrayed in Oliver Stone's *JFK* had no impact on the budding historian and politician, as best I could discern.

At Tulane, Newt developed his provocative but sometimes contradictory political ideology. An early supporter of the civil rights movement, Newt rejected the divisive racist politics of George Wallace that appealed to so many Southern conservatives. As a foe of Richard Nixon, Newt supported the moderate Nelson Rockefeller's 1968 race for the Republican nomination. The first stirrings of a libertarian streak also began to appear during his years at Tulane, a bent that today sometimes causes him trouble with the censorious religious right. In 1967, the Tulane administration blocked publication of two nude photographs in the *Hullabaloo*, the campus newspaper, on the grounds

THE ACCIDENTAL ACTIVIST

that they were obscene. ("The quantification of sex along with the quantification of everything else in our industrialized society," read the caption under the photos.)

In response, Newt led a weeklong protest. According to biographers Warner and Berley, Newt threatened to shut down classes for the rest of the semester if the administration did not relent. "It is a question of power," he warned the university president. "We are down to a clash of wills." Newt lost the battle but never forsook the cause. Yet at the same time, Newt would inveigh against feminism when the topic was broached by Jackie or his younger sisters. And by the mid-1970s he would depict the counterculture and sixties-style liberalism as the chief culprits in the "decline of Western civilization."

The sixties, however, would come to have a very different connotation for me. The decade represented the maturation of the civil rights movement, the birth of women's liberation, and the first political stirrings of the gay community. In 1969, a motley crew of teenage hustlers, drag queens, and barflies rebelled against police harassment at the Stonewall, a popular Greenwich Village gay bar. For millions of gay and lesbian Americans who came of age in the decades after the sixties, Stonewall would come to represent the freedom to be who we are.

Except for the antiwar demonstration, though, the social upheavals of the sixties had little effect on the Gingrich family. While he supported the war, Dad never let on much as to his opinions on the politics surrounding it, except to say that the brutality of the conflict was heartbreaking. Though Mom has never considered herself a feminist, I don't remember her ever criticizing either women's rights or civil rights. Dad was a loyal Democrat until switching parties to vote for Ronald Reagan in 1980. Dad, like Newt, speaks reverently of Roosevelt and Truman. Dad especially likes to tell the story of the time Truman came to Fort Leavenworth, where our family lived for a while. Asked if he would have made the decision to drop the A-bomb on Hiroshima again, the president responded, "Hell, yes." That kind of buck-stops-here certitude in politicians appeals to Mom and Dad. It's no coincidence that Newt comes across that way. Compared to the "triangulating" Bill Clinton, they see Newt as a politician with principles.

Mom and Dad moved to the right with the rest of the country. While they supported many elements of the New Deal, they were wary of the left and what they saw as the extremes of the antiwar and freedom movements; they would surely have been puzzled by gay liberation,

40

had they heard about it. As the seventies wore on, I remember that they were increasingly fretful about high taxes, the size of the federal bureaucracy, and the seeming permanence of the welfare state. Still, despite their reliable Republican voting habits, Mom and Dad hardly fit the presumed ideological profile for parents of the current House Speaker. As elderly voters who rely on social security and medicare, they are opposed to indiscriminate Republican budget slashers.

According to Mom and Dad, the cold war gave a hard edge to Newt's conservatism. Traveling from installation to installation, Newt became fascinated with military history and the power of politicians to mold history to their own designs. Susan reports that the crumbling ruins of faded European empires made him aware of the transience of empire. The great precariousness of wealth, power, and domain was thus drummed into him. Susan says what many people see as Newt's sentimental concern for the survival of "Western civilization" is genuine concern embedded in these memories.

As legend has it, Newt decided on a political career during a treacherous ride home from Europe on a military transport plane. Instead of seeing politics and public service as a vocation, Newt began to see it as a calling to save America from hostile forces both inside and outside the country. "I want to shift the entire planet," Newt once said of his political ambitions. Weaned on the military's us-versus-them philosophy, it was easy to translate international divisions to national ones.

My own political consciousness, by contrast, was formed in the waning days of the cold war. With the security of the United States assured, my generation tended to be more concerned about justice and fairness inside the country. Though I respected Dad's career, the lessons I learned had more to do with the military's ability to tear families apart, engender the worst in masculine traits, and foster nepotism—rather than with saving the nation from hostile foreign powers. I noticed these features most strikingly from 1972 to 1974, when we lived in Panama. When we arrived there, I had just celebrated my sixth birthday.

Far from serving as a vehicle for justice, the military reinforces unfairness. The Canal Zone, which was then under U.S. military control, was divided along racial lines. The armed forces, of course, have often been a positive force for racial integration since Truman desegregated them in 1948. In Panama, however, it often felt as if white Americans were imposing themselves on the dark-skinned inhabitants. Dad,

I think, was conscious of the divide. I remember with pride how well he spoke Spanish, the respectful way he would speak to our Panamanian maids, Blanca and Chachi, and his befriending of a black couple, the Pooles. Dad and Mr. Poole would go deep-sea fishing. At their place, we would eat a breakfast of grits and eggs. Military politics would rear its ugly head from time to time. After Mom beat the skirts off the other officers' wives in a golf tournament, the general's wife refused to show up at the posttournament party.

But at my young age, military life in Panama was nothing but a tropical paradise. We lived in a tidy little town house in the center of the Ft. Amador Army installation in the Zone, directly across the street from a meticulously manicured eighteen-hole golf course. The backyard was overgrown with coconut, banana, and mango trees. Whenever I was hungry for a snack, all I had to do was walk outside to our own private produce department. The ocean was three blocks away, as were an Olympic-size swimming pool and a well-kept playground, built specially for military rug rats like me. At night we could hear the coatimundis, giant raccoonlike creatures that swam in the sewers and made loud bullfroglike sounds. Their songs provided plentiful fodder for childhood nightmares. (Maybe the coatimundis explain my affinity for Stephen King's *It*, about an evil clown that lives in the sewers.) During the day, Mom would sneak me onto the golf course for private lessons. Already a budding tomboy, I was soon taking mighty clouts, though not always connecting with the ball.

It was wonderful being part of a loving, supportive family and an extended military family as well. Unbeknownst to me at the time, however, Dad was not feeling so warm and fuzzy about the Army brass. After sacrificing a possible career as a physician for the military, Dad's prospects for advancement meant a lot to him. Though he was about as good and honorable an officer as you could find, Dad kept getting passed over for bump-ups. Mom says he's bitter to this day that he didn't make general, or at least full colonel.

Expecting to succeed the old-fashioned way through hard work and a demonstrated record of accomplishment, Dad refused to kiss his superiors' behinds to secure promotions. That's where it first became crystal clear to me that people should be rewarded not for whom they know or how nice they are or their race (a natural extension would also include sexual orientation), but rather purely on their records. I learned from Dad that brownnosing is no way to earn rewards, no matter how much you might want them. Slighted one too many times, Dad retired from the military at the young age of forty-nine in 1974.

By this point, Newt had the security of a teaching post at West Georgia College in Carrollton, a small town not far from Atlanta. (One of the environmental studies courses he taught was titled "Alternative Lifestyles.") As we prepared for our final move, back to the Harrisburg area, Newt announced his first campaign for the House seat from Georgia's Sixth District. The political fallout from Watergate, however, made for an uphill battle. He lost. Badly.

We returned to Harrisburg to put down some roots and to be close to Susan and Roberta, who'd settled here. Mom and Dad bought a bilevel, prefabricated house in a brand-new development in Dauphin, a small town of eight hundred a short car ride from Harrisburg. The house had three bedrooms and a huge family room downstairs, where I hung out for the privacy. My room was soon decorated with sports posters and my hated doll collection, which well-meaning family members had forced on me as presents.

We were financially set. Thanks to a generous military pension, thriftiness, and careful saving, Mom and Dad were solidly middle class. I'm still not quite sure why he retired so early, but it quickly became apparent that Dad missed his military career. Without a career to help him organize his life, he went through a series of unsatisfying jobs: collecting tolls at the Gettysburg interchange of the Pennsylvania Turnpike, carpentry, security guard, and later, a bartending job at the local American Legion post.

The flip side of Dad's restlessness was that he had plenty of time to lavish attention on me, from which I benefited greatly. Arriving home from school each day, I would spend time with him just hanging out. He'd sit at the dining room table and wrestle with his beloved crossword puzzles, while I did my homework. On cold days, Mom would make the three of us cookies and hot cocoa. It was exactly the comfort and security I needed to venture out into the larger world, which I was just beginning to explore.

CHAPTER FOUR

TOMBOY

No one can make you feel inferior without your consent.
—ELEANOR ROOSEVELT

Once I had my feet planted, it didn't take long to unleash the real me. Harrisburg suited me fine, as long as I had plenty of tomboy stuff like kickball and building tree forts to keep me occupied. For Newt, the early seventies were spent laying the groundwork for a high-powered political career, but that was the farthest thing from my mind. I was too busy being me, which, as you'll see, was no simple enterprise.

The summer before third grade, I started telling all the kids my name was Tom. I assume I got the name from Mom and Dad, who called me a tomboy because I liked the same things boys did—playing sports and roughhousing. I didn't cotton to dolls and make-believe tea parties. One of my playmates, a nice neighbor kid named Brent, who would become my soul mate, didn't even realize I was a girl until I answered to the name Candace during attendance on the first day of school. When he found out, he didn't mind. At that age, kids don't care a great deal about gender distinctions. Besides, I had one of those Bobby Brady bowl cuts that were so popular at the time. Freckles and all, I was the spittin' image of Mike and Carol's youngest son.

And the Bobbys of the world have it better. During childhood, boys tend to get treated better than girls. While things may slowly be changing for the better, boys are the little lords, encouraged to follow their heart's desire, while girls get herded into home ec. For budding gay kids, this isn't the case. Little boys who like to play with girls and put on dresses (for whatever reason, including creativity and the sheer defiance of taboos) have it pretty tough. Many parents who can afford it immediately send sissy boys to therapists in misguided—and usually abusive—attempts to make them more masculine. If they can't afford or don't believe in therapy, parents often call in the clergy. They fear that if they don't intervene early, their boys will grow up to be homos. What they usually fail to consider is that such attempts at suppression often leave deep scars and teach little boys to hide and lie about themselves. When the church is involved in trying to make little boys more masculine, it's not what I'd call a very warm initiation to religion.

The way I see it, as kids we don't have much say in the matter. A spate of genetic research has shown that we are the way we are by nature. To change someone's nature is to do violence to them. For some reason, parents usually don't crack down as hard on girls. They are allowed to go through a masculine stage, hence the temporary connotation of "tomboy." Maybe it's because studies have indicated tomboyish girls are much more likely to "outgrow" such stages and turn toward traditional gender roles after adolescence than are feminine boys, who often grow up to be gay. Girls get into trouble only if they don't "grow out" of the "stage" by the time they hit puberty, when they are suddenly expected to don a dress, lipstick, and other accoutrements of femininity to prove attractive to boys. At this point, some parents react to their tomboy daughters as they would to stereotypically sissy sons. (Gay boys, of course, are not necessarily any more feminine than straight boys.)

Robert and Kathleen were great; they pretty much let me do what felt right for me, even when I inexplicably failed to outgrow the tomboy "phase." At that young age, instead of worrying about pleasing my parents, I was thinking, "How can I keep this tomboy thing going?"

Sports fit the bill, and as I soon learned, they also made it easier to be a little disobedient about prescribed sex roles. Athletics came naturally. I started playing softball when I was eight and mastered every position, including my favorite, pitcher. In slow pitch, the mound was mine. In fast pitch, I moved behind the plate to catcher. My only problem came with batting—I wasn't a very strong hitter. A little tyke even then, I lacked the power of the bigger girls to regularly send searing drives to the outfield.

Living in Panama, where Mom taught me golf, I'd become a great hardball fan. I'd ride my bike over from our house to watch the local adults play on cracked clay diamonds under the blistering tropical sun. I eventually found softball and golf both a bit sedate and took up rugby, the ultimate roughhousing sport. For me, sports were not just about exercise and fun. Sports represented the freedom to be whomever I wanted, without regard to gender or social status or race or any of those other things that can get in the way of living life to its fullest.

On the playing field, everyone is equal. Tatum O'Neal, the fire-balling pitcher who took on the boys in the film *The Bad News Bears*, served as a role model for girls my age who wanted to tear down barriers between boys' and girls' sports. The only fissure in my idealized view of athletics came when I realized that as a girl I would not be allowed to play football. I had dreamed of playing middle linebacker in Pop Warner football, knocking the running backs to the ground with well-timed hits. That dream would have to wait for college and the rugby field.

My enthusiasm for sports did not translate into coursework. By the time I entered the third grade in Dauphin, I'd already become a disaffected student. Partly due to my devotion to sports and partly due to good old-fashioned laziness, I never really excelled the way my older siblings had. As usual, I was the lavender sheep of the family. No matter how hard I tried, I could never really focus on what the teacher was saying. I always longed to be outdoors, playing sports, and wreaking havoc. Yet I was also pretty advanced for my age, and I always interacted well with the teachers—so much so, in fact, that some of the other kids would call me "brownnoser" and "teacher's pet." But I wasn't doing it for grades; I just found older people more interesting. Except for phys ed, where I earned A's, I got mostly B's and C's.

My poor academic performance may have had something to do with the legacy of the constant moving. I was forced to adjust to new demands, standards, and curricula, not to mention time zones. It was just easier to concentrate on the ballfield. The rules of the game and the dimensions of the fields never changed. The social nature of sports helped me make instant new friends. These are important considerations for a kid living a nomadic life.

The less than stellar grades didn't stem from lack of ability. In a November 1995 interview with the Harrisburg metro daily, the *Patriot-News*, Mom told a story I had never heard. As I was beginning the third grade in Dauphin, she got a call from my teacher, Miss Nelson. Given what Mom knew about my proclivity toward insolence, she immediately assumed that I was in some kind of trouble. Instead, Miss Nelson informed her that I had tested at 143 in the intelligence test, well above average, and asked for her permission to put me on an advanced track in school. Pleasantly surprised, Mom gave her the go-ahead.

Last year, I received a letter from Miss Nelson, now Mrs. Nelson Kastelic, saying she didn't usually see her former students on television and congratulating me for speaking out. "These are not easy times for our country and unfortunately tolerance of difference doesn't seem to be on the increase," she wrote. "I remember you as a bright and 'spunky' third grader and it was fun to see that same twinkle in your eye."

It was a treat to hear from her because Miss Nelson was one of my favorite teachers, and I've always felt a little guilty that I failed to make the most of my God-given ability in the classroom. It shows that you can never give up on kids because you never know when they will come into their own. That's one of the great things about our educational system. Unlike in some countries, where you are put on rigid tracks from an early age, it's never too late for American kids to make the most of their opportunities. In America, high school dropouts can become billionaires, a feat almost unheard of in the rest of the world.

I don't feel too much regret about my mediocre academic record. I wasn't just sitting around on my duff. I compensated for my lack of bookishness by living a full, active life. Too active, some might say. Harrisburg was my oyster. In the summers, free from the burden of school, there were an abundance of trails on Peter's Mountain and Blue Mountain to explore. After a hike, my friends and I would cool off down at the community pool, just walking distance from my house. Sometimes we'd wander down to the ballfields for pickup games. Once a week or so, we would convince one of our moms to drive us to the arcade at the mall, where we would hang out drinking sodas, playing video games, and generally wreaking preadolescent havoc.

The kids in town thought of us from Dauphin as hicks because we were bused to school over the mountain. They made fun of the flannel shirts, jeans, and leather hiking boots that many of us wore like a uniform. (I like to joke that I grew up wearing boots because I was from Dauphin, but I later realized it was because I'm a dyke.) The city kids' view of us helped me understand from an early age how false class distinctions can be. We lived in a brand-new housing development in Dauphin, and most of the kids making fun of us came from families who had lower incomes than we did. It was also obvious how artificial racial divisions were. As you might expect, the Dauphin kids were mostly white, while a higher percentage of the city kids were black. A teen group calling itself Dauphin Rebels Effort Against Disco (D.R.E.A.D.) formed to scrawl racist graffiti on public buildings. The two races rarely mingled, except when they were thrown together on a sports team. Inevitably, friendships blossomed and white football players or track athletes could be seen hanging out with black ones.

Today, the "Gingrich family as country bumpkins" fallacy lives on in the media's depiction of us. Radio shock jock Don Imus declared that we had a rusting car in our front yard, as if we were something out of the movie *Deliverance*. Maybe he was thinking of rural Georgia, where the family once lived, but Dauphin is more Orange County than Mississippi Delta. (On the same show, the infantile Imus also employed a graphic description of me that I can't repeat in polite company.)

Hick or not, I had long been something of a daredevil. One of my favorite pastimes was hiding behind the bushes in front of our house and throwing small rocks at passing cars in the 35-mph zone. That fun ended when a driver I had nailed stopped, got out of the car, and knocked on our front door while I hid trembling behind the house. I remember being upset not because I'd done it, but that I had been caught. In his sternest drill-sergeant voice, Dad told me never to do that again. I learned my lesson. But, hey, I was a tomboy, I had good aim.

That wasn't the extent of my transgressions. In my fourth-grade art class, we were making papier-mâché caterpillars and I drew an extra line on mine. Examining my creation with a frown, the teacher asked, "Candace, what on earth is that?"

"A butt crack," I responded honestly. She made me make a new caterpillar.

Politics was just beginning to enter my little world. In 1976, when I was ten, Newt lost his second attempt to win a House seat. Already the political nomad, he garnered endorsements from the liberal environmental group Sierra Club and the right-wing Committee for the Survival of a Free Congress, which would later become Paul Weyrich's Free Congress Foundation. Newt was also beginning to develop the anti-Washington rhetoric that would serve him well in his rise through the Republican ranks. "I'm running for Congress because I'm fed up with the politicians, bureaucrats, and special interests who run this country at the expense of working people," he declared in announcing his candidacy. Georgia peanut farmer Jimmy Carter's coattails proved to be too much for the young Republican firebrand, who lost by a mere two thousand votes.

Newt's loss was particularly hard on our doting mother. With a wife and two children to support, Newt was vacillating among politics, academe, and unsuccessful book writing. It was not at all clear he would become an unqualified success at anything. Just two years later, in the 1978 election, Newt would make Mom proud. Casting himself as a family-oriented everyman, Newt raised more than $200,000 for the campaign, a huge sum for those days. "Newt's family is like your family," read campaign literature, which featured photographs of the happy Gingrich clan. "We know what it is like to choose between macaroni and cheese and hamburger at the grocery store."

But what cinched the election for Newt was his turn to the right. Realizing that he lived in the midst of one of the most conservative districts in a conservative state, Newt backed away from his support for environmental causes in favor of his now-famous attacks on welfare. "If you love welfare cheaters, you'll love Virginia Shepard," one piece of campaign literature read, referring to his Democratic opponent. In the predominantly white rural district, the tactic worked. Newt was headed to Congress; Mom could rest easy.

As I went about my tomboy adventures, this drama was nothing more than a minor amusement. It meant little more to me than when Roberta or Susan got a promotion at work, except that it had something to do with running the country. I remember thinking, "Newt's got a new, high-paying job in Washington. Good for him." But that was about the extent of my interest. My complacency did not begin to change until 1980, when Ronald Reagan crushed Jimmy Carter. In January 1981 we traveled to Washington to celebrate with Newt Reagan's inauguration.

Shivering in the arctic cold, we listened to boring speeches at the Washington Mall. Afterward, happy to be out of the cold, we watched news coverage of the political change in Newt's huge, wood-paneled office. Newt gave me a big hug. In the midst of the jubilation of Newt's family and friends, however, a short news story about the happy ending to the Iranian hostage crisis flashed on the screen. The story reported that critics of the newly elected president were questioning the timing of the release of the hostages and whether Reagan had arranged a secret arms-hostage deal to render his inauguration even rosier. No one in the room paid any attention to the allegations, but I had an uneasy feeling that they just might be true. I wondered why Newt and Mom and Dad were not taking them more seriously. "This is no time to celebrate," I thought to myself.

It was about this time as a teenager in the early eighties, still milking my tomboy stage for all it was worth, that I began adding an unarticulated liberal political slant to my mischief. My high school friend Donine was my partner in crime. Fortunately for our friendship, we both had really cool moms. Every month or so, we would talk them into writing us dental- or doctor-appointment notes so we could sneak away from school and have lunch together. During one of those illicit lunches, we hatched a daring plot.

It started innocently enough. In twelfth grade, as the liaison to the Harrisburg *Patriot-News* for Central Dauphin East, I would contribute to the school page where students wrote in about sports, exchange students, teachers back from sabbaticals, and science fairs. I'd applied for and received the job because I had good writing skills. What the editors at the newspaper didn't realize was that I was also lazy, apathetic, and prone to procrastination. When I wasn't playing field hockey, softball, or touch football with the guys, I was hanging out in the parking lot with a big group of friends. Who had time for writing articles that would not even count toward graduation? For the entire four-month period I held the job, I may have turned in two articles.

Coincidentally, it was also homecoming semester. In fall 1983, the previous year's homecoming queen was crowning the new one, who happened to be her sister. As this was the first time such a peculiar circumstance had arisen in the school's history, I was expected to write about it. But already something of a budding feminist, I made my protest against this sexist ritual by inexplicably failing to write it up for the paper. Even had I been swept up in the event, I would probably not have written anything about it anyway. Thanks to my talent for stalling, I had a built-in defense: "I just didn't get around to it." (Thus sensitized to sexist traditions, I would secretly applaud when I heard about regular feminist protests at Miss America pageants, which included a bra burning and a brigade of bikini-clad women with raw meat hanging from their bodies.)

Anyway, there was this teacher in school, Mr. Reichlin. Notorious for saying that women belonged in the home, Reichlin might as well have had horns, as far as I was concerned. I avoided his class like the plague. Given his zealous support for pom-pom–waving homecoming queens, however, I guess it was okay for women to leave the house long enough to fulfill their role as cheerleaders. The notion that women should stay home sounds severely outdated today, but at the time it was undergoing something of a resurgence in popularity. The president had recently declared that unemployment wouldn't be such a big problem if women would just stay in the home, where they belonged. This all rubbed me the wrong way, so I certainly wasn't going to do a puff piece on the tiara-passing at my school. After this story somehow failed to appear in the local paper, Mr. Reichlin called me into his classroom.

"Now, Candace," he began as I fidgeted in my chair, staring at the worn linoleum floor. I knew exactly what he was going to say. "I know you're the liaison to the paper. You should have written an article about those wonderful sisters. It's the first time it's ever happened in the history of Central Dauphin East."

Being an expert at apathy, I played clueless. "I'm sorry, Mr. Reichlin, I had too much homework," I said somewhat disingenuously since I rarely took school work home. "I just didn't get around to it." The procrastination defense, however, didn't hold much water with that old stickler.

"I know the real reason you didn't write about the homecoming," he intoned. "You're part of that anticheerleader clique at Central Dauphin East. That's it, isn't it? You just hate cheerleaders."

By this point I was incensed. "I don't hate cheerleaders," I said, getting up to go. I didn't hate cheerleaders. I hated that they were another example of the objectification of women. The way their fawning over the football players demeaned women—and made stinky adolescent boys into some kind of idols! But that was beside the point. For me, football games were about drinking Budweiser, getting buzzed, and hanging out with my friends. Mr. Reichlin, who was not even my teacher, had no business telling me what to write. I left, slamming the door.

Vengeance—tomboy style—was just around the corner. The next week as Donine and I embarked on our lunch outing, we stopped by the local Democratic headquarters and picked up several of those red, white, and blue Mondale-Ferraro bumper stickers. After lunch when everyone was back in class, we placed them on the bumper of Mr. Reichlin's Caddy, which sat conspicuously in the school parking lot, almost as pompous as its owner. As far as I know, Donine and I were never suspects. All I do know is that I was right about his politics—and that the bumper stickers held true to their union label, proving tough to remove. Mr. Reichlin had two cars, the Caddy and another big, gas-guzzling thing. For the rest of the week, the Caddy stayed home, safely hidden in Mr. Reichlin's garage.

CHAPTER FIVE

GROWING UP GAY

I shall be telling this with a sigh
Somewhere ages and ages hence:
Two roads diverged in a wood, and I—
I took the one less traveled by,
And that has made all the difference.

—ROBERT FROST,
"The Road Not Taken"

Rebellious feminist politics was not all I was exploring at a young rage. Sexually, I was what my parents and their contemporaries would call an "early bloomer." At age ten in fifth grade, I discovered to my surprise that the warm water from the bathtub faucet felt intensely pleasurable when it splashed against my midsection. Not knowing what a clitoris was, I just thought of it as an undefined region of my body "down there."

All I could discern was that it was a sensation akin to the physical joy of a hot meal on a cold day, the first spring sunshine beating down on my face, or a warm shower after an exhausting softball game. But this pleasure was especially neat because it was something I could create on my own. I didn't need the cooperation of others, at least not at that young age. It was wonderful but strange: What exactly was this mysterious feeling? Despite my precociousness, I had never heard the word *orgasm*. I sought an explanation wherever I could.

Adults were little help. In the sixth grade came the notorious "boys in one room, girls in the other room" talk. For budding gay kids like me, that was their first mistake. Middle Paxton Elementary School in Dauphin organized a parade of teachers, nurses, and social workers to inform us of the mysterious hormones that were coursing through our little bodies. Trained to approach sex education in a cold, clinical light, the nurse, who wore far too much makeup, explained that the girls would be getting periods soon, failing to realize that I and some of my friends had already begun menstruating.

Shy about frank discussions of sex, Mom and Dad told me little of these bodily functions. They figured the school would take care of the birds and the bees. When it came time for me to menstruate, Mom gave me a hand-me-down "garter" belt with a space for a sanitary pad that one of my sisters had used many years earlier. It looked like some kind of medieval chastity belt. Mom, who had by then gone through menopause, didn't realize that there had been a revolution in feminine hygiene since my sisters were teenagers. Finally, my sister Roberta came to my rescue with a box of o.b.s.

I heard about another kid who had an even worse experience. She had heard that one of the symptoms of cancer is excessive bleeding. So when she began to experience a blood flow, she was convinced she had a terminal disease and began making peace with the Lord. Fortunately, a friendly teacher came to her aid, assuring her that the bleeding was perfectly normal. Heaven could wait.

Not understanding the changes taking place in my body led me to some bizarre misperceptions of my own. When the nurse informed us that vaginal yeast infections create discharges, the blood drained from my face. I had been masturbating for some time, and a by-product of stimulation was a vaginal secretion I couldn't identify. Were those sexual sensations I was experiencing in the bathtub evidence of some hideous infection? Compelled to inquire, my hand shot up in the air.

"Are there any other kinds of outbursts?" I blurted out innocently enough. The other girls broke into uproarious laughter and I hid my head in shame. Embarrassed herself, the nurse ignored what in hindsight was a perfectly legitimate question. Any possibility of an honest discussion of sex was effectively over. The message we took away from these sessions was that when it came to information about sex, we were on our own.

If instruction about sex and adolescence was poor, information about sexual orientation was nonexistent. I knew that some kids—I among them—were beginning to experience same-sex attraction. From elementary school to high school, I can recall a couple of effeminate boys who were bullied and ridiculed relentlessly on the playground during recess. They became the outlet for the boys' insecurities about their own masculinity. If you beat up a queer, the logic seemed to go, you certainly couldn't be one yourself.

Dauphin likes to think of itself as an upright community. Profanity and racial epithets in the classroom and playground were usually stomped out. But antigay epithets such as *queer* and *faggot* were considered acceptable. The male phys ed teachers even used them as motivational tools: "You run like a queer, Jones, get your butt moving," and so on.

It saddens me to think that I failed to come to the defense of these boys. Even then, I knew the harassment they received was wrong. But sticking up for them was something no one seemed to do at that age. Still, that doesn't justify my silence. I guess I just lacked the courage of my convictions. I hope my activism today provides some compensation.

I was somehow spared the schoolyard taunts. By the time I reached East High, I was pretty well liked. From the jocks to the burnouts, I was a member of just about every clique. It was hardly a conscious strategy, but it seemed to immunize me against ridicule. The jocks didn't mind that I was still a tomboy. Obnoxiously witty, I was welcomed by the brains and class clowns. Before school I'd hang out with a bunch of hippie kids in the parking lot. With their long hair, sideburns, dirty jeans, and biker jackets, they were grunge before there was such a thing. The burnout kids, who smoked dope and drank beer, were the least likely to cast judgment on anyone, especially jocks like me who hung out with them.

Though spared the abuse heaped on some of the gay kids, I felt an unarticulated longing for more information about sexual identity. As far as I could tell, the junior high and high school libraries had an unofficial ban on the subject. Books like *Heather Has Two Mommies* and *Gloria Goes to Gay Pride*, today excluded from many school libraries, did not even exist in the early eighties. At that time, the media still engaged in a virtual blackout of the subject. The Harrisburg *Patriot-News*, which prided itself on being a "family" newspaper, rarely touched the subject.

The sex ed instructors were no help either, blithely blundering ahead with the assumption that everyone was feeling the same heterosexual urges. As usual, the gay kids were left to twist in the wind with their fears, and straight kids, lacking accurate information, were similarly deprived and disappointed. It was like a seminar on race that assumed that everyone was white. For Dauphin and even Harrisburg, AIDS was still a crisis looming beyond the mountains, not yet the catalyst for discussions of sexuality it would later become in many parts of the country.

When it came to AIDS, I was fortunate. It was the sexually active gay boys for whom the dearth of information could prove potentially fatal. Many had no knowledge of how to protect themselves from HIV infection, which was beginning to take hold in the more established gay male community, especially in major metropolitan areas. I'm sure there were gay guys in Harrisburg who made surreptitious trips to the bustling gay bars of Philadelphia, just a hop, skip, and a jump away by train. With proper information about safe sex, those kids might have been more likely to look back on such trips as a fun and exciting way to meet other people like them. Instead, memories of those trips now sometimes carry an undercurrent of tragedy.

Pedro Zamora is a case in point. The handsome MTV *Real World* star who died from AIDS in 1994 at age twenty-two was infected in the early 1980s in Miami just as he was coming out as a teenager—and before the gay community's prevention campaigns had really kicked in. Distraught over his mother's death, Pedro sought comfort in the arms of older gay men, some of whom took advantage of his vulnerability. Like the vast majority of gay men who've tested HIV-positive, at the time of his infection Pedro had no idea that HIV even existed.

After his diagnosis in the early nineties, Pedro spent the rest of his time on earth touring the country teaching young people, gay and straight, the dangers of unprotected sex. He's a perfect example of an accidental activist. Thrust into a difficult situation not of his choosing, Pedro made the best of the calamity by helping others avoid his fate. He lives on through the contribution he made to others.

At least Dauphin stayed away from the right-wing curricula such as "Sex Respect" and "Teen Aid," which swept the country in the 1980s. Funded by grants from President Reagan's Department of Health and Human Services, the curricula sought to modify adolescent sexual behavior through fear. Not only did the material, adopted by several hundred school districts nationwide, for the most part ignore homosexuality, but it cast it in a negative light. "Sex Respect" declares that AIDS is nature's way of "making some kind of comment on sexual behavior," a cruel and inaccurate message to send to young gay men.

Not coincidentally, my first stirring of attraction for other girls was at about the same time I started having those mysterious "outbursts." At age ten in 1976, I attended Girl Scout camp at Camp Lycogis in the Northern Appalachians, where my sister Susan had once worked as a counselor. Mountain streams meandered through the pine forest where the camp was situated. A large, shimmering lake, where we were required to take frigid swims each morning, lay near the center. The tents where we slept were raised on stilts to keep out rain and critters.

I shared a tent with a lithe girl of eleven whose brown locks were bleached blond from days spent under the sun and in the pool. I immediately noticed how much I treasured the time we spent alone together, just giggling and jumping around. One night Stephanie and I played that silly game kids who are experimenting like to play. We would put our hands over each other's mouth and pretend we were necking. Only for me, it wasn't just play. It made me feel warm and happy; I wanted to move my hand and kiss her for real, smack on the lips. As a young jock, I'd been in close physical contact with guys plenty of times and it had never felt anything like this.

The proverbial lightbulb didn't flash in my head. After we returned home for the summer, I forgot all about what had happened. I lacked the information to understand the ramifications of what I had felt for another girl. If Stephanie had gone to my school, it might have been different. Maybe her presence would have forced me to confront my feelings. I might have erased the whole incident from my mind if lightning hadn't struck again a few years later. This time, my attraction to another girl made me consider for the first time how unfair it was that I could not express openly the feelings I was having for another human being.

The year before I started at East High School in 1981, I attended field hockey camp at Maple Lake near the Poconos. I fell head over heels for a star senior on the team, Martha, whose hazel eyes, sharp sense of humor, and aggressiveness on the field were irresistible. That she was kind and didn't treat me like a rookie simply deepened my feelings. By now, however, I was painfully aware that to let on about my secret crush would be a kind of athletic suicide for me. Even at that young age, the stigma of lesbians in sports pervaded every move we made, every conversation. From locker room jokes about cute guys to dating men, our athletic lives were structured to give the appearance of universal heterosexuality. As the new kid on the block, there was no way I was going to break through that seemingly impermeable barrier to tell a senior that I had a crush on her—no matter how right I felt my feelings were.

I don't remember crying about Martha, but I had a visceral reaction to the unfairness of the situation. My friend Caroline, now an adult living in Harrisburg, has never recovered from the presence of homophobia in high school. Small things can make gay or lesbian kids self-conscious. In the car on the way to the ABC Bowling lanes near school, where Caroline and I competed together on an East High intramural team, I suggested we listen to some tapes. When I opened the glove compartment, several tapes of the lesbian icon Anne Murray fell into my lap. Engaging in a subtle form of homophobia, I laughed at her for having the tapes. "Interesting choice of music," I said half-jokingly, half-seriously. (My boss at the Human Rights Campaign, Elizabeth Birch, actually ran away from home as a young teen specifically to attend an Anne Murray concert.) Caroline and I laugh now about how I contributed to her closetedness back in high school.

This is not to imply that Caroline is today an "out" lesbian. When my interview on *Eye to Eye with Connie Chung* aired in 1995, Caroline jokingly told me she had plans to take her parents out to dinner so they wouldn't be around to watch it. Her fear was that if they knew I was a lesbian—surely they know by now—she'd be guilty by association. As adults, adept at partitioning our lives to avoid the adverse judgments of others, we sometimes carry our self-consciousness about being gay to outrageous lengths, sparking honest cries of "I never knew!" when we finally identify ourselves truthfully. Though Caroline has contributed to her situation, no one should have to live that way.

At that age, girls weren't my sole romantic interest. Boys occasionally caught my attention. I met Robert Frost in the Linglestown Junior High choir just before we graduated to high school. His parents had given him the name of the famous poet, but we all just called him Frosty. Actually, he was anything but frosty. He was this warm, bright, funny, cute guy. I'm not sure exactly what he saw in me. I was still not much more than a pint-size hellion. But we had an intense connection that went well beyond our mutual passions for music and sports. Unlike with my other male friends, I could talk to him about more than just sports and partying. He would actually listen to what I had to say.

Soon after we met, we started "going together." "Where are you two going?" people would ask us as we prepared to head off for an outing. "Together," we would answer. Frosty would come watch my softball and field hockey games. He was a talented musician and a marvelous athlete, equally gifted in basketball and track. He was also black.

Frosty's race, I'm sorry to say, didn't sit well with the mostly white and stuffy Harrisburg-area crowd, as I discovered the hard way at a dance we attended together. Held in the basement of Saint Mark's Church in Colonial Park, with the obligatory punch bowl and boxed-cookie assortment, the dance was chaperoned by parents who cringed when we slow-danced together. They didn't say anything to us directly, but their disapproval was transparent. The worst reaction I had was from some Dauphin kids who derided me as a "nigger lover." If I'd only read Gloria Steinem earlier, I'd have been able to refute their small-minded cries with the classic line, "Are you my alternative?"

Even my own parents didn't think our dating was a good idea, though they never actually forbade me from seeing him. Little did they know at the time, interracial dating would be the least of their discomforts with my love life, such as it was. Actually, I think they were genuinely more concerned about the social stigma I might experience from having a black boyfriend than from the fact that he was black. I soon came to see this argument—an excuse for apartheid—as a cop-out for intolerance on race as well as sexual orientation, even if people make it "in good faith." My experience with Frosty only reinforced my fledgling belief that people who made arbitrary distinctions based on race, sexual orientation, or anything else were the ones with the problem. It was a conviction that would make my own coming-out that much easier.

When Frosty came to our house to meet my parents, we were both nervous that it would be tense. As usual, Mom and Dad came through with flying colors. Dad made a point of shaking Frosty's hand the minute he stepped across the threshold, and Mom fed him cookies. As people of their generation used to say, a good time was had by all. Mom and Dad really had nothing to worry about. Frosty and I never slept together. The most we did was neck at dances and parties. As strong as my feelings were for him, they were nowhere near the intensity of what I would feel for Martha at field hockey camp. I felt affectionate toward Frosty; Martha struck a chord deep in my soul.

Our romance would come to an end a few months later when we went to different high schools. The feelings we had for each other were not strong enough to overcome the boundaries imposed by school districts. But I have to admit that Frosty was not my only boyfriend. From the time we moved to Harrisburg in 1974, one of my best friends had been this neighborhood kid named Brent, to whom I'd introduced myself as "Tom." When he learned that I was a girl, he didn't hold it against me.

In fact, as we hit puberty, he became extremely grateful for my gender. As kids do, we had been fooling around for several years, touching and comparing our bodies. It was all very innocent; more experimental than sexual. It was no fault of Brent's that I viewed our activities quite objectively. I knew then that I did not share the other girls' passion for boys.

I do have at least one thing for which to thank Brent. Like many of his male friends, Brent was already a devoted *Hustler* reader. He was smart enough to know better than to show that sexist crap to me. But one day in 1982, he came across a really gross cartoon depicting Newt's head on an asshole. He thoughtfully passed the magazine on to me. The cartoon depicted Newt as a censorious jerk. It was really the first time I realized that Newt was becoming a national figure, and a despised one at that. (The less-than-respectable *Hustler* was the least of Newt's problems with the press. Two years later, the left-wing magazine *Mother Jones* published a sensational exposé claiming that in 1980, Newt, who was already boasting of his family values, had asked his wife, Jackie, to sign divorce papers while she was in an Atlanta hospital recovering from a second operation for uterine cancer. Newt later confirmed parts of the story.)

On the Kinsey scale of one for completely hetero and six for completely gay, I think of myself as a six. But as my relationships with Frosty and Brent show, human sexuality cannot be reduced to numbers and does not adhere to linear scales. Most people go in three dimensions, depending on a variety of circumstances. Some people will tell you, "It's the person, not the label." I'm not willing to go that far. I think that when pressed, most people will acknowledge leaning one way or the other.

Having found men sexually unsatisfactory and women taboo, I spent the rest of my days at East High in a sexual stupor. Not that it mattered. I was too busy keeping up with all my friends to find the time for dates. I went to the prom with my friend Tim, who was a really nerdy guy whom I knew would never try anything with me. We spent most of the night sneaking into the bathrooms to drink Jim Beam from a silver flask. More than anything, I hated wearing a dress. I'd have felt a lot more comfortable in Tim's tuxedo.

While I didn't wear my sexuality on my sleeve, my real affections weren't entirely invisible, either. My coach, Bee, who had befriended me, must have noticed that something was up because she took me aside for a cautionary tale. Four years earlier, she explained, two women on the team had fallen for each other and begun dating. When the other girls on the team found out, they ostracized them completely. The couple was made to feel so unwelcome that they ended up quitting the team. Apparently, the openness with which the girls displayed their affection for each other hit too close to the bone for the supposedly hetero girls, some of whom might have been struggling with their own latent lesbian yearnings.

Coach, who would go on to become a school principal, was telling me, in so many words, "Watch your back." She didn't want me to make any decision about coming out without carefully considering the potential repercussions. That's a message a lot of young people—in Harrisburg and throughout the nation—internalize, preferring the closet to the "or else" that threatens to derail family support, friendships, career ambitions, and even personal safety. In high school, at least, it was a message that I, too, took deeply to heart.

CHAPTER SIX

LIFE
AND HOW TO LIVE IT

I am human and I need to be loved
Just like everybody else does.

—The Smiths,
"How Soon Is Now"

The biggest difference between high school and college can be summed up in one word: freedom. Away from the restraining influences of parents and small-town mores, college life encourages students to assess the choices available in life and how to make the most of them. This newfound openness allowed me for the first time to explore my true identities, sexual and otherwise.

Back home in Dauphin, gay kids and adults alike had a lot at stake in staying in the closet. I, for one, was dependent on my family and friends for physical and emotional support. As wonderful as Mom and Dad were, I never quite knew how they might react to the *big* revelation. None of us gay kids could really afford to risk losing the support of our parents, which could mean getting kicked out of the house and ending up on the streets. That's why the support of friends and faculty often allows what might be called the floodgates of homosexuality to open wide in college. Indiana University of Pennsylvania, or IUP, was no exception to this rule.

I landed there in the fall of 1984, the year Reagan defeated my beloved Mondale-Ferraro ticket in a legendary landslide. Dad packed all my stuff in the back of the truck and dropped me off two weeks before the start of school, so I could attend preseason hockey camp. I'd like to say I was accepted everywhere I applied, and I chose IUP because I really wanted to go there. The truth was my grades ruled out most prestigious colleges, and IUP was the only college to which I even sent an application. Since it was a state school, Dad could afford the tuition. And having lived in the lively college town as a little girl, I felt at home there. In addition, Roberta had graduated from the school in 1972. If she could handle it, I figured, so could I. It was so comfortable, in fact, that I managed to prolong my stay for five glorious, fun-filled, beer-soaked years.

You would think that Indiana, Pennsylvania, would be a pretty conservative place. And in a lot of ways it was. But like most college towns, it had a wild, libertarian streak that allowed students to explore life to their heart's content. For me, the intellectual, sexual, and even spiritual exploration was taking place both inside and outside the classroom—and, as usual, on the playing field, where I was nominated all-American goalkeeper one season in field hockey. Granted, I wasn't the most serious student in the world, but I did know a good class when I saw one. I started out freshman year intending to study psychology. When I realized that entailed passing probabilities and statistics class, my enthusiasm for the subject quickly waned. I picked sociology instead.

One of my favorites was "Introduction to Sociology" with Brooke Grant, a Grateful Dead–style throwback to the 1960s. The disheveled professor, who was sharp enough to remember teaching my dad the same course two decades earlier, looked as if he had stepped out of Woodstock and into the classroom without coming down from his LSD high. Because Professor Grant had a reputation as a somewhat less than exacting grader, the class was composed of me and about fifteen hulking football players. He used to tell us that finding your "center" through the martial art tai chi was one of the keys to happiness. It was Professor Grant who turned me on to the Buddhist thinker Ram Dass's book *Here and Now.* Along with *Zen and the Art of Motorcycle Maintenance,* this book and the pacifist philosophy it espoused would forever change my outlook.

The essence of Dass's philosophy is that we must all learn to let our troubles evaporate. Some people would simply call this forgiveness, or even laziness, but for Dass it implied some work. Though we may be the products of our past, we should strive not to be its prisoners. "Where are we?" Dass asks rhetorically. "Here," we respond. "What time is it?" "Now." Sounds obvious and corny, but the truth is we don't always live our lives according to these basic tenets. Starting out in college, I never imagined I would become so "woo-woo," as they refer to New Age philosophy in California.

As clichéd as it might seem, Dass's philosophy has really helped me live a happier life. I can't say I had ever been inclined to depression, but I was prone to bouts of anxiety. Since that class, I've led a virtually stress-free life in some pretty stressful times. I learned to say "So what?" if someone derisively calls me a dyke or a bitch. I've learned to let a lot of the criticism I've received for taking on Newt roll right off me and into the gutter where it belongs. My outlook helped me start without major emotional upheavals a new life as a high-profile activist. It's also kept my blood pressure at ninety over sixty and my pulse at sixty-three. Some people, particularly ex-girlfriends, accuse me of being so self-contained as to be unemotional. But it's not that I don't feel things deeply; it's that I don't hold on to bad feelings for long. Since I have pretty good control over my emotions, I rarely get pissed off. Anger is one of the most destructive emotions, unless it's carefully channeled into something productive, like politics. Newt's certainly made it into an art form.

Professor Grant's sociology class coincided with the start of my formal coming-out. While I had been inching out of the closet since Girl Scout camp a decade earlier, I was beginning to take my first steps toward actually articulating my sexual orientation to myself and to those close to me. It helped enormously that I was never ashamed of it. I felt no internalized homophobia; I genuinely loved being who I was. After coming out, many feel a need to make elaborate arguments about why it's okay to be gay. I didn't have to provide evidence; I just knew deep inside me that it was right.

At about the same time, I started a class titled the "Sociology of Human Sexuality." If Professor Grant was Jerry Garcia, Dr. Chauncey Rawleigh was a leprechaun posing as a college professor. His name, one of my all-time favorites, only added to the magical impression. When we entered his class in the spring semester of 1988, Rawleigh had us pull our chairs into a big circle and distributed a sex and perception survey. The questionnaire dealt with our views on everything from male and female role models to same-sex relationships.

That survey opened a Pandora's box. During the first few weeks of class, as part of exercises in talking about our sex lives, two women came out as lesbians. One, a criminology major, wore blue jeans, short-cropped hair, and boots—a typical trendy-young-dyke outfit. The other, sporting a pink jumpsuit, had longish curly hair and stereotypically feminine mannerisms. The difference between the two effectively broke down any remaining stereotypes the class, myself included, may have harbored about the appearance and demeanor of lesbians. Accustomed to derogatory references to homosexuality, I reveled in the nonjudgmental manner with which the rest of the class handled the women's disclosures. Maybe it was possible, I thought, to be accepted as a lesbian.

It's a funny thing: from my Girl Scout kiss at age ten, I had suspected that I was attracted to women. Hearing these women talk so candidly and unashamedly about their sexual orientation should have provided the opening I needed to declare my own. I couldn't have asked for a more supportive environment. Yet something was still holding me back from echoing their revelations. For most people, coming out is a very personal and unpredictable process. Some kids feel perfectly comfortable declaring their homosexuality at age twelve. By contrast, Marvin Liebman, the prominent conservative organizer who was a close friend of William F. Buckley Jr.'s, did not come out publicly until his sixty-seventh birthday. Others go to their graves with their secrets. My own coming-out was more process than declaration; more brook than waterfall.

Despite my reticence, Dr. Rawleigh's provocative sex questionnaire gave me a definite nudge in the right direction. As I answered the questions, it became increasingly clear to me that I was destined for dyke-dom—and soon. My responses to nearly every item about emotional or sexual stimulation and fantasies leaned heavily toward the female. The survey helped me to become more specific about my feelings instead of wandering aimlessly in a haze of self-doubt.

Understanding my attraction to women was not all I took away from the class. It also sharpened my comprehension of the connection between sex and politics and formed the basis of a philosophy that would deepen as I made my full-time leap into gay activism. One of the best exercises we did was thinking up slang words for the male and female anatomy. As we would shout them out, Dr. Rawleigh would scribble them on the blackboard. The point was to show that slang words are often used in a sexist manner. The penis, for example, has dozens of cute and ironic synonyms for it—*willie* and *trouser hoagie*, to name just a few—while the clitoris and the vagina have very few, most of them crude and derogatory.

Another formative class was Professor Thompson's "American

Women and Sport." By this point I was pretty much out to most of my friends at IUP. The three-hour class would meet every Wednesday night. After class, a bunch of us, sometimes including Ms. Thompson, would go to the Gazebo, a restaurant off campus. Over pizza and beer, we'd sit at a huge mahogany booth and discuss women's issues and politics late into the night. The combination of intellectual conversation, close friends, and the warm pub atmosphere made those some of my most exhilarating nights in college. Much to my relief, the subject of Newt never came up.

Had I taken more traditional political science courses, I would have realized that Newt was making some astonishing political gains during my college years. In 1987, for instance, he launched a campaign to unseat House Speaker Jim Wright by charging him with a series of House ethics violations, including converting $100,000 in campaign funds to personal accounts and receiving an inflated advance for his book, *Reflections of a Public Man*. Amid diminished support from the Democratic majority, Wright resigned in June 1989. Three months later, Newt was elected minority whip by his Republican colleagues, laying the groundwork for his ascension to the Speakership.

But far from these dramas in Washington, D.C., I was experiencing crucibles of my own. My writing assignments were beginning to reflect my growing confidence in my sexual orientation. In the "Psychology of Human Sexuality" with Dr. Maureen McHugh the semester before graduation in 1989, I wrote a paper on my sexual attitudes in which I identified myself as a lesbian. "I am proud that I am a woman identified woman, and the important people in my life know that and still accept me," I wrote. "It has been one of the best feelings in the world knowing that I'm comfortable with myself."

The right wing argues that such classes reflect a liberal bias, contribute to promiscuity on college campuses, and cause a plethora of other supposedly grievous social problems. But I see them as providing to young people a clearer understanding of the world, helping them to recognize the power vested in language and the tilted state of the sexual playing field. Maybe students who opted for classes like these— over self-congratulatory history courses such as the ones Newt taught as a college professor—would pass on fewer harmful ideas about sex to their children.

Even the relatively simplistic discussion about pet names for sex organs is a good example. We often attach nicknames to objects that provoke discomfort. But for kids, the use of euphemisms simply reinforces discomfort. When parents teach their two-year-old son, for instance, that he has a "wee-wee" instead of a penis, it mystifies his anatomy in a way that may affect him throughout his life. What happens when the boy hits puberty and doesn't understand how his body is changing and why? Diminution of the penis may help parents deal with their son's body, but it doesn't help the boy ask questions about sex and sexuality honestly and without shame.

That's why I was such a big fan of former surgeon general Dr. Joycelyn Elders for saying that masturbation is "part of something that should be taught" in the nation's schools as an HIV-prevention measure. It's also why I was so disappointed when President Clinton, bowing to pressure from the newly elected Republican majority in Congress, gave her the boot in late 1994. (Asked where Newt, who was one of those calling for her ouster, might fall in studies showing that 90 percent of Americans masturbate, she responded, "He might be in the other ten percent." Thankfully, that's a question I can't answer.)

Elders was also famous for saying that "gay sex is good, gay sex is wonderful," and for endorsing same-sex marriage. Statements like these earned her a spot in the magnificent mural on the women's building in San Francisco, alongside other female heroines, such as Eleanor Roosevelt and the African-American lesbian writer Audre Lorde. I couldn't agree more with Dr. Elders that both parents and teachers should teach that masturbation is okay. Kids need to understand their own bodies before they share them with others. Going into the dating world without sex ed, especially in the age of AIDS and widespread teen pregnancy, is like owning a gun without taking a safety course first. It's a recipe for disaster.

The mystification of sex hurts everyone, I think, but does particular disservice to women and girls. It never ceases to amaze me that there are thousands of women out there, both gay and straight, who have been having sex for decades without achieving orgasm because they don't know what makes their body feel pleasurable or because they don't know the terms for discussing it. But the problem is certainly not exclusive to women. A straight male friend at another college could achieve orgasm only through vaginal penetration. Once he learned how to ejaculate through masturbation—with his own two hands, so to speak, as instructed by a gay male friend—he felt an enormous sense of relief, literally. No longer did he feel compelled to spend his nights mindlessly chasing women from whom he wanted only one thing. I'm sure his cast of female sex partners was equally relieved.

The other advantage we onanists have is that knowing what feels good helps us to better understand a partner's needs. This, of course, is particularly true of lesbians and gay men because our sexual responses are usually more familiar to one another than opposite-sex partners'. As a *Seinfeld* episode suggested, it's easier to operate a machine if you already know the equipment.

There's an outdated health book, once distributed to college freshmen, that claims that lesbians can't really enjoy sex because "zero plus zero equals zero." It's one of those old antilesbian canards, suggesting that since there's no penis involved, sex between women must not be any fun. It also reaffirms the myth of vaginal versus clitoral orgasms. Men don't want to believe that women can have orgasms without them simply by stimulating their own clitoris or having another woman do so. When it comes to sex roles, straight people have a lot to learn from gay people. (It can, of course, work the other way around as well.) I know I'm biased, but I can't think of anything more beautiful than two women making love.

There's something especially nonviolent and noncompetitive about it when you compare it to the more conventional types of heterosexual lovemaking. There's repetitive motion involved, but neither partner is subjugated, as is sometimes the case in hetero intercourse. Neither are there preassigned roles. In political terms, it's democratic sex. Of course that's only part of the story. There certainly are lesbians who like to mimic heterosexual roles using sex toys. I don't think there is necessarily anything wrong with that either, as long as both partners are aware of what's going on. And I don't mean to imply that hetero relationships can't be democratic, too. My bet is that a lot of opposite-sex couples rely on oral sex or mutual masturbation in ways that are little different from what same-sexers do in bed. Women these days are much less likely to allow themselves to be the sexual property of their husbands or boyfriends. They know they deserve pleasure as much as men do, and there's little pleasure in forever being passive.

(Newt seems to understand sex-role reversals. In the uncorrected galleys for Newt's novel *1945*, he describes a graphic sex scene between John Mayhew, a treasonous presidential aide, and his sexy girlfriend, a Nazi spy named Erica von Strasse. "Suddenly, the pouting sex kitten gave way to Diana the Huntress," my big brother writes. "She rolled onto him and somehow was sitting athwart his chest, her knees pinning his shoulders." Okay, Newt, whatever turns you on!)

The equality of sex roles often translates into the durability of the relationship. That's one reason I object so strenuously to the "family values" crusade's emphasis on the style of a family over its substance. Nothing about a "traditional" heterosexual unit makes it better than a "nontraditional" homosexual unit. What counts is what goes on inside the family. Are the relationships within it based on values like love, compassion, and equality? If you judge people exclusively on the way they treat one another, it becomes much more difficult to make distinctions along gay-straight lines. Using that standard, I believe, would benefit us all.

PART TWO

AWAKENINGS

CHAPTER SEVEN

"IMAGINE MY SURPRISE . . ."

Women are thick and rich and full of hidden treasures.

—RITA MAE BROWN,
Rubyfruit Jungle

When it came to actually knowing how to perform in bed, I'm embarrassed to admit that I got my first lessons from a surprising source: the racist, misogynist, antigay late comedian Sam Kinison. In my feminist sociology courses, we read all these wonderfully highbrow feminist authors such as Carol Gilligan, Adrienne Rich, and Gloria Steinem. But no one spoke about the actual mechanics of sex, let alone the comparatively exotic nuances of lesbian sex. Even Lonnie Barbach's enlightening health book *For Yourself*, which teaches women how to enjoy sex and their bodies, was silent on the subject.

On our road trips to field hockey games in the beat-up school van, we would spend hours listening to tapes. Usually, we would listen to bands like R.E.M., the Grateful Dead, or whatever happened to be popular at the time. I don't know if the left or the right will be offended by the confession that we would sometimes take a kind of perverse pleasure in listening to Sam Kinison's rants. His irreverence, when we were able to overlook his many prejudices, fit our outlook on life as rowdy college jocks. His most hideous joke at the time was about starving Ethiopians. "You live in a desert," he would scream at the top of his lungs. "No wonder you don't have any food. Move!" The absurdity of it was part of what made it funny to us. You could never quite tell if he was ridiculing or endorsing racist stereotypes.

But Kinison's skit about going down on his girlfriends especially caught my attention.

"You do the alphabet with your tongue," he said. "A, B, C, D—oh, they love Mr. T. 'Oh, Sam, do the letter *T* again,' " the women would respond, Kinison joked. Since I still had not even gotten to first base with a girl, Mr. T was still far in the future. But one day, I knew, Kinison's joke would come in quite handy.

April 16, 1987. I recall the date precisely because I considered it my official coming-out kiss. My friends Bob and Allie and I took a short road trip to Bob's hometown, about a forty-five-minute drive from Indiana. We were to stay at Bob's apartment there. With me in the middle, we all sat in the front of Bob's beater of a car, which we affectionately dubbed "Motel Hell." As with most college kids, road-tripping was one of our favorite things to do, so we were all in a giddy mood. For no particular reason, we'd often drive for hours in search of those fabled covered bridges indigenous to Pennsylvania. Along the way during this particular trip, we stopped at a grocery store so Bob could buy some pretzels and chips.

When Bob returned to the car, she found Allie and me all over each other, kissing and necking passionately. In my excitement, I didn't know who initiated the kiss or how Allie knew I was attracted to her, since I hadn't even told her I was a lesbian. All I recall is the sweet taste of her mouth and her overpowering cologne. Kissing Allie was one of those "wow" experiences that blew my mind. It felt like my first kiss with Frosty years before, only more real and permanent. And like my masturbation experience more than a decade earlier, I knew that sex with women was something that would never grow dull, at least with the right woman. Getting into the car, Bob, who had long suspected I was a lesbian, exclaimed, with a huge smile on her face, "Imagine my surprise . . ."

Later that night at Bob's, Allie and I made a drunken attempt at sex, which went nowhere. In what Dr. Ruth would describe as tribadism, we groped around a little bit, rubbing up against each other for stimulation, the kind of tentative sex that kids often have as teenagers. Since Bob was sleeping on the floor in the same room, our movement was severely limited. As we were both fully clothed, the whole thing didn't amount to much. Obviously not meant for each other, Allie and I went our own ways after that night.

The truth, as the saying goes, had finally set me free. I went home that summer of 1987 and informed all my friends of my discovery. Nine out of ten of them said, "What took you so long?" or "It's about time" or "Why didn't you tell me earlier?" I don't think I got a single negative reaction. Bob, who was already out, guided me through this period with aplomb. In that dizzying summer, my lesbian friends and I spent a lot of time at the D-Gem, the local women's bar.

Somewhat unintentionally, I soon came out to my parents and sisters as well. In my excitement over finally coming to terms with myself, I began buying gay and lesbian periodicals such as *The Advocate*, the *Washington Blade*, the *Baltimore Gay Paper*, and anything else I could get my hands on at a women's bookstore near the city. Cleaning my room one day, Mom found the *Lavender Letter*, a Harrisburg periodical that described events in the local women's community. When I returned home from work one day, she confronted me with her discovery. Mom's initial reaction was not one of unconditional acceptance. She said all the stereotypical things like "It's my fault" and "You just haven't met the right man" and other comments like that.

But since Mom is a very tolerant and loving person, it didn't take her long to come around to my side. Though I'm still not sure she understands exactly what it means to be a lesbian, she has been very supportive. (In 1995, she was quoted saying, "I accept Candy . . . But I do wish that she would be—how should I say it?—*natural*." I was miffed until I realized it came more out of ignorance than anything else.) One of the best clues that everything was okay with me was that I was happier than I'd ever been. I literally sailed through the summer. In the end, my happiness was what mattered to Mom and Dad.

My sister Roberta was more confused than anything else. For the first time in her life, she realized that she knew nothing about homosexuality. She tried to be supportive, although she later told me that she would have been better prepared if I'd said I was having sex with the entire football team. Roberta and Susan quickly got up to speed. It wasn't long before Roberta was telling my nieces Emily and Susan, not yet ten, about me and assuring them that "some people love the opposite sex, and other people happen to love the same sex, but we are all just human beings."

Not long afterward, Mom informed Newt about my declaration. Like my sisters, he reacted with love and support. According to Mom, Newt said, "That's fine. Candace should live life the way she pleases." As Mom pointed out, on a personal level, Newt has always been nonjudgmental.

Unbeknownst to me at the time, however, Newt was already building bridges with the Christian right, which was beginning to assert itself as a force in the Republican Party after years of underground organizing. The Christian Coalition would not be founded for two more years, but like the astute politician he is, he had identified an important element in the conservative constituency he hoped would one day make him Speaker of the House. To be frank, I don't know whether he thought of my revelation as a threat to his ties to religious conservatives.

It wasn't long before I was immersed in my first full-fledged relationship. That April, I met Ann Ashley at rugby practice. I noticed right away that she was cute, had a great sense of humor, and carried herself with the confidence of the good athlete she was. Still, I didn't spend much time thinking about her or arranging amorous meetings. For me, at least, it wasn't love at first sight because I don't believe in that so-called phenomenon. That whole concept is a lot of crap. People may feel lust at first sight, but not love. A person needs to know an awful lot about someone to really find love. I've never even been able to find someone physically attractive enough to sleep with until I knew what she was like as a human being, not just as a body. I know that may sound old-fashioned, but that's just me. That's one of the reasons it took me so long to find the right person with whom to share my body. Sex for me is not about genitalia; it's about comfort, security, and love.

Lest I sound like the lesbian version of Lou Sheldon, I want to make it clear that I would never pass judgment on people who choose to behave different from me. I openly admit that I'm a bit reserved when it comes to sex and my choice of partners. Plenty of people—gay and straight—are more driven by lust than I. As long as consenting adults practice safe sex and respect each other's limits, whatever happens between them is none of anyone else's business. Sexual choices are intensely private; only a person knows what's right for herself. There's nothing inherently wrong with exploring sexuality to one's heart's content. Many people go through periods in life, especially in youth, when casual sex is an important part of their identity. The only caveat I suggest is that the sex be safe and that both partners understand that it entails no enduring bond; that neither is under the illusion that the other is in love. This is when people get hurt unnecessarily. As to why people behave in so many different ways when it comes to sex, I'll leave that to Masters and Johnson and Shere Hite.

Upon our return to campus in the fall of 1987, Ann and I began dating. We used to have parties at an apartment a bunch of us frequented at R-1136 Philadelphia Street or "Ho"—as in "Homo"—Central as we called it. One night, after everyone had left, Ann and I were left alone on the couch. Fully clothed, we rolled around. Let's just say that Ann was more successful than I. Once again, I was proceeding cautiously; too cautiously for Ann, who pursued me relentlessly, professing true love.

Succeeding only in heightening the expectations of us both, I would barely let her touch me for three full months. I guess I felt a little intimidated. Ann had been sexually active since she came out at sixteen, while I was still a "virgin," at least with women. I was afraid that if I really let myself go, I would make a fool of myself in front of her. By Christmas break, we still hadn't really had sex, just more awkward tribadism. Finally, I relented and we consummated our relationship: another "wow" experience. All I can say is that Sam Kinison was right.

More important than the sex, though, was the feeling of family we were able to bring to each other's life. There's an old joke about lesbian dating:

"What does a lesbian bring to her second date?"

"A U-Haul."

(The twist on the joke goes something like this: "Why is that joke about lesbians and moving in together a lot of nonsense? No self-respecting lesbian needs to *rent* a truck. She already *owns* one!")

Looking back, I think Ann and I lent some credence to the joke. Ann's family lived on a small farm in Indiana County. During my senior year in 1989, we slept almost every night in a single bed in her childhood bedroom at her family's cluttered and cozy, ranch-style home. The room had a sweeping view of the vast countryside, where we could see deer graze on wild grass. Since I was investing little in my studies, I had plenty of time to help them shovel snow in the winter and mow the lawn in the summer.

For years, Ann had had her share of emotional unhappiness. Suspecting that their daughter's problems stemmed from her sexual orientation, Mr. and Mrs. Ashley sent Ann to Doctor Edgar, a specialist in "reparative therapy" who they hoped would "cure" her. In his Freudian psych class at IUP, Dr. Edgar taught that male homosexuality is the result of a smothering mother and a distant father. Whatever he believed the cause of lesbianism to be, he was no help to Ann. The treatment, in fact, was worse than the symptoms. Ann remained a lesbian, only she felt worse about it than when she began. To their credit, Ann's parents quickly realized that her problems had nothing to do with her sexual orientation. Once they realized that it was not a "phase" and simply accepted her for who she was, they more readily accepted me into their lives, as well.

The Ashleys seemed genuinely grateful I was there to provide a calming influence on their daughter. Ann and I would go play bingo at the local church with Mrs. Ashley. On Sundays, we'd settle into the living room to watch an afternoon of football with Mr. Ashley. It was an idyllic life, a kind of never-ending lesbian episode of *The Waltons*. But like all good things, our life together would eventually have to come to an end.

CHAPTER EIGHT

"JESUS CAN'T PLAY RUGBY"

[Sports are] the ultimate metaphor for life.

—BILL BRADLEY,
U.S. senator and former
pro basketball player

Pacifism may lower your blood pressure, but I don't think Gandhi ever played rugby. There is a time and place for controlled violence, and that's on the playing field. During coed phys ed classes back in high school, we were often presented with two choices of activities: volleyball with the girls or flag football with the guys. As a big fan of contact sports, I, of course, chose football. In one of my few shining academic moments, I received an A from my phys ed teacher, who watched me repeatedly dive headfirst for fumbles. As for pent-up stress, there's no release valve quite like rugged physical contact on a playing field.

So I guess it's no surprise that I would become fanatical about rugby, the most aggressive sport of all. (A popular bumper sticker reads GIVE BLOOD, PLAY RUGBY.) One day in the fall semester of 1986 at Indiana University, on my way to field hockey practice, I was running past the women's rugby practice and saw several women smashing one another ferociously. I was transfixed. One of my housemates, Colleen, a rugby player, motioned me over to join them on the field. I had to get to hockey practice, which suddenly seemed hopelessly tame by comparison, but I knew I would be back.

That spring, I was the first to sign up. I was so excited that I jogged a mile from my house through the rain just to get to the first practice. I didn't realize how complicated the game really is: the official rugby rule book has over two hundred pages to memorize! (Not that anyone ever does.) Rugby originated in 1823 on the playing fields of Rugby School, England, when a student picked up a soccer ball with his hands and began running downfield, only to be tackled by teammates. The game is a mixture of soccer and American football. A player may pass the ball only to the sides or to a receiver behind herself. Unlike American football, play is virtually continuous.

My progression through positions on the field corresponded to my growing expertise. As a beginner, I played wing, one of the less demanding positions. Later, I played hooker, whose job it is to "win" the ball in scrum. There's often a presumption in athletics that if you are small, you must be fast, like the diminutive basketball player Muggsy Bogues, who can practically run between the legs of bigger players. I prove this presumption wrong. I was, and continue to be, *slow.* What I lacked in speed and agility, I made up for in aggressiveness and determination. Basically, I would play anywhere and do anything, including sacrificing my body, to help the team. Actually, the idea of players sacrificing their bodies in rugby is redundant—because that's what the game is about.

From rugby, I learned an important lesson that I would later bring to my jobs at United Parcel Service and my political activism. Hard work and aggressiveness can overcome perceived weaknesses and even the most daunting of odds. When friends and family fret over the physical danger inherent in being a well-known lesbian activist, I remind them that I played rugby and am inured to pain. It's going to take a lot more than mere threats to take me away from activism.

The irony of rugby is that it frustrates truly violent impulses with restraints imposed by the rules. Rugby isn't as dangerous as American football, but it's not exactly safe either. From broken fingers to hamstring pulls to a dislocated shoulder, I was always playing through pain. Once, I was running with the ball when a woman from the opposing team tackled me hard but clean, and we both landed with our combined weights on my right shoulder. It felt as if someone had hammered a railroad spike through it. When the shoulder popped right back into the socket, I figured it was just a bad bruise. Downing a couple of Motrins, I played three more games that day. I could move my arm up and down, it wasn't making any noises, and nothing was poking out of my shoulder. In retrospect, playing was stupid, but my motto has always been that I won't leave the pitch voluntarily.

As I was showering after the postgame party later that night, I noticed that my entire shoulder had turned black-and-blue. I said, "Gee, that doesn't look very good," and Ann insisted on driving me to the hospital immediately. As the Washington Bullets basketball star Chris Webber, who has lost the better part of two seasons to a shoulder separation, has discovered, full recovery can be tricky. Because the shoulder had immediately returned to its normal position, the doctor prescribed rest, more pain suppressants, and physical therapy. At that time, I was working part-time at UPS, which required heavy lifting. When I discovered the company's health insurance didn't cover physical therapy, I rehabilitated my shoulder quite nicely by lifting thousands of fifty-pound boxes. It was soon as good as new.

While violence may not find an easy outlet in the play itself, it often gains expression after the whistle blows, especially when teammate loyalties are involved. Taking my cue from Bob, I earned a reputation for fierce loyalty and scrappiness. But I would never fight—unless pushed to the limit. During a game at Penn State, an opposing player stomped on Ann's stomach in the middle of a ruck, obviously on purpose, with malice. As soon as play was halted, I tackled the offending player—though I refrained from pummeling her—to make the point that no one takes cheap shots at our players. With a few exceptions, I spent a lot more time breaking up fights than initiating them. Bob, who's twice my size, served as the team enforcer. Women's rugby tends to be a lot less violent than men's because women recognize that it's about skill, passing, and timing. We liked to leave the gratuitous displays of physical superiority—and outbursts of brutality—to the guys.

There's a saying among rugby partisans: "It's not just a game, it's a way of life." Even better than the game itself was the camaraderie of the players during and after it. It was like being in the best sorority on campus, only we did more than just waste time, woo boys by looking pretty, and throw splashy parties. After games we would shower and hit the pubs for a night of drinking. In rugby, there is a postgame ritual known as the third half. Players spend the first two halves trying to physically dominate their opponents, and the third half bonding with them.

I must admit that in our enthusiasm we sometimes mimicked the worst adolescent pranks most often associated with male athletes. During a tournament at Slippery Rock near Pittsburgh, Ann injured her back. We all clambered into a big old station wagon and followed the ambulance to the hospital in Grove City. To relieve the boredom of waiting for her release, we made human pyramids in the parking lot and took photos. One of our teammates, who was more than a little inebriated, got caught stealing a holiday decoration. The hospital sent a letter to the IUP dean complaining that we were doing "acrobatic pyramids and stealing decorative pumpkins." Duly chastened, we apologized in a letter to the dean, but we laughed for years about the rather stilted description of our antics. We were never as outrageous as the male team, which got caught stealing cadavers from the science lab and placing them on the field before the opposing team arrived for the game. (There's a saying that rugby players "eat their dead." I'm not sure what the guys did with the bodies, but that's the saying.)

I even had a couple of scraps with the law. Every spring IUP students would barricade an apartment complex, back in a beer truck, and throw a huge, all-day block party. One year a bunch of us from the rugby team were enjoying the free flow of beer when the police, who had received complaints from townies, arrived to shut down the festivities. In my first act of civil disobedience, I stood in front of the beer truck, blocking its departure. After debating with the kind officer the consequences of an arrest on my already dubious academic future, I abandoned my protest and headed off to the pub with my friends.

Rugby has an extra-special place in my heart because so many of the players I met were lesbians and were extremely comfortable with who they were. At that point in my life, I'd never met a group of people who were so matter-of-fact about their sexual orientation. The confidence they had gained from their accomplishments on the field made them equally fearless off it. Without their support and example, my protracted coming-out would have been prolonged even further.

Led by the outspoken Bob, the gay and straight women on the team had zero patience for the antilesbian stereotypes that dominate women's sports. More than just about anyone, Bob helped me gain the self-confidence to stick up for myself. From defending teammates on the rugby field to her fierce loyalty for her friends in everyday life, she was the kind of woman anyone would want on her side. Instead of giving in to the stereotype by trying to hide from it—as so many gay and nongay women athletes do—she reveled in it. She seemed to understand instinctively what it's taken me years to understand in a political context. To hide your identity is to be complicit with the very people who would keep you down. When you stand up to the bigots, it robs them of their power. "We're lesbians, deal with it" was the attitude she took. That strategy came in handy when a straight teammate tried to wrest control of the club away from us.

In the fall of 1988, we received word that someone had applied to organize a women's rugby team. Since we had already formed a team and begun practice, we were puzzled. We soon learned that the team treasurer, Tracey, had made the request. When we confronted her, she complained to the assistant director of student affairs that lesbians had "taken over" the rugby team. Apparently she had been traumatized by the sight of two women from the team holding hands at a rugby party. Outraged, we demanded that the team remain under our control. The faculty adviser reassured us that the sexual orientation of the players was of no concern to the school, and since it was obviously Tracey who had the problem, the team should stay as it was.

We figured that the lesbian-baiting may simply have been a convenient cover for her attempt to gain control of the team. That homophobic attacks often get used as diversions in conflicts over power control was a lesson I would carry with me into activism. That incident was also one of my first brushes with practical politics. If the adviser had not satisfied our demand to honor our team and have Tracey removed, Bob and I were ready and determined to come out to the school newspaper and begin a political crusade on the team's behalf.

That was the last we ever saw of Tracey. She probably graduated and joined Concerned Women for America. We got our revenge by incorporating her into the rugby song, sung to the tune of "The Battle Hymn of the Republic," and passed on to us by St. Bonaventure's rugby team. The lines are recited at the beginning of each stanza to "Mine eyes have seen the glory . . ." The chorus is "Three cheers for all the ruggers," instead of "Glory, glory, hallelujah."

> *Jesus can't play rugby because the ball goes through his hands . . .*
> *Jesus can't play rugby because he wears illegal headgear . . .*
> *Tracey can't play rugby because she is a homophobe . . .*

While we vanquished Tracey with relative ease, most antilesbian innuendos die hard. During a game at Penn State, we were being shellacked by the Nittany Lions, our then archrival, by something like sixty-five to zero. Frustrated, we were hitting a little harder than necessary, playing to the hilt the role of schoolyard nasties. Walking off the field after the game, we overheard one of the Penn State mothers, sitting in a lawn chair, say, "At least our girls wear nail polish." All we could do was look at one another in disbelief at such a farcical challenge to our femininity. Still, the combination of the humiliating loss and the numskull comment meant that we went out of our way not to schedule a Penn State game the next year. Though arguably more talented, they didn't deserve to share a field with us.

Of all the women's sports, rugby has generally been the most accepting of lesbians. The reasons are pretty obvious. For one, the ruggedness necessary to play rugby makes it a lot harder to put forward an archetypically "feminine" image. Second, since rugby is not yet a big-time National Collegiate Athletic Association sport, with budgets, advertising, and high-stakes recruiting, there is less temptation to play into the prejudices of some athletes, parents, and conservative fans. Few are concerned about lesbians' ruining the image of women's rugby because it doesn't really have an image in the first place, with the possible exception of the "macho" one that some male players have given it.

Such a tolerant attitude makes rugby the exception to the de facto lesbian ban in big-time college sports. Penn State women's basketball coach Rene Portland, one of the winningest coaches in college basketball since taking over the team more than a decade ago, is also one of college sports' worst bigots. In March of 1991, the *Philadelphia Inquirer* reported that Portland does not allow lesbians to join her team, *ever*. According to an unnamed source quoted in the paper, Portland "tells you, flat out, 'I don't have any appreciation for the homosexual life-style and I won't have that on my team.'" The story was especially believable because in 1986 Portland told the *Chicago Sun-Times,* "I will not have [lesbians] in my program." During recruiting visits, she said, "I bring [the ban on lesbian players] up, and the kids are so relieved, and the parents are so relieved. But they would probably go without asking the question otherwise, which is really dumb."

What's truly dumb is that Portland would make recruiting decisions based on something besides sheer ability. Let me get this right. If Nancy Lieberman, Martina Navratilova's former trainer and flame, who was one of the best women's basketball players ever, had tried out for Portland's team in her prime, she would have been cut. "Sorry, Nancy, I know you would probably assure Penn State a national championship, but because of what you do in the privacy of your bedroom, we simply can't have you around," Portland would have told her.

Rather than supporting women's basketball, Portland was dragging it into the gutter. Judging women on their sexual orientation rather than on their athletic ability undermines women's athletics generally and promotes baseless fears.

The other glaring gap in Portland's logic is that she has no idea which of her players are in fact lesbians. All she is doing is making sure that her players, many of whom are surely still coming to grips with their sexual orientations, hide their identity from their coach, who is supposed to provide leadership and support. What's even more galling is that Portland has a national reputation as a leader in the fight for equality between men's and women's athletics. The use of antilesbian prejudice to justify unequal treatment for women's sports is totally lost on Portland. Whether she is able to hide the lesbian presence in college sports is of little consequence to critics of women's sports. The absence of a Penn State policy forbidding this type of antigay bias has made it more difficult for the school to put an end to Portland's abuses, once again demonstrating how vulnerable gays and lesbians are to discrimination without explicit protections in force.

As liberal as its participants tend to be, women's rugby is not entirely immune from the same mentality. According to the November 1995 edition of *Rugby,* a newspaper published in New York, a New Mexico team was debating bucking tradition by wearing skirts instead of shorts with their team uniforms to more firmly establish their "femininity." As a smart reader pointed out, it would have been more honest for the team to replace the word *femininity* with *heterosexuality.* I had always been attracted to athletics because it offered a refuge from prejudice: on the playing field, more than anywhere else, everyone was equal. The idea that the higher someone goes in sports, the more likely it is that fairness will fall victim to appearances was a hard one for me to swallow.

Maybe that's why professional team sports still lack a single openly gay or lesbian athlete. While Martina Navratilova, Olympic gold medalist Greg Louganis, and most recently, Muffin Spencer-Devlin, a veteran golf pro, have broken down barriers in individual sports, team sports have made little progress. Dave Pallone contends that he could field an entire team, coaching staff, and front office with the gay men he knows from his days as a major-league baseball umpire. I don't doubt it; rumors have swirled for several years about certain stars in several sports. Chicago Bulls forward Dennis Rodman, who has spoken in interviews of putting a dollar in the G-string of a go-go boy at a gay club, has probably come the closest, though no one quite knows whether the man with the pink hair is actually gay or just teasing the press. Then there is that Dallas Cowboys star who always seems on the verge of holding a press conference. (Not Deion Sanders, I'm sorry to say.) Someday, the team sports barrier, too, will fall. I just hope it happens in my lifetime.

I'm not holding my breath. I'm too big a pro-sports fan to spend all my time fretting about the plight of closeted gay athletes with million-dollar contracts. My favorite athlete in the world is Neon Deion, as he is known to aficionados everywhere. Over his career, I've collected every scrap of Deion sports memorabilia I could lay my hands on—his Kenner figurine in an Atlanta Braves uniform; his Nike Air Diamond turf sneakers, which feature a miniature likeness of Deion in the bubble on the sole; a Falcons jersey with SANDERS emblazoned on the back. I've got a big green binder with plastic-covered slots for just about every Deion trading card ever made. In it are Deion's rookie card, cards from his stints with the Yankees, Braves, Falcons, Reds, Giants, and finally, Cowboys. If I ever had a baby boy, I'd seriously consider naming him Deion.

My obsession with Deion has become so obvious that Mom has started calling him my "boy" and my "boyfriend." During Mom's trip to Georgia to help out on Newt's reelection campaign a few years ago, she brought me back a sharp red, black, and gold Nike jacket, with a gold DEION emblazoned across the back. Mom was clearly hoping against hope that my enthusiasm for this athlete would mean that I wanted to start dating men. (This is just more wishful thinking on Mom's part, but I have to admit she's come a long way. After discouraging me from dating Frosty, she now apparently thinks that dating a black man is better than dating any kind of woman.)

People may rightly wonder why on earth a serious lesbian activist would idolize a pampered pro athlete who publicly brags about his $35-million contract and rarely makes a peep about politics. For one thing, I admire the fact that he has been able to achieve a two-sport career. As someone who has tried to perform in multiple sports myself, I know how hard it is to excel in one sport alone. To succeed in not just one but *two* pro sports is nothing short of amazing. My feelings for Deion are not unlike my feelings for Newt. Despite the fact that I disagree with a lot of what he says, I have to admire his ability, his drive, and his commitment to succeed.

Though Deion is prone to shameless boasting, he's actually the consummate team player. When the young lefty Steve Avery, who came into the leagues as a country bumpkin, showed up as a rookie with the Braves several years ago, Deion took him under his wing, spiriting him around town and showing him how to dress like the star he would soon become. Deion's always sacrificing·his own stats for the sake of the team. That's why he's played on so many winners. Success, as far as I'm concerned, rests more on teamwork and collaboration than on self-interest.

Believe it or not, I've actually had a few brushes with Deion. Two years ago, Newt generously got me tickets at RFK Stadium in Washington to see the Redskins play the Falcons, for whom Deion played at the time. (I hope the whole family doesn't take similar advantage of Newt's generosity. After Newt took Mom to a Braves World Series game in Atlanta last year, she asked him, "So when do we go to the Super Bowl?" Newt could only shake his head.) After the game, in the hope of snagging an autograph from Deion, I hung out with a bunch of fans by the tunnel from which the players depart. As we were all standing there, a couple of kids who couldn't have been much past sixteen were bad-mouthing my hero.

Fed up, I told them to shove it.

One of the kids responded, referring to me, "What does this little boy think he's going to do? Kick our butts or something?"

I shot back, "I'm a woman, twenty-seven years old, and you don't want to know." That was, I'm proud to say, the end of that.

Another brush came last year when I was staying at some fancy uptown Manhattan hotel, compliments of *Good Morning America*, on which I was making one of my first nationally televised appearances. I'd worked at the Harrisburg UPS plant until one in the morning, showered, hopped in a limo sent by the show, grabbed an hour or so of sleep during the drive, and arrived at the hotel. By six-thirty in the morning, I was in the lobby with a public relations guy, waiting to be picked up and driven to the studio for the taping.

Suddenly, a huge entourage of extremely well-dressed people appeared in the lobby. In the middle stood Deion, dressed in an autumn brown leather jacket with gold jewelry everywhere. I knew he was in town because he'd appeared on *Saturday Night Live* two nights before. I was so nervous I could hardly talk and ended up blowing my chance to ask him for an autograph. The PR guy, misinterpreting my mood swing, asked me what the matter was. Was I suddenly nervous about the show?

"No," I said, pointing toward the entourage. "I'm nervous because that's Deion Sanders over there." Not being a sports fan, he didn't get it. With regard to the autograph, neither did I. Second chances are hard to come by, and that, I vowed, would be the last one I'd ever squander.

CHAPTER NINE

WORKING FOR A LIVING

> I stand here ironing,
> and what you ask me
> moves tormented back
> and forth with the iron . . .
> There is all that life that has
> happened outside of me, beyond me.
>
> —TILLIE OLSEN,
> "I Stand Here Ironing"

It had taken me five years, but I finally did it. The combination of good old-fashioned slacking off, frequent road trips for field hockey and rugby matches, and flunking Dr. Edgar's antigay psychology class (among others) had made my academic life something of an adventure. Nonetheless, in May of 1989, Indiana University of Pennsylvania bestowed a B.A. in sociology on me.

The actual ceremony was anticlimactic, since most of my friends had graduated on time the year before. Still, it was a brilliant spring day at the university football stadium, where, appropriately enough, the ceremony was held; I'm embarrassed to admit that, having had a few too many celebratory beers, I can't even recall what VIP delivered the commencement address. With the exception of Newt, tied up as usual with Capitol Hill business, my entire family was on hand to celebrate with me. Always the thoughtful older brother, Newt sent a sweet card with a check.

The nicest thing about the weekend was that my family finally had an opportunity to meet the Ashleys. Ann's parents invited us to their farmhouse for a small celebration. In the days leading up to the party, Ann and I fretted that our families would be uncomfortable and awkward with each other and the unusual situation. In-laws are hard enough to deal with. It's not every day that parents have to face the family of their offspring's same-sex lover. As it turned out, all four parents did their best to put our fears to rest. The whole thing felt relaxed and natural, as if Mom and Dad and the Ashleys were old friends. Roberta, her husband, Dave, and Susan also enjoyed themselves. Emily and "Baby" Susan, my nieces, ran around chasing the cat. After everyone left, Ann and I talked about how fortunate we were. Many gay or lesbian couples never get to have their parents meet each other in such a supportive atmosphere.

The exuberance of completing school, however, soon gave way to the reality of earning a living. Ann had taken a year off from school to help her family financially when her father lost his job as a union worker. As she still had some coursework to finish, I packed my stuff into the back of Dad's truck and moved back to Dauphin to live at home. Mom and Dad were great, giving me free rein to come and go as I pleased. They refrained from the great temptation of parental prying. Still, I felt constrained living with them, especially since I was broke and couldn't afford a car of my own. I needed wheels to drive into town for nights out with my friends, rugby practice, and weekend trips to Indiana to visit Ann.

Since I had already been working summers at Nevada Bob's, a golfing supplies store in Harrisburg, I increased my hours to full-time. Within a month, I applied for and received a full-time job at the United Parcel Service hub in Harrisburg, where I had already been working during school breaks. The wages were great—starting at $8 per hour with full benefits and the opportunity for merit raises. Soon I could afford the monthly payments on a little teal green Toyota Tercel. By the time I quit my job there in February 1995, I was making $12.83 an hour. The noisy plant was filled with otherwise unemployed college grads. Compared to the $5 an hour I made at Nevada Bob's and at a video distribution store in which I briefly worked, it seemed like a fortune. Later I took a $10-per-hour day job doing word processing for my sister Rob at the state Department of Education, where she ran the Family and Consumer Sciences division. For a young person in Harrisburg, the $18,000 a year I was bringing home was hardly chopped liver.

But the reality of the work made me feel like table scraps. At first, Nevada Bob's was a lot of fun. It was great to hang out with a bunch of guys talking about golf, one of my first loves in life. I got a great discount on equipment, too. Gradually, however, the male-chauvinist attitude of a lot of the customers started to grate on me. There I was, a woman in my midtwenties, and these idiots were calling me "son" and "young man."

When they said something dumb like "Thank you, son," I got a measure of revenge by responding, under my breath, "You're welcome, ma'am." "I have breasts," I felt like saying. "They may not be big, but I do have them."

Working at Nevada Bob's for five years made me something of an expert on its inventory. Guys would come up to me with a question about golf clubs. As I'd come out from behind the counter to help them out, they'd often say something like "Aren't you going to get someone to help me?"

"No, I'll help you myself," I'd insist.

Some customers would immediately see that I knew exactly what I was talking about. Others, no matter how hard I'd try, refused to listen to a boyish, short-haired woman tell them about golf clubs. The same situation, I've learned, holds true in general with gay activism. There's a small but hard-core group of Americans who are determined to disapprove of homosexuality and refuse to listen to opposing points of view. The vast majority, though, can be won over with the right argument.

The combination of two jobs meant long hours and little time for rugby, hanging out with my friends, or spending time with Ann. Yet I enjoyed the sense of pride I developed from doing hard, honest work. It also kept me out of trouble, at least during the workweek. While I was something less than a dedicated student, I've never shrunk from physical labor. Like rugby, there was something therapeutic about the toil, which intellectual work always lacked.

My family tends to be highly educated and hold down professional jobs. Dad has an advanced degree in counseling, Susan, a master's in education, Rob has worked toward hers, and Newt, of course, owns a Ph.D. in history. As a result I've often felt a little like the kid in a Monty Python skit that I once saw. The parents, elegantly dressed, await their son's arrival for the holidays. Much to their dismay, he shows up in a dirt-stained coal miner's uniform. The parents rag on him, saying, "Oh, college is too good for him." In almost Gingrich-style sarcasm, they add, "He doesn't like working in an office like Dad does." The way I saw it, there are lots of jobs in this country that need to be done that aren't necessarily prestigious. What they lack in éclat they make up for in integrity and sheer discipline of will.

No one in my family ever said a word about my choice of work, for which I am grateful. One of the best things about the Gingrich family is that we are in no way judgmental about someone's occupation. We have seen enough hard times to know that people have to do whatever it takes to get by. The years Dad spent in the Army—which is as close as this country comes to a classless society—bred a contempt in us for income-based divisions and political elites. After Dad retired from the military in 1973, we lived modestly but comfortably on his savings and generous military pension. To keep busy and bring in extra income, Dad did a series of odd jobs. Though I think he was less than satisfied with them, he never once complained that they were beneath him.

To this day, Mom works part-time at a Camp Hill department store. She likes nice stuff for the house (recently purchasing a new cherry dining-room table), but Mom and Dad share a distaste for material excesses, which I've inherited. Their house in Dauphin is an extremely modest two-story tract house, which they now feel is too big for their needs. Because Mom's failing vision has forced her to give up driving, they're looking for a small condo somewhere near a mall. They want a simple place where Mom can watch *The Young and the Restless,* do her knitting, and gab on the phone all day while Dad completes an endless stream of crossword puzzles. Although Newt has earned a small fortune for his book (even after forgoing the $4.5-million advance), I know Mom and Dad would never accept a cent from him, even if they needed it.

Manual labor strengthened my liberal pro-union position. Without the UPS union, for instance, I'd have been working for minimum wage without benefits. Without federal occupational safety standards—which Newt and his Republican allies have sought to eviscerate—factory workers would be burned, cut, maimed, and poisoned. Factories are not naturally safe places, and "the market" won't make them any less risky. Governments and businesses have a joint responsibility to ensure their safety. Even with its strong union, UPS is constantly battling its employees over work rules. The *New York Times* reported recently that work-related injuries have increased there as management, under fierce competitive pressures, has upped productivity goals.

People don't realize the stamina it takes to survive the backbreaking labor at UPS, especially for someone as diminutive as I. Every week I was required to attend a meeting with a dozen people who were hired at the same time as I was. Slowly the workers began to disappear. After two months, I was the only woman left, and all but two of the guys had dropped out. What saved me was my determination to prove that I could do it and the fact that I was assigned the night shift, when it was cooler and thus less exhausting. I began my stint with the hardest assignment of all, loading trucks. The goal was to move six hundred boxes per hour. As I was a good deal shorter than most workers, I was slowed by having to use a load stand, which is basically a footstool, to reach the top of the truck.

I was fortunate enough to have a supervisor who was willing to work with me, rather than against me. Though they would never admit it, many of the male supervisors (very few are female) don't believe that women should work at UPS and do everything to undermine their presence. The sexism at work opened my eyes to why women need protections against employment discrimination as much as gays and lesbians. (The difference, sadly, is that women already have them enshrined in law.) Gradually, I began to build the muscles I needed to perform the job routinely. It never gets easy; one just becomes accustomed to it.

After a year of loading trucks, I was transferred to small sort. My boss figured that my productivity would improve once I was free of the physical demands of loading. I guess it could be called a demotion of sorts, but a welcome one nonetheless. I was liberated from the hell of lifting seventy-pound packages, four to five hours a day. Small sorters work equally hard, but it's nowhere near as taxing. They are required to sort packages into thirty to sixty different bins with small doors on them, organized by zip code. Though we were required to sort eight hundred to nine hundred per hour, it was a zillion times easier than lifting boxes. The trick to small sorting is memorizing zip codes, of which there are literally thousands. At the end of the night, several of the small sorters would go up and help in the local sort, which was fun because I got a chance to joke around with the guys up there. They knew what was up with me and Ann, but it didn't faze them at all. If they respected a colleague's work, that was all that mattered.

The company had a lesbian supervisor, Martha, who used to look after me because she appreciated my work ethic. She was always shouting, "Get Candace to the outbounds," where I would help load the trucks when they were overwhelmed. Most of the small sorters hated being called out to lift boxes, but I didn't mind at all. I saw the others as slackers. Why should I resent heavy lifting when some people had to do it full-time?

Besides the money, physical labor suited my needs at the time. I sorely lacked long-term career goals and ambitions. In the back of my mind, I dreamed of one day landing a job as a women's studies instructor. I occasionally allowed myself to imagine that teaching other women and enlightened men about feminism and politics would be just about the best thing a person could do in this world. But the reality was that I lacked the requisite motivation, not to mention the grade average, to qualify for a top graduate school. I figured I'd salt some money away while allowing time to elapse so that schools might overlook my less than stellar C-plus GPA.

I don't regret for a second the six years I spent at UPS. But if I ever went back to that line of work, I might try FedEx first. Not only does it not seem to have a glass ceiling for women, but the work rules and wages are far more generous. As I've moved into activist work full-time, I've realized that my blue-collar days have provided me an invaluable perspective from which to carry on my activist work. For one thing, it's helped me appreciate just how fortunate I am to have landed where I am today. To be paid a living wage to travel the country speaking to people about gay rights and encouraging them to become voters and activists is a dream come true. Toiling away in the trenches of the shipping business, I never imagined I'd have such an opportunity. I feel like Cinderella, hoping midnight never comes.

CHAPTER TEN

CANDYFRUIT JUNGLE

A city on the river is a girl without a dream
—R.E.M.,
"South Central Rain"

Harrisburg rises on the eastern shore of the Susquehanna, a wide, mournful river that winds into the city from central New York and the foothills of the Poconos. The river has an especially eerie quality since sitting in its midst a few miles downstream is the notorious Three Mile Island nuclear power plant. Every decade or so, heavy rains cause the Susquehanna to overflow and flood the expensive homes on Front Street, the avenue that runs along its bank. Over the years, as flood insurance has become prohibitive, the homes have been converted to office and entertainment spaces. One of those old brick buildings became home to the D-Gem—for years the city's only lesbian bar.

After graduation, this incongruous riverside nightspot became a second home. Following my brutal sixty-to-seventy-hour workweek at UPS and various odd jobs, Ann and I would spend Saturday nights in its comfortable confines. The D-Gem was a safe haven for hundreds of women in the Harrisburg area who had no other place to be themselves. We met so many people there that whenever my friends and I would spot a familiar face at the mall or on the street, we would joke that we must know her from the club. Because the women who hung out there would see one another only occasionally, the bar had the feel of one long, joyous reunion.

Our long nights there were festive and exuberant. Women from their late teens to early fifties would dance to pulsating disco music

95

ranging from Gloria Gaynor to the M-People, shoot endless games of pool, drink beer from the bottle, and swap gossip and the latest local news around the bar late into the night. Every month or so an older lesbian DJ, whose specialty seemed to be scratching records, would mix in lesbian kitsch like Peggy Lee between the dance tunes. Free of the dangers from AIDS then afflicting our gay brothers, those were giddy times. It was not unusual to see a few women leaving with a different woman every night. Lesbians, we all assumed, were at the lowest risk for HIV of any group, including heterosexuals. (If, in the minds of religious conservatives, AIDS was God's punishment for homosexuality, why was he favoring lesbians?) Even for the women who had heard of protective dental dams, they were somehow associated with those far-out lesbian activists from the New York chapter of ACT-UP.

Since I was usually with Ann and had always lacked interest in cruising other women, I passed the time chatting amiably with my old friends and acquaintances from the club. After the long workweek, it was a chance to celebrate and let what there was of my hair down a little. With the exception of an occasional fight that would break out around the pool table, most of our nights there were pretty tame. Once a year, my friend Sherri and I would celebrate our birthdays, which were less than two weeks apart in June, by going on a bender. We would go shot for shot until one of us would end up under the table. Last time, the game ended abruptly when she made me drink a shot of peach schnapps and I ordered ouzo, an oily anise-flavored drink popular in Greece. Despite the stamina for alcohol we had painstakingly developed at IUP, the disgusting drinks cured our appetite for drinking games until our next birthdays.

When Americans imagine gay life, they tend to think of wild gay pride parades in New York's Greenwich Village or San Francisco's Castro district. But my hunch is that Harrisburg's cautious and often closeted gay community is far more representative of gay life in America than that in the nation's great urban centers. Gays and lesbians flock to the cities to take advantage of the plethora of gay bars, cafés, restaurants, community centers, political organizations, and film and cultural festivals. But with its population of just over fifty thousand, Harrisburg has few of these amenities and little in the way of a gay "community." It boasted two small gay male bars, the Neptune and Stallions. Harrisburg even lacked a red-light district where closeted (and married) gay men have traditionally gathered for anonymous sex.

The annual gay pride festival, held at Reservoir Park, was more like a cultural event than a political demonstration. I would spend most of the day enjoying the music, slathering sunblock on my pale skin, and playing Hacky Sack with my friend Calvin. Later in the summer, Stallions would sponsor a picnic for the fledgling community. The pride committee, in fact, was one of the few gay organizations in the town. Most of us showed up for food and fun; politics was the farthest thing from our minds. Though Philadelphia was home to an aggressive statewide gay rights group, the Philadelphia Lesbian and Gay Task Force, led by longtime lesbian activist Rita Addessa, national gay organizations rarely sent anyone to encourage participants to get involved in gay politics.

Besides the D-Gem, my lifeline for gay news was a women's bookstore called Her Story, which is located in York, a small town not too far south of the city. When I came out two years earlier, I personally liquidated the store's stock of books and magazines to satisfy my voracious appetite for reading material about gay life and feminism. Except for the monthly *Lavender Letter*, a six- to eight-page bulletin of gay and lesbian events that had been published for years, Harrisburg's gay community lacked a regular flow of the information vital to building a gay community. For news, we would turn to national publications such as *The Advocate* and regional publications such as the *Washington Blade*, the *Baltimore Gay Paper*, and the *Philadelphia Gay News*.

It was at Her Story that I bought my copy of Rita Mae Brown's *Rubyfruit Jungle*, which still sits, dog-eared, in my bookcase. York has a special meaning for me because Molly, the spirited lesbian protagonist in *Rubyfruit*, grew up in this working-class town. Later, in search of more information, my friends and I would make the hour-and-a-half drive to Giovanni's Room, a gay bookstore in Philadelphia with a huge selection of gay and lesbian literature. That's where I became addicted to *Hothead Paisan*, Diane DiMassa's comic about a homicidal lesbian terrorist with her sidekick, a mangy cat named Chicken, and Allison Bechdel's comparatively tame *Dykes to Watch Out For*. Despite my ravenous appetite for knowledge, I was still consciously avoiding anything that might remind me of Newt's politics.

Some of our most valuable news about the community was gleaned at the D-Gem. When it closed down in early 1993 due to flagging bar receipts, for all practical purposes the lesbian community ceased to exist. Without a focal point to gather at, we were dispersed throughout the city and its suburbs. As condemnatory as many religious conservatives are of gay and lesbian bars, they should imagine their sadness if a favorite church were forced to close. In Harrisburg, as in many small cities and towns, the closing of the local watering hole is the loss of a crucial meeting place.

In the wake of the D-Gem, we would meet for small dinner parties and brunches, or at the pride celebration. My friends and I took to doing what the most closeted people had done prior to the bar's closing—we drove to the nightspots in Philly, Baltimore, or even Washington because it decreased the chances of being recognized. But affection and nostalgia for the D-Gem never died, and in early 1995, a new women's bar called B-TL'S opened on the other end of Harrisburg.

The lack of a social life and news of the nation's greater gay community translated into a dearth of political activity in the city. In this regard, I was one of the prime culprits. I cared enough to vote for my favorite Democrats, including Jesse Jackson in the 1988 primary. Beyond pulling a lever in the voting booth, however, I contributed little. Given the long work hours, my comfortable life with Ann, and the lack of advocacy groups, I had little to motivate me politically. Despite my friends' increasingly persistent kidding, I remained in deep denial about Newt's role in the religious right's emerging antigay strategy.

One reason millions of Americans remain politically apathetic is that they have little idea of the extent to which happenings in Washington affect their lives and aspirations. But it's not just a matter of complacency. In many cases, the lack of accurate information about national politics contributes to false or flawed political conclusions. The left-wing political scientist Noam Chomsky makes the point that if average Americans could analyze politics with the sophistication without which they discuss sports box scores, liberal democracy would flourish. But the media pays more attention to batting averages than to important political trends and statistics. Had I, for instance, been able to overcome my denial about the antigay shenanigans in which my brother was already engaging, I might have spoken up earlier than I did.

The evidence of his turn to the antigay right was going largely unreported, especially in Harrisburg. In 1989, the year I graduated from IUP, televangelist Pat Robertson founded the Christian Coalition, which would go on to become a major force in both Newt's congressional district and national Republican politics. As my boss Elizabeth Birch at the Human Rights Campaign has pointed out, the Christian Coalition was built in part on antigay and antiabortion fund-raising appeals. Their ascendance to power helped persuade Newt, the onetime libertarian, to begin pandering to the themes that at the time of his first race in 1974 had been largely the terrain of the social-conservative fringe.

After Newt knocked off Jim Wright in 1989, for instance, he employed the far right's gay-baiting to go after Wright's successor, the liberal Washington Democrat Tom Foley. Karen Von Brocklin, one of Newt's aides, began disseminating the rumor that Foley, who had been married for twenty years, was a closeted homosexual with a taste for teenage boys. Von Brocklin's campaign came to an abrupt halt when gay Democrat Barney Frank threatened to publicly identify closeted gay Republicans if it continued. In her October 1995 profile of Newt in *The New Yorker*, Connie Bruck reported that Newt resisted calls for Von Brocklin's resignation from members of his own party on the grounds that he considered the episode "essentially a minor transgression." If playing on antigay prejudice to defame a widely respected member of Congress is a "minor transgression," I'd really like to know what my brother considers a major one.

Perhaps Newt's reluctance to sanction his staffer has something to do with the fact that he took part in the gambit himself. Addressing Republican congressional candidates not long after the Von Brocklin incident, Newt instructed them on the power of code words in the nation's cultural wars. "Notice the power of the word *gay* versus the word *homosexual*, and notice how it changes the whole dynamic of the discussion," he said. "Where we believe in the importance and power of the traditional family, the left . . . feels relatively comfortable talking about homosexual couples adopting children." What Newt didn't tell his fellow right-wingers was that his own Republican family felt perfectly comfortable talking about his lesbian sister adopting children.

As I was blithely going about my small-town life in Harrisburg, Newt was laying the groundwork for his next step: the Speakership. When President Bush withdrew the nomination of John Tower for secretary of defense amid allegations of public drunkenness, he tapped House minority whip Dick Cheney of Wyoming. Not only did the move put Newt next in line for Cheney's position, but it opened the doors for the national gays-in-the-military debate. As secretary of defense in 1992, Cheney set off a furor when he termed the security rationale for the ban on gays in the military a "bit of an old chestnut" that he had inherited from his less enlightened predecessors.

Newt's prominence, however, wasn't making for foolproof reelection bids. Things got so bad that in 1990, Mom traveled to his district to hit the campaign trail with him. He fared little better in 1992, again calling in Mom, who's great with the blue-haired-lady vote, to help him out. In both elections, he won by razor-thin margins. In 1991, Newt worked to secure a Georgia political district that would allow him the freedom to concentrate on his national aspirations. His opportunity came in 1992, when redistricting by the Democrat-controlled state legislature left him languishing in a predominantly black district. The always astute Newt turned the tables on the Democrats by moving to a new district north of Atlanta in predominantly white, affluent Cobb County, home to a vocal mix of religious conservatives and, later, the site of a major gay rights controversy.

Back in Harrisburg, Newt's machinations weren't even a blip on my radar screen. Contributing to my own political complacency and that of my gay and lesbian friends was that we actually had it pretty good, despite the lack of cultural and political institutions. As conservative as it was, Harrisburg was hardly Cobb County. In fact, the state capital lacked the hostile presence of an organized antigay constituency until the early nineties. Our adversaries emerged only after the staunchly pro-gay mayor Steve Reed, who once dated my sister Susan, led the city to add sexual orientation to its antidiscrimination ordinance. It's become an axiom of American politics that interest groups thrive on opposition.

Alas, the legal protections hardly meant that discrimination ceased to exist in the city. Most gay people I knew remained fearful enough to stay deeply in the closet, particularly to their employers, upon whom they depended for their livelihood. Gay people are loath to test such ordinances even when they feel the brutal fist of bias. Since the enactment of the legislation, fewer than a dozen people have filed claims under it. And since Pennsylvania is one of forty-one states without legal protections for gays and lesbians, those who happen to live outside city limits are out of luck. As the state with the largest rural population, it's imperative that the state pass legislation to protect everyone.

In a celebrated 1990 discrimination case in Camp Hill, an upscale Harrisburg suburb where my sister Rob lives, Dan Miller, a highly regarded accountant on his way to partnership in a management-consulting company, was fired when his boss saw him interviewed on TV discussing antigay hate crimes. To justify his action, Miller's boss used a clause in Miller's contract that stated that "homosexuality" was "just cause" for termination. This boss then informed several clients as to Miller's sexual orientation, hoping to erode their apparent loyalty to his former staffer, who set out to start his own business. To make matters worse, when several of the company's clients followed Miller, his former boss won a $130,000 suit against Miller for violating the non-competitive clause of his contract. Under Pennsylvania law, Miller had no legal recourse for the discrimination he faced. At the conclusion of the case, one of the jurors was quoted in the paper as saying, "It was outrageous to hear intolerance like that in a court of law, where people come to seek protection from intolerance, but the law was silent."

At the time, I remember reading about the case in the *Patriot-News*. In my self-imposed state of ignorance, I was far angrier at Miller than at the company. I thought it was stupid of Miller, being gay, to sign the contract. What I didn't realize was that even if he hadn't signed the contract, he could legally be fired for being gay. In many areas of the country, people are forced to sign such contracts to gain employment. And in most states, people wrongly assume that antigay discrimination is against the law.

All I can say in my defense was that my own little world was very secure. My family accepted me without question. To supplement my income and pay off debts, I took advantage of my connections to work extra hours doing data entry for Roberta, who headed up the Family and Consumer Sciences division of the state Department of Education. Susan, who oversaw funding for the Department of Health concerning AIDS, abortion, and single-mother services, also worked in the upper echelons of the state bureaucracy. With their support and high-level contacts, I couldn't imagine losing my livelihood.

My life had an almost ethereal feel. I spent a lot of time at Roberta's cozy, wood-paneled Victorian house in Camp Hill, where we had regular family cookouts. Ann and I baby-sat for Roberta and Dave's two young daughters, Emily and Susan. In the summer, we would take the girls to the Hershey amusement park for cotton candy and roller-coaster rides. Emily took to calling me "Aunt Dandy" because she had a hard time pronouncing her hard *c*'s, as in Aunt Candy. Baby Susan, who was two years younger than Emily, followed suit.

I'm not suggesting everything was perfect. When Roberta and Dave were going away for vacation, I asked if I could drive their vintage 1976 VW Beetle convertible while they were away. I was surprised and a little hurt when they said no. Later, I found out that Dave was concerned that the Bug might be spotted in the parking lot of the D-Gem, thus associating him with my still-secret "vice."

We've come a long way. Today both of my nieces are old enough to call me Candace and be completely comfortable with my being a lesbian. (I'm not suggesting that either are budding Democrats. When Emily's second-grade teacher asked her to name a saint, Emily responded, "George Bush.") Following in the other great Gingrich family tradition, little Susan is already something of a tomboy. To my horror, she recently considered trying out for the cheerleading squad. I held my tongue. Fortunately, she abandoned the idea when she discovered that the cheerleaders' schedule conflicted with her beloved soccer practice. We Gingrich girls always did have our priorities in order. There's great hope for Emily, too. She has already demonstrated acuity on the softball diamond, hitting with far more power than I was ever able to muster.

My sister Susan lived with her fuzzy cats in a ranch-style house with a big yard on the outskirts of Harrisburg. In her own quiet way, Susan, whom I as a child named "Snow" after Snow White, was as supportive as Rob. I always admired that she was perfectly happy as a single professional woman. In 1994, at the age of forty-eight, she married Jim Shurskis. (Much to my relief, Jim turned out to be a registered Democrat, not to mention a former rugger.) But she didn't do it just to get married. She waited for the right guy to come along. Snow is definitely someone who did not depend on a man for her happiness and sense of self-worth. It gave the two of us a common bond, despite our sexual differences.

Whenever we'd get together, Susan and I would swap stories about our jobs or talk about state politics. That she was a Republican and I was a Democrat made for some spirited jousting. We both crossed party lines in 1990 when Democratic governor Casey, whom my friends and I labeled Pope Casey III for his strict antigay and antiabortion views, was challenged by pro-choice Republican Barbara Hafer. Our political discussion became more heated, however, when Snow inexplicably joined the Christian Coalition in 1995. As hard as I've worked to inform her of the evils of the organization, her membership in it serves as a reminder for me to avoid stereotyping the group's membership. Like gays and lesbians, Christian Coalition members are everywhere. They are us.

My life with Ann was equally comfortable. When Ann began substitute-teaching in the fall of 1990, we were able to afford an apartment together in Fort Hunter, a historic area north of town, situated equidistant from Dauphin and Harrisburg. We found a great two-bedroom place in a red-brick converted mill built in the 1800s. The extra bedroom was for show; Ann wanted to make sure that if she got a regular teaching job and had to entertain superiors, she could demonstrate that we were nothing more than roommates—one of those small accommodations to convention that gays and lesbians are often forced to make.

The huge arched windows in the living room overlooked a creek; we could hear its gentle music as we fell asleep at night. For two years, we lived there in a kind of marital bliss. Nongays sometimes think that same-sex couples adopt sex roles that mimic their own, with one partner playing butch and the other femme. One of the fantastic things about some same-sex relationships—and enlightened opposite-sex ones—is how the division of labor does not fall along traditional gender lines. There's a genuine "from each according to her ability, to each according to her needs" aspect to the relationships. Ann did most of the cooking because she was great at it. Since I was already a semivegetarian, she came up with a great veggie lasagna as well as beer-batter onion rings. In return for her cooking, I did the lion's share of the housework. Vacuuming is one of my favorite relaxation techniques.

Keeping us company were the cats. We got a charcoal gray feline on June 17, Newt's birthday, so we named him after my conservative brother. Figuring that Newt must be lonely, we soon went to the no-kill shelter and adopted a little orange tiger. I knew he was right for me when I bent over to pet another cat and he came up behind me and bit me right in the ass. We named him Ripley, after the strong and sexy Sigourney Weaver character in *Aliens,* one of my all-time favorite movies. Our third and final cat we named Bishop, after the android character in the same movie.

My times there with Ann were deliciously run-of-the-mill. During football season, we'd invite a bunch of friends over to watch football and enjoy Ann's tangy chicken wings. We shared a similar sense of humor, and many common interests. When we were not up for the D-Gem, we'd spend cozy weekends in front of the television set indulging our mutual passion for films. By this time, I'd outgrown a habit Snow is fond of recalling: how as a little tyke I'd throw an afghan over my head and watch scary movies through the tiny holes. In the winter, we'd make popcorn and hot chocolate.

The movies we saw truly ran the gamut. My favorites were horror classics like *Texas Chainsaw Massacre.* The scene in which the dead guy jumps out of the freezer is the best. I also liked Clive Barker's *Hellraiser* films because they had real plots, not just a bunch of crazy people who escape from the asylum. *Night of the Living Dead* and *Dawn of the Dead* were great for their camp value. In the second of these films, a guy in a motorcycle gang who's having his blood pressure taken in a shopping mall gets torn off the machine by some ghouls, but the gooey arm stays behind, hanging limply. Now *that's* great special effects! I assume his blood pressure took a dive. My favorite explanation for why people make such outlandish movies comes from filmmaker John Waters, who once admitted of his bizarre cult films such as *Pink Flamingos,* "If I didn't make films about people doing crazy things, I'd probably do them myself."

During the weekend days, Ann and I would either play rugby or attend sports-trading-card shows, another shared passion. We could spend hours on a Saturday morning, sorting, evaluating, and pricing what soon grew into a pretty impressive collection. The shows themselves, held at local fire halls or hotel conference rooms, were a trip. We'd lay out our wares on long banquet tables for the other collectors, mostly men or little boys, to peruse. They had no idea what to make of us. But it didn't matter; we had a reputation for being particularly well-organized and stocked with goodies. Guys would come around looking for a complete card set, or something special like the Topps 1993 Steve Young Most Valuable Player card. We loved bantering with collectors about the value of cards.

Collecting became something of a third job, except for the fact that it was ultimately a net financial loss. I'd spend anywhere from $20 to $100 per week on cards, most of which ended up on my four credit cards, which were soon maxed out. It was the start of a financial slide from which I'm only now recovering. In retrospect, it's sad I wasn't better at handling my hard-earned dollars.

When we weren't watching movies, playing rugby, or attending card shows, we'd head out to Riverside Stadium to watch the Harrisburg Senators, the Montreal Expos' Triple-A affiliate, who were Eastern League champs two years in a row in the early nineties. We got to see future major-league stars such as Rondell White and Curtis Pride, who I believe is the only deaf player to reach the major leagues.

But as contented as our life together was, there were storm clouds gathering. Ann, whose degree was in physical education, was having a hard time nailing down a full-time teaching position, which took a toll on her self-esteem and put stress on our relationship. There were simply a finite number of openings for phys ed instructors in the area. Despite our weekends, it was difficult to find enough time to spend together. My work hours were long. I worked from eight-thirty in the morning to five for Roberta at the Department of Education. Exhausted, I'd come home to a hot dinner Ann would have waiting for me, nap for an hour or so, head off to work at UPS from ten at night until around three in the morning, come home for a few hours of sleep, then start the whole grueling process all over again.

For all our good times, Ann and I gradually began to grow apart. Out of respect for Ann's privacy, I won't get into the specifics of our problems. For whatever reason, we were never able to work through our differences. Reluctantly, we gave up the apartment and split up the cats and the card collection. I moved back in with my parents in Dauphin and Ann moved back to her parents' farm.

After seven years together, the breakup was painful. In the beginning, I carried around what felt like a hole in my heart where she once resided. To be honest, the whole dismal thing was probably as much my fault as it was hers. Like many people, I'd assumed my first love would be my last. What I'd failed to countenance was that people change during their relationships. It's a human failing that when they begin to change, they don't or can't always tell each other. I failed Ann by not recognizing that my feelings for her had changed well before we actually split.

I'm sure what happened has something to do with the fact that I didn't really begin dating until I was in my early twenties. Lacking examples of flourishing same-sex relationships, we were left to figure things out for ourselves. Like a lot of same-sex couples, I think we probably maintained the relationship longer than we should have because the comfort and familiarity of it was a buffer against the potential hostility of the outside world. It was another form of complacency that was plaguing my life.

As our relationship disintegrated in 1994, I began building a relationship with a new player from the Harrisburg-area rugby team that my friends Bob, Ann, and I had founded after college. Jolene, as in the Dolly Parton song, was taller than I, with brown hair and matching eyes. Wonderfully androgynous in appearance, she was a ferocious rugger, which, of course, impressed me to no end. After the practice at which we met in '92, we smoked a joint together in her car. My Department of Education gig with Roberta, which replaced a job as a distribution coordinator when Artec Video Distributors moved to Vermont, brought me downtown every day. Since Jolene also worked downtown at the courthouse, we'd meet for intimate lunches. In the spring, we'd buy sandwiches at the deli and sit outside at City Island, a pretty key in the middle of the Susquehanna.

If I'm going to hold Newt accountable for the flaws in his personal life, I have to admit that I began seeing Jolene before Ann and I had officially broken it off. Then again, I've never pretended to be a moral paragon. Though Jolene and I had a prolonged flirtation with each other, I did wait more than two years to act upon my feelings. In the late summer of '94, shortly before Newt was promoted to Speaker, I bought tickets to an Indigo Girls concert at Radio City Music Hall in New York City. Ann was unable to go, so I asked Jolene to accompany me.

On the way up in my new Tracker, I admitted to Jolene that I was deeply attracted to her and wanted to sleep with her. For the rest of our trip, it felt as if we were one. She fed me M&M's as we blasted the Indigo Girls' *Swamp Ophelia* cassette on my car stereo. Upon our arrival in the city, we met my friend Karen at her apartment in Manhattan, and the three of us proceeded uptown on the subway. Radio City is a neat place to see a concert; the acoustics are flawless and everyone gets a clear view of the band from any seat. As we were milling about in the lobby before the concert, Jolene put her hand on mine, giving me a serious case of butterflies.

The concert was equally electric. Amy Ray and Emily Saliers, the reluctantly open lesbians who are the Indigo Girls, played an intense all-acoustic show for almost two full hours. (Too bad they, like many entertainers, don't seem fully ready to realize the power they have as role models to educate Americans about gay issues.) When we returned to Karen's apartment, still high from the music, Jolene and I fell into each other's arms on the futon Karen had set up for us. Sadly, the rest of our relationship failed to live up to that magical night.

We saw each other sporadically until April of 1995 when I moved to Washington, D.C., to begin my fifty-one-city tour across America for the Human Rights Campaign. Still, whenever an Indigo Girls song plays on the radio, I think of that night and what might have been. In their song "The Power of Two," they sing that our "legacy" is to love one another well. At the end of my relationships, I'm not sure I lived up to that noble sentiment.

The English language can be cumbersome when it comes to affairs of the heart. Some emotions are impossible to express except in a song. There's a Mary-Chapin Carpenter ballad "Where Time Stands Still" that evokes how exhilarating my time with both Ann and Jolene was and why it could not last. The song describes the "fear and the thrill" of passion that is doomed to end prematurely.

As sappy as it may sound, I left a piece of myself with those two women.

FEEDING FRENZY

I'm not willing to be tolerated.
That wounds my love of love and liberty.

—JEAN COCTEAU

The epiphany that finally jolted me from my apathy came on Thanksgiving Day, 1994. Mom had prepared a turkey dinner with all the fixings, which she displayed proudly on her new dining room table. The entire family was in a particularly festive mood because Newt had just achieved his lifetime goal of becoming Speaker of the House after spearheading the Republican congressional takeover. My sisters and I were awestruck that our big brother was suddenly perhaps the most powerful politician in America. The only damper on our celebration was the fact that Newt, tied up in Capitol Hill business, was unable to join us. As it turned out, it was probably a good thing for my relationship with Newt that he didn't.

As we sat down to enjoy the feast, Roberta asked innocently if I had seen Newt's comments about homosexuality published that day in the Harrisburg *Patriot-News*. In my usual state of ignorance about my brother's increasingly scary politics, I hadn't even noticed them. Rob, who's always been very supportive of my being gay, explained that while invoking the principle of "tolerance"—a term I despise because it implies pity—he had compared homosexuality to alcoholism and declared that it would be "madness to pretend that families are anything other than heterosexual couples."

Rob's news flash struck like lightning. How dare my older brother deign to "tolerate" my existence. What right does he have to decide whether I'm acceptable or not? I would never consider "tolerating" him. Whether I like what he does or not, it's his life. It's not up to me to make value judgments about it. I might judge his political actions, but certainly not his personal decisions. One tolerates a leaky faucet or a dog's barking, not a fellow human being. As for family, wasn't I sitting in the midst of one he had blown off once again to satisfy his political ambitions? When I'd brought Ann to spend a previous holiday with Newt and the family, he'd never given any indication that we were any less a family than he and Marianne. If that's what he was thinking, he certainly didn't have the guts to tell me to my face. As for the equation between homosexuality and alcoholism, all I can say is that Newt must have had a few too many Guinnesses when he came up with that one.

I'm glad I didn't have food in my mouth because I would have spit it on Mom's shiny new table. I felt physically ill. For the rest of the dinner, I didn't make so much as a peep. Concerned, Rob asked if I wanted to talk about it. But knowing how much the family admires Newt, I felt intimidated and couldn't find the words to express my anger. I didn't dare say what I was thinking: that my own brother seemed bent on the destruction of *my* community. To make matters worse, he hadn't even had the decency to seek my views on gay-related issues. In retrospect, I think my physical symptoms sprang from a powerlessness that I hadn't experienced in the seven years since I'd come out to my family and friends.

Maybe Newt needed to hear from me, too, without the family to filter my message. I just couldn't allow him to defame me and my gay and lesbian brothers and sisters any longer without at least having to deal with me. I was finally so angry that I no longer cared what my overly protective Republican family thought. Nor would I defer to my own misgivings. Though I'd come out to the Associated Press shortly after the November 8 election, more activity on my part was clearly called for. The little excuses I had allowed myself for years began to evaporate.

In the past, I had always told myself that the Democrat-controlled Congress would protect the gay community from the excesses of the right. I had tremendous confidence in liberal stalwarts such as Ted Kennedy in the Senate and Pat Schroeder in the House. That was a mistake, I realized, because no single politician, no matter how skillful or powerful, can protect us from attacks. Only we can protect ourselves. For the first time in my life, I was beginning to think I could muster the inner strength to take on Newt publicly. After all, it was the political equivalent of self-defense. He had fired the first salvo. In fact, with antigay comments and a hostile voting record dating back at least a decade, he'd fired the first, second, and third rounds. It was time to begin my activism.

Shortly after Thanksgiving, I unearthed the source of Newt's quotes, a lengthy interview published in the November 25 edition of the *Washington Blade*, one of the finest gay weeklies in the country. Highlights of the interview had gone out across the country on the AP wire. Though I knew this was not the first time Newt had run his mouth off about gay rights, I hoped to God that his quotes in the *Patriot-News* had been taken out of context.

When I located the paper, a huge photo of Newt's round face jumped out at me from the pink-and-green cover. Conducted by gay journalist Chandler Burr, the interview had taken place in a bar at the La Crosse Radisson Hotel in Wisconsin, where Newt had just attended a fund-raiser for Wisconsin Republican Steve Gunderson's reelection campaign, which had been imperiled by antigay activists. The right-wingers were angry that Gunderson had recently announced what had long been an open secret: that he was a gay man. A leader of the moderate wing of the party, Gunderson had served as Newt's deputy until the 1992 Republican National Convention in Houston, when he quit the leadership post to protest the incendiary antigay tone that dominated the convention and frightened much of the nation.

As it turned out, Newt's views were in fact a bit more complex than what the *Patriot-News* account indicated, but only a *bit*. His lengthy comments were frustrating and confusing. I could see flashes of brilliance, genuine loyalty to Gunderson and his partner, Rob Morris, and creative thinking about public policy. Equally on display, however, were a penchant for speaking before thinking, pandering to right-wing stereotypes, viewing life in strict hierarchies, and invoking moral absolutes.

The backdrop for the interview was a rowdy demonstration by a small group of sign-toting antigay activists outside the fund-raiser. Newt, whose fondness for Gunderson is well-known, was obviously angered by the protest. For an evening, at least, Newt stepped into the shoes of gays and lesbians who find their life under siege, leaving him in a contemplative mood. He began his remarks by declaring that Bob Dornan, the antigay Republican from Orange County, and conservative commentator Pat Buchanan were "not representative of the future [of the Republican Party], they're just noisy—like the three [antigay] guys who were picketing tonight, that was perfect." The Gingrich sarcasm sparkled.

Since becoming Speaker-elect, Newt had downplayed his flame-thrower image in favor of a more statesmanlike demeanor. "My Republicanism is a much more open-to-ideas Republicanism than you would normally assume if you said, 'I got this guy from Georgia whom [former House Speaker] Tip O'Neill denounced and Jim Wright hates . . . ,' " he said. "I realize that you have to reach beyond the Republican Party, which is why I talk to Ross Perot and Jimmy Carter and try to reach out to people who come from a lot of backgrounds."

However much he decries his far-right GOP cohorts, he's not above playing good cop to their bad cop. Because it's an improvement over Dornan's and Buchanan's "hate the sin, hate the sinner" routine, Newt said that gays should be grateful for his own "hate the sin, love the sinner" philosophy. "You can say of something that it's wrong and yet not condemn the person doing it," he explained. "Our position should not be promotion and it should not be condemnation. I don't wanna see police in the men's room, which we had when I was a child, and I don't want to see trying to educate kindergartners in understanding gay couples. I think where we're moving towards as a society and in our party's position is that consenting adults can have private relations without in any way the political system being involved."

I wondered whether this meant that Newt opposed *Bowers v. Hardwick*, the infamous 1986 U.S. Supreme Court ruling upholding the constitutionality of sodomy laws. The case had originated in a legal challenge to Georgia's law, which prohibits sodomy between *consenting* adults. Since Michael Bowers, the Georgia state attorney general who defended the law, is a close Gingrich ally, I somehow doubted Newt was going to put his money where his mouth was.

After insisting that he did not support "condemnation," Newt proceeded to condemn gay and lesbian families. "But where, I suspect, Steve [Gunderson] and I deeply disagree is that it is madness to pretend that families are anything other than heterosexual couples. *I think it goes to the core of how civilization functions,*" he said. (Italics, I confess, are mine.) Burr asked Newt how he could hold such a position in light of the fact that he knows Gunderson and his partner, Rob Morris, are a family—as much of a family, I might add, as Newt and Marianne or any other heterosexual couple.

Newt wriggled out of that corner by terming his friends "anecdotal exceptions" and comparing their relationship to that of a heterosexual male pederast. "I believe it's possible for some fifty-year-old men to fall in love with some ten-year-old girls and have wonderful Shakespearean moments," he explained. "I think as a matter of public policy that should be called statutory rape. Over time, we want to have an explicit bias in favor of heterosexual marriage." "As opposed to the one we have now?" I thought. Sorry Newt, Rob and Steve are not the exception, they are the rule.

Newt then proceeded to undermine his own argument about favoring heterosexuals in public policy by acknowledging that under the skin, gays and straights are essentially alike. "On most things, most days, the vast majority of practicing homosexuals are good citizens," he said. "I know a number of practicing heterosexuals who I believe are more decadent and more corrupted by a good margin than many of the homosexuals I know personally. So then why would I condemn a person who in most things I agree with and think is an honorable decent person . . . ?"

Since most of us "practicing" homosexuals, not to mention heterosexuals, don't really need practice anymore, Newt should probably drop that term from his vocabulary. But on a more serious note, what was I to make of this conglomeration of confused ideas? Once Newt had admitted that it's irresponsible (indeed impossible) to differentiate among human beings on the grounds of something as superficial as sexual orientation, he had gone a long way toward accepting the idea of full legal equality for gays and lesbians.

Yet at the same time, Newt clung to the bigoted notion that gays and lesbians somehow undermine "how civilization functions," and that society should "have an explicit bias in favor of heterosexual marriage." Aren't gays and lesbians a contributing part of civilization? Steve and Rob certainly are. I'd always labored under the assumption that I was. Who would it hurt if our relationships were treated equally to my brother's?

In another article, in the December 9 edition of the *Blade*, I found evidence that Newt's remarks were not merely the indiscriminate ravings of a confused politician. The new Speaker's views, no matter how ill-informed, had a political dimension that was damaging to a community of people to which I belonged. Apparently, Newt's interview with the *Blade* caused quite a stir among religious conservatives. Despite the clear expression of decidedly antigay sentiments, he was pilloried for saying that gays and lesbians were welcome in the Republican Party, as long as they didn't expect to be treated equally, and that he supported tolerance. A pattern was emerging. Whenever he would be quoted saying something sympathetic, however remotely, about gays and lesbians, he would be back in the papers the next day trashing them.

In an interview on NBC's *Meet the Press*, reprinted in the *Blade*, Newt declared that employers should have a right to fire gay employees. "I don't think the Christian Coalition feels betrayed," he said. "Let's say someone walks in and says, 'I really want to be a waitress, but I insist on wearing my hair in a way that nobody's going to want me to wait on their table.' There is a point here where there has to be some relationship between functionality—not protected class, not legal status, but functionality."

Something ugly lurked below this strange comparison. The analogy between firing (or not hiring) someone because she or he is gay, which has no effect on job performance, and firing someone with long hair, which can sometimes interfere, was lost on me. As usual, Newt hadn't bothered to specify how being gay can hurt job performance. In my past apathy, I'd failed to grasp an important point. Newt, I now realized, was determined to halt efforts to add sexual orientation to federal antidiscrimination statutes.

What shook me most about both interviews was the fact that he was able to pontificate endlessly in this bizarre, breezy fashion without having to answer for his lesbian sister. I wanted to add my name to the short list of people who could personally keep the soon-to-be Speaker accountable for his antigay views. It wasn't enough to be out of the closet. I had to take an active role in confronting him. As much as I loved to imagine myself as David slaying Goliath, I realized I could hardly go it alone. I needed to be part of a movement of people who could first check his excesses and ultimately reverse them.

After all, it wasn't just Newt I was worried about. He commanded an army of freshmen Republicans who were among the most reactionary the country had ever seen, including one who insisted that homosexuality deserved the death penalty and another who opined that homosexuals were responsible for the decline of Greek civilization. As a fellow House Republican, Gunderson had scant ability to confront the most powerful member of his own party. By contrast, the only thing holding me back was excessive fealty to family ties.

I resolved to take my newfound activism as far as it would go, regardless of what my family thought. But unschooled in practical politics and the media, I had no idea of where to turn. Should I call a gay rights group in Washington? In Newt's district? As it turned out, my worries were academic.

After the AP story was picked up in the *New York Times,* all hell broke loose. The press knocked on my door. In early January, I appeared on the *Eye to Eye with Connie Chung* segment in which Connie used sleight of hand to get Mom to tell her that Newt had called the first lady a "bitch." Newt and the family were furious at Connie for supposedly taking advantage of Mom's naïveté, but I didn't see what the big deal was. I actually got to like Connie during the day she spent with the family at Mom and Dad's place. Off camera, Mom told Connie that Newt had called the press, by which he means the "liberal press," a "bunch of snakes." Connie laughed and said, "Yes, I guess we are."

I braced myself for the inevitable question about my decision to come out. "There has been some question about your sexuality . . . ," she said to me during the interview. "There's no question about it," I thought. "I'm definitely a lesbian." Asked if I would vote for Newt, I hesitated, laughed, and admitted, "Probably not." I was careful, though, to keep the mood light and steer clear of personal attacks on Newt, which were becoming all too commonplace in some quarters. When Connie asked whether being a lesbian generated friction with my brother, I replied, "He's probably more embarrassed that I'm a Democrat." (I should acknowledge my friend Bob for providing me with this one-liner the week before.)

The next call came from Peter Freiberg, a *Washington Blade* reporter, who wrote a polite profile of me in the January 13 edition. Much to my surprise, *The Advocate* put me on the cover of the March 7 edition posing in my Capital Area Women's rugby shirt with Newt's angry face looking out from television monitors in the background. That story led to an invitation to appear on *Good Morning America* in early March.

Sipping coffee in the greenroom minutes before my appearance, Charlie Gibson, the show's host, introduced me to California House speaker Willie Brown, the future mayor of San Francisco, who was going on after me. Charlie, who's got a good sense of humor, said, "Mr. Speaker, I'd like you to meet the Speaker's sister." "Brother," I said, shaking Willie's hand. "My long-lost sister," he shot back. I should be so lucky. Like Newt, Willie has earned a reputation for arrogance in wielding power. But unlike Newt, he has demonstrated a profound sympathy for those less fortunate than he. Growing up the son of poor African-American sharecroppers, Willie worked his way to the top of California politics without resorting to denigrating the already disenfranchised. Early in 1996, as mayor, he made headlines by serving as master of ceremonies at a mass same-sex wedding in San Francisco.

Before long, there were too many interview requests to keep track of, and since I was still working full-time, many fell by the wayside. It was, I must admit, more than a little overwhelming. Suddenly I could understand why Newt often felt badgered by the press, and my coverage, come to think of it, was usually far more positive than his. Still, the important thing was that I'd lost my reticence about speaking out and was daily going about building the confidence I needed to challenge my brother's politics in a sustained fashion.

In fact, I quite enjoyed most of my contact with reporters. I felt like Deion Sanders at a post–Super Bowl press conference. Like my parents and sisters, I'd never imagined that the nation would care so much about what I had always assumed were my inconsequential views of the world. I didn't fully comprehend why the press was so excited by my story. I was neither the most outspoken lesbian in the country nor the only gay relative of a famous politician. One reporter explained to me that the media's dual fascination with Newt and homosexuality made the story irresistible.

During this frenetic period, I tried to contact Newt every time news leaked out about the antigay plans of the House Republicans. My intentions were honorable. I wanted to tell him that my decision to speak to the press had a political, not personal, motivation, and that I hoped he understood this. After all, I was expected to understand that *his* views weren't personal. I wondered whether he'd be willing to sit down with me sometime and hear me out. I especially wanted to know from where on earth sprang his views on homosexuality. Maybe, I thought, a polite conversation could clear up what I felt was a growing, but unspoken, animosity between us. We'd still never had a face-to-face discussion about my sexual orientation.

On December 16, I faxed Newt my annual handwritten note requesting Redskins tickets, but I added a political twist. I registered my objection to his decision to allow congressional hearings on a bill that would deny federal funds to school districts that adopt some form of pro-gay curricula. "Was just curious about some of the scary things I read about Rev. Sheldon, and hoped you could confirm or deny this info," I wrote. Wishing him "Peace and Christmas cookies," I tried to conclude on a lighter note: "If we're so far apart in years, how did our handwriting end up so similarly poor?"

At the time, the papers were reporting that the hearings were a favor he was granting Lou Sheldon, the Traditional Values Coalition leader who had created a cottage industry of antigay invective. I got the tickets, but no response to my request to talk, the first of many I would make to him over the next year. Several calls to his office and to his answering machine at home also went unreturned. I know that between his new job, book writing, and family life, Newt had to be one of the busiest guys on this earth. Nonetheless, I was beginning to take his snubs personally. It was, I would soon realize, just the beginning of Newt's avoidance of me and the difficult political questions my presence raised.

We finally hooked up for a few minutes at Newt's January 3 swearing-in ceremony in the House chambers. The whole family had traveled to Washington for the occasion. Dropping his tendency to blame liberals for the decline of Western civilization, Newt made a moving speech in which he invoked the legacy of FDR and scolded his fellow Republicans for having obstructed the path of the civil rights train. "Here we are as commoners together, Democrats and Republicans, liberals and conservatives—but Americans all," he said, his voice thundering throughout the cavernous chambers. For a moment at least, I thought that the high ground Newt was staking out might enable us to one day bridge the troubled waters of our political differences.

Looking back, I was naive, but infused with a genuine fondness. Despite my antipathy for the incoming class of right-wing Republicans, I was caught up in the excitement of the day. I don't think I've ever seen Mom happier. You could see the pride in her eyes for a son who had come so far from such troubled beginnings. It was true: in America, anything is possible.

But underneath the conciliatory rhetoric of the Republicans, I detected a deep reservoir of contempt for any political opposition. The sore winners in the crowd were chanting, "Newt, Newt, Newt," but what they really seemed to be saying was, "We beat the Democrats, ha, ha." It wouldn't take long, however, for the boasting to turn to whining as the country resisted the imposition of Newt's strident Contract with America.

After the ceremony, Newt gave me a big hug and we chatted for a few moments. He told me that he was concerned that now that I was out in the press, people would invade my privacy and make my life miserable. At the time, I thought his sentiments were genuine. In retrospect, I realize that they could just have easily spoken to his own ambitions—and desire to keep me quiet—as to any concern for his little sister. *I know,* I told him, *but it's something I have to do.* And Newt, after all, should have been familiar with this sense of purpose.

CHAPTER TWELVE

"THE PERFECT HUMAN BEING"

He that is without a sin among you,
let him first cast a stone at her.

—JOHN 8:7

My world had not come to an end. Speaking out had brought an enormous sense of relief and none of the adverse consequences I'd imagined. My family hadn't disowned me. In fact, they seemed to enjoy the attention I was getting. Instead of one politician child to brag about, Mom now had two, even if she didn't quite understand what it meant to be a gay activist. As she kept reminding me, they didn't have "those" kind of people in her generation. My sisters, who felt neglected by comparison, had mixed emotions about the attention I was receiving and the way in which the media was pitting brother against sister. Nonetheless, they were as loving and supportive as always. Life was good.

Still, I had no concrete idea of what to do with my newfound celebrity. Starting in November and ending in February, I'd spoken to more reporters than I could count. I figured my proverbial fifteen minutes were just about up. Yet I was ready for a big change in my life. I was beginning my sixth year at UPS, my relationship with Ann had gone south, and frankly, I was more than a little bored. There was nothing to keep me in Harrisburg. It was a comfortable, even honorable life, but I have to admit that I longed for something bigger and brighter, even if it was for just a short time. As I sorted boxes at UPS, I imagined what life might be like in Washington, D.C. Like Molly in *Rubyfruit*

Jungle, I knew that if I didn't leave soon, I'd spend the rest of my life in the midsize town.

At the same time, I had no idea how to translate the apparent interest in what I had to say into any kind of long-term action. As much as I wanted to make a difference on a bigger scale, I was resigned to continuing the workaday routines of my life in Harrisburg. I had no delusions of grandeur. I'd made my point to Newt and the family. And I'd made it clear I was willing to continue speaking out when necessary.

Then the gay movement came knocking. It arrived in the form of an early-January telephone call from David M. Smith, the communications director for the Human Rights Campaign Fund, the country's largest gay and lesbian political group. I'd heard of the group—derisively dubbed the Champagne Fund by its critics—from reading the gay press. Yet, like many gays and lesbians, I had associated it primarily with well-heeled gay white men and the exclusive black-tie fund-raisers it held across the country. I couldn't see why on earth they'd be interested in a left-wing, blue-collar rugby dyke like me.

Recent changes within the organization, however, had pushed it in a new direction. The group had just named as its new executive director Elizabeth Birch, the dynamic former board member of the more grass-roots National Gay and Lesbian Task Force. As the former legal counsel for Apple Computers, Elizabeth hoped to lead the Campaign Fund into what Newt would call "the information age." David asked if he and Elizabeth could drive to Harrisburg to meet me for lunch. Over veggie sandwiches, Elizabeth explained that they'd like me to attend their March leadership conference and lobby day and to be their spokeswoman for National Coming Out Day, an annual celebration of gay identity. "How fascinating it is that Newt Gingrich has a lesbian sister," I recall her commenting. If all went well, Elizabeth hinted, we might be able to work out a long-term partnership.

But family loyalties and ties to friends made a quandary out of a godsend. Miraculously, I'd found the outlet for which I'd been looking. Yet all of a sudden my decision didn't seem nearly so obvious. When it came down actually to moving, giving up what I had suddenly seemed more painful and dangerous than I'd ever imagined. Life in Harrisburg was all I knew. I'd miss the close proximity to Mom and Dad, Rob and Snow, Emily and Susan, and all my old Harrisburg friends. And I'd be descending into the great unknown of gay politics, where the dangers of exposure and retaliation were real and the long hours and frequent setbacks harsh.

Immersed in work, family, and friends in Harrisburg, I could keep my distance from the meanness of Washington politics and the mistreatment of gays and lesbians in America. I could avoid thinking about how AIDS was still cutting a wide swath across gay (and nongay) life; how gays and lesbians were being beaten and killed in the streets; how, in the name of Christianity, conservatives had established a multimillion-dollar industry based on hysterical antigay propaganda. Most of all, I could pretend that my own flesh and blood had never played a role in any of this insanity.

In the end, however, my hope—and ambition—overcame the fear, and I headed south to take David and Elizabeth up on their offer, at least for one weekend. The March 5 political conference was named for Randy Klose, a gay businessman who had left a small fortune to the organization after his death from AIDS. I spent most of the weekend just listening to people talk at workshops on a range of issues, trying not to let my political naïveté show. At this point, I just wanted to absorb as much information about gay politics as I could. Ignorant of the basics, I had miles to go. To be honest, I wasn't even sure how one went about lobbying Congress. My advocacy experience was limited to sending pleading faxes to Newt's office.

David asked me to make a few remarks at an awards reception for the group's largest donors on Saturday night. Obsessing throughout the day on what I was going to say, I felt nervous and embarrassed. Feelings of inadequacy rolled over me like whitecaps. I was haunted by Mom's words as I'd left for the trip to Washington: "You're just going down there to talk about Newtie and drag his name through the mud." Her ferocious loyalty to Newt had caused her to lose sight of my legitimate concerns. I assured her that I was going to speak out only for gay rights—not against Newt. As protective and proud as she is of Newt, I could forgive her hurtful words. But they played directly into fears I was already experiencing about my legitimacy as a spokeswoman for a cause I'd never thought much about. In retrospect, I was putting far too much stock in my critics who said that I was merely capitalizing on Newt's notoriety.

When it came time for me to speak, a cold sweat spread over my body. I stumbled through a few sentences before I pulled out of thin air the accidental-activist line that would become my mantra during my travels across the country: "I'm glad each of you has not waited until your brother became Speaker to get involved." The phrase broke the ice. Everyone clapped. I was especially relieved I had to speak only briefly because I had just met Mary Fisher, the eloquent AIDS advocate who electrified the 1992 Republican National Convention and who was scheduled to speak the next day. Mary, whose clarion call for an end to discrimination and prejudice seemed to fall on deaf ears that night in Houston, is such a powerful speaker that she would have overshadowed even the most experienced activist.

On Monday, I took part in the Human Rights Campaign Fund's annual lobbying day. Members from across the country descended on Washington to lobby their representatives, many of whom were newly elected conservatives visibly discomfited even by being in the same room with a gay person. I spent the day lobbying the Pennsylvania delegation, Senators Rick Santorum, a freshman Republican, and Arlen Specter, a veteran GOP moderate who later undertook an abortive run for his party's presidential nomination. I also visited Rep. George Gekas, a right-wing Republican who represented Dauphin and a favorite of the Republican wing of the Gingrich family.

During my Capitol Hill visit, the media's Gingrich frenzy was at its apex. Newt was everywhere, and I—like it or not—was not far behind. The attention we were getting just blew my small-town mind. As I walked down the aisles of Congress, I was trailed by a horde of reporters, photographers, and cameramen. Being a complete political novice, I had no idea what to say to them. They were all after that sound bite that would bring the political tension in the Gingrich family into high relief or a chance encounter between me and Newt. I was happy to disappoint.

I had made a pledge not to attack Newt personally, and no amount of badgering was going to change my mind. I was there to fight for the gay community, not to denigrate my brother, I repeatedly reminded the reporters, who clearly did not know what to make of me. I recall trying to explain rugby to one reporter who was walking backward taking notes. It's hard enough to understand rugby without walking backward at the same time. Somehow I don't think those were the quotes that he was seeking. But I must admit, they were all extremely practiced at that particular reportorial skill.

The meetings were eye-openers. Escorted by David Smith and Nancy Buermeyer, a senior HRCF lobbyist, we began our rounds of the Capitol. Senator Santorum was out of the office, so we spoke to his aide, Will Sears, a pleasant guy who put me at ease. Of course I'd have been much happier to meet with Harris Wofford, the liberal Democratic senator from Pennsylvania who'd been edged out in the Republican groundswell. I reminded myself that it was critical to confront the new political reality and not to waste time longing for the past. And even though Santorum was no friend of gays, he had a reputation as something of a maverick. He'd signed on to HRCF's nondiscrimination pledge for his Senate office. On the other hand, he ended up siding with a number of insidious antigay amendments offered by Sen. Jesse Helms of North Carolina. Somewhat awkwardly, I told Will about the widespread discrimination faced by gays and the need for federal protections. He promised he'd speak to Santorum about my concerns.

Our next stop was Senator Specter's office. I was predisposed to disliking Specter for his dishonorable role in the Anita Hill–Clarence Thomas episode three and a half years earlier. During the Judiciary Committee's hearings, the distinguished senator proved that there was no sexist slur or unproved insinuation that was too low for him. Two years later, after women voters in the state nearly ousted him from office in favor of feminist Lynn Yeakel, he'd said he regretted his posture in the hearings and his vote to confirm the clearly unqualified Thomas. To Specter's credit, he'd also begun a personal crusade to expose the bigoted fringe of the Republican Party, going so far as to call for respect for diversity in front of a Christian Coalition gathering in Iowa, a rare act of political courage for which he was rewarded with a generous round of boos and catcalls.

The senator's respectful behavior toward me went a long way toward allaying my reservations. When I arrived at his office, he'd just flown in from Pennsylvania and gone directly to the nearby headquarters of his presidential-campaign exploration committee. Specter had instructed his staff in advance to escort us over to his other office. It was one of the first times that the currency that comes with the Gingrich name really hit home. A Republican presidential candidate had dropped everything so he could meet with the Speaker's lesbian sister. Apparently, Specter had foreseen a photo opportunity for his subsequent campaign, which was already beginning to woo gay Republican voters. That I was a die-hard Democrat and Clinton loyalist hardly seemed to matter. He was smart, witty, and appeared earnest in his bid to rid the Republican Party of wild-eyed hatemongers. (He didn't say whether he included my brother in that ever-widening category.) I suggested it would be far easier to simply switch parties. I asked him to cosponsor the Employment Non-Discrimination Act, or ENDA, which would ban sexual orientation–based discrimination in the workplace. Specter explained that as a general principle he doesn't cosponsor legislation of any sort, but he would probably support the bill.

Our final stop was Gekas's office, where we were informed that the representative was taking part in a debate on the House floor. His aides took us to a finely upholstered waiting room just off the House floor, where Gekas took a few minutes to meet with us and smile for the photographers. Aware that he was already on record opposing ENDA, I asked him to consider at least signing the nondiscrimination pledge for his House office. Forgetting that HRCF had sent him a copy nearly a year earlier, he said he'd never sign anything without scrutinizing it, but he'd get back to us. To no one's surprise, he's not signed it yet. When I got home from the trip, everyone in the family wanted to know what our representative was like. Was he as smart as Newt? As conservative? All you need to know, I responded, is that in 1992 it was Gekas who proposed the amendment to strip sexual orientation from the Hate Crimes Statistics Act of 1992, which was ultimately signed into law by President Bush. For Gekas, apparently, there was no political stigma attached to being soft on crime as long as gay people were the victims.

At the end of the day, Newt's staff tracked me down for a brief reunion at his office just hours before I was to head back to Harrisburg for my sacred rugby practice. We chatted amiably behind closed doors about how bad the Redskins are before he invited me to join him for an impromptu press conference. In the outer office, Newt made a snide comment to Elizabeth Birch to the effect that HRCF's "making Candace famous." Since gay activism had never made anyone famous, Newt was so far off I could have picked him off with an underhand toss. Elizabeth shot back, "Candace is doing it herself—she is quite capable." Almost as an afterthought, Newt sputtered, "Don't get me wrong, I'm proud of her." If anyone had made me famous, it was Newt himself because of his famous political gay-bashing. At any rate, my motivation was not about notoriety—it was simply to use my stature to remind Americans that gays and lesbians deserve an equal place in society, free of violence and discrimination. It was hard for my Machiavellian brother to accept that my motives could be pure. Rob, who was also in town, joined us. We sat on his office veranda with its sweeping view of the Capitol Mall while posing for photos and aswering questions. "I love my sister, period," Newt said simply. "I don't mix my family with my politics."

Newt sure has a funny way of showing his love. I bit my lip when he delivered the coup de grâce: "I consider Candace a sinner, but she considers me a sinner, too. I don't walk around Georgia looking for the perfect human being." I was dumbstruck. If this was what he considered love for his little sister, he had another think coming. I've never considered Newt a "sinner." As an agnostic, I don't even view the world in those Old Testament terms. And with the shabby way he treated Jackie during the divorce, no one would ever mistake Newt for a "perfect human being," if such a person exists. All I'd ever said is that I thought his politics were wrongheaded, even cruel. But that hardly qualifies him, in my mind, as a candidate for eternal damnation. Purgatory, maybe.

All this and more raced through my mind. But overawed by the surroundings, I couldn't put my objection into words. I hardly wanted to get into a spitting match with my brother during our first public appearance together. Even if I had, how could anyone come up with a sound bite to express the profound sense of betrayal I was experiencing? Asked by a reporter about Newt's statement backing "tolerance" for gays, I could only mumble, "My position is that tolerance is not enough."

Love and family, apparently, have a temporal meaning for Newt. After receiving yet another spanking from the far right, he told reporters the next morning at his regular Tuesday press briefing that gays should not be afforded federal protection from job discrimination, attempting to burst ENDA's balloon before it even got off the ground. Just for good measure, he delivered another stunning blow: "I'm very cautious about the idea that you want to have active homosexuals in junior high school and high school explaining to young people that they have all these various wonderful options." As an "active homosexual," I can assure my big brother that the "wonderful options" humans have are to make a choice between honesty and hiding, love and hate. Sadly, it seemed, he had chosen the latter.

After our meeting, Newt did make several halfhearted efforts to welcome me into the political arena. "It's great to see my sister get active," he told reporters. Asked if my activities might hurt his standing among his conservative constituents, he replied, "No. It's a free country." In March, he inexplicably sent me a copy of an *Atlanta Journal-Constitution* column by Tom Teepen about our visit. "Candy, FYI. Enjoyed seeing you, Newt," he scribbled next to the article, which was sharply critical of his about-face. "Sure family is important, but, hey, politics is politics," Teepen wrote. "Just a day after a palpably warm meeting with his lesbian half-sister, House Speaker Newt Gingrich was back doing what has become Republican gay-bashing business as usual. . . . What was a pleasant embrace of family values one moment degenerated into the politics of family values the next." I couldn't have said it better myself.

CHAPTER THIRTEEN

CANDACE THE MENACE

Such a long, long time to be gone
and a short time to be there

—GRATEFUL DEAD,
"Box of Rain"

I returned to Harrisburg from Washington that early-March night with ice coursing through my veins, and it wasn't the fault of the frigid cold front that had descended on the East Coast. Newt had continued his antigay barrage, and my presence appeared to have had no impact on his words or actions. When Newt insisted that he didn't mix "family and politics," what he really seemed to mean was that he would place his political constituency above his familial bonds. From what I could tell—and Rob, to a lesser degree, seconded this view—Newt had become more Speaker and less sibling.

That's why I started thinking of him as the Stepford Speaker. His actions, it seemed, increasingly resembled those of the automaton-like women from the famous book and movie. I understood the kind of pressure he was under and the inordinate demands placed on his life, but I couldn't see him sacrificing humanity for career. What harm could possibly have come from showing warmth toward his family—or at least a willingness to sit down and hash things out with his lesbian sister? Even the most fanatical on the religious right would be hard-pressed to fault him for that.

Shortly before lobby day, HRCF had asked me to become their chief spokesperson for National Coming Out Day, a decade-old annual celebration on October 11 which encourages gay people to be open with friends and family about their sexual orientation in order to challenge stereotypes and combat hatred. Still leery of leaving behind my life in Harrisburg for the high-pressure world of the cultural wars, I struggled with the decision, especially since it entailed a grueling twenty-four-city tour culminating in a Coming Out Day press conference on the steps of the Capitol, and a stop in Los Angeles at the Gay and Lesbian Community Center later that evening. (The tour would soon be expanded to include twenty-seven more stops.)

Newt's cold behavior toward me and his continuing narrow-mindedness on the gay question helped me to understand that the opportunity with HRCF—which later in the year dropped the "Fund" from its name—was one I couldn't afford to pass up. Newt might be a lost cause, I thought, but this was at least in part because he saw nothing to lose, in crass political terms, as a result of his hostile rhetoric. And that, with some stepped-up organizing and mobilization—in Georgia and on every other leg of the tour—could change.

At the very least, I hoped my presence would encourage him to refrain from the most incendiary forms of verbal gay-bashing. The rest was up to gay activists and our nongay allies. We had to help along the ongoing grassroots movement that would one day make overt expressions of homophobia as politically dangerous as racism, sexism, or anti-Semitism. It was a tall order, I realized, but a noble one nonetheless—the kind of cause in which a twenty-eight-year-old, rugby-playing dyke could find meaning and, perhaps, a calling. At the time, I had no idea of the extent to which Newt's far-right politics and arrogant wielding of power would alienate so many Americans and serve as a rallying cry for his opponents.

As important as this goal seemed, there were the practical considerations. I was reluctant to give up my decent wages and job security at UPS, which had taken me six years of backbreaking work to achieve. Could I take a six-month leave of absence from UPS? That wasn't feasible. UPS rarely granted leaves longer than three months, and even then it was usually only in case of illness or personal crisis. When David and Elizabeth offered to make my position with HRC semipermanent, freeing me from having to job-hunt after the tour ended in October, that concern began to fade.

In thinking about their offer, I still worried about the nagging allegation that I was capitalizing on my brother's fame. To feel good about my decision, I needed to find some special contribution that I could make to the gay movement and the larger gay rights debate, something beyond being a thorn in his side. It didn't take me long to spot a niche I could fill. In speaking to reporters and gay activists and in doing an extensive survey of gay literature, I realized that my blue-collar roots had provided me something of a unique understanding of gay politics.

As a number of observers have pointed out, a major weakness of the contemporary gay rights movement is its inability to connect national groups with the grass roots. For too long, the major national gay rights lobbies have adopted an inside-the-Beltway strategy that has limited both their popular appeal and a widespread understanding of what they are actually trying to achieve. While the groups, including HRC, have had considerable success lobbying members of Congress, especially liberal Democrats, they have never been able to create the outpouring of support from the gay and lesbian rank and file or their legions of supporters necessary to create change. As a result, when letters, phone calls, or votes are needed to win on a national issue like the gays-in-the-military fight, the groups lack the firepower to influence Congress. The Christian Coalition, by contrast, seems capable of unleashing its hard-charging army at will.

From my perspective, the inability of the gay groups to connect with the grass roots is partly the result of perceived class divisions. The leadership of gay groups is drawn primarily from the highly educated professional class, dominated by lawyers, lobbyists, and communications specialists. While they are almost invariably extraordinarily bright, dedicated, and effective, they may not always connect with the majority of gays and lesbians who live more workaday existences. During my travels across the country, I have been fairly successful at translating the message of the gay groups into practical terms that large numbers of people can understand. My personal story, and the accidental nature of my activism, seem to resonate with audiences of all sorts. Describing my background, I tell audiences that if I can make a difference, anyone can. It gives me an authenticity with a skeptical public that Washington insiders sometimes lack.

Of course, being Newt's little sister doesn't hurt either. Newt is, after all, the master of the populist political appeal, even if his rambunctious rhetoric sometimes backfires. Many of the gay community's most charismatic leaders, from San Francisco city supervisor Harvey Milk, who was assassinated in 1978, to Donna Red Wing, who helped fight off statewide antigay initiatives in Oregon, have had that rare ability to connect to a wide cross section of gay and nongay Americans.

For years, class divisions have been wielded like a cudgel against the gay movement. The religious right has effectively promoted the myth that gays and lesbians are a "privileged" class undeserving of "special" legal protections. My favorite villain of this school is Lon Mabon. In a derivative of classic anti-Semitic arguments, Mabon, head of the anti-gay Oregon Citizens Alliance, has played on the fear that gays and lesbians control a disproportionately large slice of the economic pie. The argument has played particularly well in rural Oregon. Suffering from a severe downturn in the logging industry, local communities throughout the state have passed dozens of Mabon-inspired ballot measures barring gays from inclusion in antidiscrimination laws. (A state law and a court ruling have blocked the measures from taking effect.)

To bolster their erroneous claims, Mabon and other antigay leaders have used the gay business community's own propaganda against it. Citing figures from surveys of the disposable income of readers of upscale gay magazines such as *The Advocate* and *Out,* they have claimed that the income of the typical same-sex couple is close to double the national average. Gauging the income of gays and lesbians from a sampling of magazine readers is like claiming that the average income of *Fortune* readers is representative of the country as a whole. (Newt has played directly into this artificial cultural divide by anointing himself the spokesman for "normal Americans." Implicit in that characterization is the suggestion that his political foes, gays included, are somehow less normal and less American. In fact, his liberal critics are every bit as much a part of the nation's fabric as Newt and his conservative friends.)

Actually, like most Americans, gays and lesbians are much more likely to load trucks at UPS than serve as an executive at Bank of America. Billionaire Hollywood mogul David Geffen or wealthy tennis star Martina Navratilova are no more representative of the gay community as a whole than Bill Cosby and Deion Sanders are representative of African-Americans.

Mabon and other antigay ringleaders have also promulgated the stereotype of the childless homosexual. Freed from parenting, they argue, gays and lesbians have more disposable income than heterosexuals. While it's probably true that gays and lesbians are less likely to have children than their straight counterparts, we are raising them in increasing numbers, and with the same monetary concerns as heterosexuals. What about a couple like Sharon Bottoms and April Wade, who made national headlines when they were stripped of custody of Bottoms's four-year-old biological child? The couple is decidedly working class: Bottoms bagged groceries at Kmart and Wade was a chef at a Red Lobster restaurant while they raised their son, Tyler.

Indeed, a better case could be made that gays and lesbians are less affluent than their hetero brothers and sisters. In a July 1995 study in *Industrial and Labor Relations Review,* Lee Badgett, an assistant professor of public affairs at the University of Maryland, found that "gay male workers earned from 11 percent to 27 percent less than heterosexual male workers with the same experience, education, occupation, marital status, and region of residence." Badgett based her study on the 1989–91 General Social Survey, a sample that is far more representative of the general population than a few thousand well-heeled magazine readers. Because gays and lesbians face so much discrimination, they face a competitive disadvantage in the workplace. This inequity translates into lost jobs, missed promotions, and ultimately, diminished earning power.

Despite its critics, the study has lent an empirical basis to a trend that a long trail of anecdotes corroborates. Conservatives dismiss Badgett's study because she is a lesbian. But the contempt that religious conservatives heap on gays and lesbians is itself evidence of the discrimination Badgett has identified. To remind people that antigay workplace discrimination is pervasive, the HRC compiled a forty-one-page booklet detailing more than two dozen well-documented cases of antigay discrimination. The case studies range from a postal worker who was harassed and beaten on the job to a college professor who was dismissed when a student threatened her life by toting a gun on campus and declaring that God had "ordained" him to kill all homosexuals. In both cases, the employees lacked recourse because sexual orientation was not included in relevant antidiscrimination laws.

Today, only nine states and the District of Columbia ban discrimination on the basis of sexual orientation, a category that is also conspicuous by its absence from federal civil rights laws. Because the religious right has been so successful in positing gay rights as special rights, we've had little success passing legislation protecting gay people from discrimination, despite the fact that national polls have consistently found that close to three-fourths of likely voters oppose job discrimination against gays and lesbians. Equally glaring is that a majority of respondents do not realize that it's perfectly legal in most of the country to fire someone who is gay or just perceived to be.

This argument, I determined, was my ticket into the gay and lesbian movement. As a UPS veteran from Harrisburg, I was as well placed as anyone to make a compelling case to the American people. Almost overnight, I went from reluctant convert to enthusiastic advocate for gay rights, set to begin my tour of the country. I took David and Elizabeth up on their offer.

After renting a tiny apartment with a view of a small grove of trees in Wheaton, Maryland, about a thirty-minute drive from the HRC's office in downtown Washington, I packed my stuff into the back of my Tracker and headed out with my cat Mingus Khan, who I'd named after the villain Khan of *Star Trek* fame and in honor of my first Siamese cat, Ming Toi.

When I wasn't in another state altogether, my drive to and from the office was one of the few chances I had to collect my thoughts and contemplate how much my life had changed in such a short period of time. The ride up and down Sixteenth Street reminded me of a scene from Hunter Thompson's *Fear and Loathing on the Campaign Trail*, in which he describes the gauntlet of lights heading into the District as a metaphor for the treacherous terrain of American politics.

Leaving Harrisburg was bittersweet. Despite all our moving when I was a kid, the city on the river was the only place I'd ever really considered home. As the youngest of four children and an inveterate partygoer, I was accustomed to being surrounded by loving family and friends. I had no idea if the political pros in Washington would have anything to do with me, or I with them. To make matters worse, for the next six months, I'd be on the road, where it's all but impossible to make permanent friends. I know it sounds trivial, but I also hated giving up the spring rugby season. It was an inducement that had helped me get through numerous bleak Harrisburg winters.

The tour began in late April in Seattle, where, frankly, I bombed. Nervous and self-conscious, I stumbled through a short speech, disappointing the hundred or so people who had shown up to see Newt's lesbian little sister. It was so bad that David Smith, whom I was soon fondly calling "Smith," suggested on the cab ride to the airport that HRC hire a speech coach to whip me into verbal shape. I assured him that wouldn't be necessary. As bad as I was, I told him, with a little practice I couldn't help but improve. There was nowhere to go but up.

Most of the tour is a blur. There were stops in Greenville, South Carolina, which is a Christian Coalition breeding ground; New

Orleans; Las Vegas; Des Moines. In San Francisco, where I had the honor of serving as a grand master of the twenty-fifth anniversary of the city's gay pride parade, I had a chilling encounter. After the parade ended in downtown San Francisco, I hung out for a little while with an HRC canvasser who was asking people to sign up for our organization by showing them some of the scary things Newt's Congress was doing. Suddenly a skinhead-appearing young man approached and pointed to a photo of my brother. Rolling up his sleeve to reveal a swastika tattooed on his forearm, the guy said, "I want *that* man to be president." I wondered if Newt understands the kind of people his firebrand politics attracts or if he just doesn't care. As Republican Rep. Peter King once said of Newt's attacks on everyone from liberals to unionists, by the time the Speaker is done, the party will be supported only by "barefooted hillbillies at revival meetings."

For the rest of the tour, I generally managed to elude such ugliness. My hectic schedule made my sixty-to-seventy-hour UPS workweek look like a walk in the park. I would usually start the day with a 6:30 A.M. television interview that Smith or another HRC staffer had set up. From 9 A.M. to 4 P.M., I'd do as many as a dozen print and radio interviews.

After the brouhaha over *Eye to Eye with Connie Chung*, I felt that I could handle even the most wicked curveball a reporter could throw. With a few exceptions, journalists were respectful and polite, especially in comparison to the brutal treatment my older brother sometimes receives. I continued to field questions about whether I was taking advantage of my brother's notoriety. The bigger problems were usually semantic: using the term *sexual preference*, which implies choice, versus *sexual orientation*, which signifies a more deep-seated identity. Reporters repeatedly confused *equal rights*, which means the inclusion of gay people in antidiscrimination protections, and *special rights*, the religious right's dishonest term for the desire of gay people to be free from discrimination. Generally, I was content if I could get in a few quotes about how gay people lack antidiscrimination protections in most parts of the country and about the importance of coming out of the closet.

HRC maintained a huge file of clips from the tour. "Newt, Candace: A Lesson in Love," read the *Boston Herald* headline. "This Gingrich a Proponent of Gay Pride," announced the *Los Angeles Times*. "C. Gingrich: Coming out a 'vital' step," said the *Des Moines Register*. Almost all the stories were accompanied by photos of me and, less often,

Newt. In the stories, reporters tended to fixate on my diminutive size and boyish features. I'm described as everything from "elfin" to my personal favorite, "Candace the Menace."

The most problematic story of all had nothing to do with me. Gail Sheehy's September 1995 *Vanity Fair* profile "The Inner Quest of Newt Gingrich" revealed Mom's history of manic-depressive illness, which had been misdiagnosed for years. Sheehy attempted to understand Newt's ambition in the context of Mom's illness, which made little sense to me. It was painful for Mom and the rest of the family to see her personal life picked apart in a glossy magazine.

Despite its grueling pace, the tour did have a sort of rhythm. After finishing with interviews, I'd take a couple hours off to eat and nap back at the hotel before heading out to the town meeting, where I'd speak for up to half-hour and then take questions for another half an hour or so. After that, I'd chat with members of the audience, sign a few autographs, and head off to dinner with whatever HRC staff member had accompanied me. By the time I was finished, it was usually pretty close to midnight. My head would hit the pillow as soon as I was safely back inside my hotel room.

At each stop, as the usually overflowing crowds warmed up to me, I gained confidence. As the summer passed, I noticed myself speaking more assuredly and with greater depth and complexity about gay politics. The positive feedback I was getting served to reinforce my belief that I'd made the right decision in becoming an activist. Much to my shock, a Kitsap County, Washington, gay and lesbian political club wanted to name itself the Candace Gingrich Democrats.

The positive feedback made for a few laughs. In Greenville, the local Metropolitan Community Church minister thanked me for speaking and told me I was a "prophet." I was touched and humbled because I knew I was anything but. One massive ego is enough for my family, so I turned his compliment into a running gag. For the rest of the stop I called Kris Pratt, a native of the state who accompanied me on this leg of the tour, my disciple. "Get me a glass of water, disciple," I teased her. "Scratch my back, disciple."

The trip helped change my perspective about relationships. At the time, I was still dating Jolene, who was living in Harrisburg. But the good-natured jousting between me and Kris, I soon realized, was rooted in a growing affection between us. During the brief periods in which I was in D.C., I found myself spending most of my time with her. The two of us shared passions for baseball, hiking, beer, and heavy doses of sarcasm. I also found her charming, handsome, and more than a little sexy. We went out together so often that we had our own regular table at Cafe Luna, a gay restaurant in the Dupont Circle neighborhood of Washington that serves great veggie meals. But since we both were dating other women, we never acted on our feelings. Besides, as Kris constantly reminded me, I wasn't really her type, which was ultrafeminine women.

Over time, however, we both came to see each other as the most compatible person with whom we had ever spent time. So, after I ended my relationship with Jolene—and after Kris was unceremoniously dumped by her girlfriend—we gradually began dating in the late summer. We cemented our relationship during a women's vacation cruise. The lesbian-only Olivia Cruises holds regular commitment ceremonies. Though we did not participate in the event, Kris and I were a little weepy as we watched couples declare their devotion for each other and announce the length of their relationships—nine years, eleven years, thirty-four years. We realized that we could imagine spending the rest of our lives together.

The timing of the tour was uncanny. Everywhere I went, people wanted to talk about Newt, who was crisscrossing the country on his own tour to promote his new book, *To Renew America*. The combination of the controversial book tour and Newt's string of legislative successes implementing the Contract with America had put my brother in the forefront of the national political consciousness. I tried to stay, in David Smith's communications parlance, "on message" by talking about National Coming Out Day, but grassroots anger at Newt's right-wing political crusade kept cropping up anyway.

My favorite Newt protest came from the adorable blond son of a lesbian couple during a stopover at the University of Michigan in Flint. In anticipation of my visit, the budding Democrat had drawn a small poster, which he handed me with a big grin on his face. NEWT, YOU ARE NOT THE KING! NICK—7, FLINT, MI., it read. I couldn't agree more.

It was in Charlotte—without Kris—that I also faced the first and only anti-Candace protest. A bunch of students from the Republican Club at the University of North Carolina at Charlotte held aloft placards that said things like THE REPUBLICAN PARTY IS PRO-MORALITY, NOT ANTIGAY; CANDACE IS A POLITICAL OPPORTUNIST; and WE WANT NEWT. In the question-and-answer period that followed, one of the guys wanted to know if I was taking advantage of my brother's celebrity. By that time, however, I had my response down. "Why is it that you only accuse the liberal relatives of politicians of opportunism? Why don't you ask Jeb Bush and George Bush Jr. the same question?" I said, referring to the politician sons of former President Bush. The guy stared back at me blankly.

In New Orleans, I marched at the head of a candlelight vigil through the heavily gay French Quarter to commemorate World AIDS Day. The somber march impressed the tourists, and bar-goers who lined the sidewalks wore mournful expressions on their faces. When the march was finished, I milled around the Quarter a bit, chatting with some of the participants. A young man who could not have been older than twenty approached me with a funny story that shocked me because it illustrated how well-known I'd become in such a short time.

As the young man told it, he was sharing a house with a young woman who had named her pet parrot after her political hero, who happened to be Newt. "Hi, Newt," she'd say as she entered the room. But when the woman neglected the bird for long periods, the young man took it upon himself to teach it some phrases more to his liking. The next time the woman said, "Hi, Newt," the bird shot back, "My name's Candace, bitch." He said they both got a good laugh out of that one, as did I. In some homes, apparently, I was not just a household name; I was a birdcage name.

In one of my last stops, I attended the Gay Day at the Texas State Fair in Dallas, where I spoke at a rally with Chastity Bono—the daughter of now Representative Sonny Bono and pop icon Cher—who had just come out in an interview. Our common bond of having conservative relatives made us fast friends. Months later, Chastity went on to interview her famous conservative father about gay politics for a gay magazine, something I hoped I'd be able to do with Newt for this book.

One morning Jolene called the bed-and-breakfast at which Chastity and I were staying. The operator accidentally put her through to Chastity's room. Chastity promptly connected her to my room, but Jolene accused me of being in bed with Chastity because she had answered the phone. It was the beginning of the end for me and Jolene. To this day, Chastity and I laugh about the hotel operator's confusion. Who can tell all us lesbian children of Republican politicians apart?

Spending time with Chastity was one of several high points of the Dallas stop. Much to my surprise, the state-run fair actually sanctioned a gay picnic at the fairgrounds. All the straight guys in cowboy hats milling around knew exactly what was going on and didn't seem to mind in the least. It really felt like the "family outing" that was the theme for that year's coming-out day.

One of the most exhilarating stops that summer was the day I took off in June to attend a Grateful Dead concert at Robert F. Kennedy Stadium in Washington with Jolene. It was one of the Dead's last concerts before Jerry Garcia's tragic death in August. Appropriately enough, Bob Dylan opened up the concert. The crowd ranged in age from gay sixteen-year-olds in baggy jeans and grungy T-shirts to straight sixty-year-olds in tie-dye and ponytails. I realized about halfway through the concert that it was the safest I'd felt in my life in a large group of people.

The concert had a special meaning for me, in the midst of my own tour, because the Dead embodied so many of the ideas I wanted to get across to audiences. While Newt and his prohibitionist friends have accused the band of fostering a drug-induced "culture of irresponsibility," their concerts, for all the drug use, are really nothing like that. For nearly three decades, Jerry Garcia has encouraged millions to be open to human diversity and new experiences in life. That's the profound legacy, I realized, of Garcia's life—a legacy that no amount of right-wing revisionism can take away from him.

My summer of speaking engagements and press coverage triggered an outpouring of letters and cards to the HRC, many of them heartbreaking. "Your brother's politics scare me!!" one mother wrote. "Your courage makes me hopeful. I have two daughters—one straight, and one gay. They are both wonderful. My straight daughter was born with rights. My gay daughter has to fight for them."

Another mother related the death of her beloved son, Daniel, from AIDS-related complications. She described Christian Gays and Lesbians for Justice, an organization Daniel had left as his legacy to the world. "Members of this organization are attempting to inform and send the message to the closed minds of Christian leaders, employers, and others who are persecuting the gay movement," she wrote.

A gay person in Denver wrote to ask for my help in stopping Colorado for Family Values, an antigay group that had just unleashed a diabolical plot to blame the Holocaust on the supposed gay presence in the Nazi leadership. " 'Macho' homosexuality inspired the ruthlessness of an entire regime," the group announced in its April '95 newsletter. "Please help stop such vile actions by the radical right," the young man wrote. "They are declaring war on us." "If only I had the power to answer his prayers," I thought.

The tour concluded back in my new home of Washington, D.C., with a well-attended press conference on the Capitol steps. The only glitch came when the ubiquitous Lou Sheldon held a simultaneous press conference at the other end of the Capitol, which he dubbed National Coming Out of Homosexuality Day. He imported the usual assortment of religious crackpots, "ex-gays," and antigay psychiatrists to attack the idea of feeling good enough about yourself to come out of the closet. To Sheldon's dismay, only a handful of reporters showed up.

That afternoon, I flew to Los Angeles for a celebration with an assortment of openly gay celebrities such as Dan Butler of *Frasier* and Sheila Kuhl, the *Dobie Gillis* star who was now a member of the California legislature. Like a bad odor, Sheldon followed us to set up another poorly attended demonstration a few blocks away from us in the heavily gay enclave of West Hollywood. I suppose I at least have to give him credit for perseverance.

At the end of the joyous night, back in my hotel room, I felt a combination of exhilaration and exhaustion at the thought of what I'd just completed. I felt as if I could sleep for a month straight, yet I was also eager to get on with the task of educating America. The day ended with a tinge of sadness, though. Rob Eichberg, who had founded National Coming Out Day more than a decade ago, had succumbed to AIDS not long before. I vowed to see his dying wish—a world without closets—fulfilled. Rob's death was a reminder to us all not only of how far we had traveled, but of how far we still had to go until we were home—free.

CHAPTER FOURTEEN

THE HOEKSTRA HOAX

That these "culture wars" with their "pro-family" emphasis turn those same families into mini-Gettysburgs,
with close to 10 percent of the children MIA or worse,
killed by friendly fire, is political exploitation at its
most cruel and cynical.

—LINNEA DUE,
Joining the Tribe

Talk about out of the frying pan and into the fire. After returning to
Washington in October 1995 from my grueling fifty-one-city
tour of America for the Human Rights Campaign, I barely had time
to catch my breath before being thrown into the middle of a congressional inferno with the religious right. This time, Brother Newt was
providing a taxpayer-supported forum to attack gay and lesbian youth
to "Rev. Lou," as Lou Sheldon, chairman of the Traditional Values
Coalition, affectionately calls himself.

This was one fight I relished. The minute Newt announced plans for
hearings on a measure to discourage school districts from adopting
gay-friendly curricula, I imagined what I would tell the committee
were I permitted to testify. I hoped to inform its members in no uncer-
tain terms that if they passed such a law, it would contribute to the pain
and suffering that gay and lesbian kids already experience in the
nation's schools. It would drive some of them over the edge and into
suicide. I would tell them that it's agonizing to see my brother have
anything to do with such an ugly agenda.

The battle had begun nearly one year earlier, in December 1994—
just as I was coming out publicly—when Newt, according to Sheldon,

agreed to Sheldon's request to hold hearings on the minister's allegations that gay activists were "recruiting" in the public schools through gay-positive curricula. In the December 19 edition of the *New York Times,* Sheldon explained that Newt told him he did not want "kindergarten children or elementary school children being taught, where federal dollars are involved, that the homosexual lifestyle is just another kind of diversity."

Hearing this, I fired off one of my patented faxes to Newt's office requesting a face-to-face meeting with him. Attaching a copy of an article about Sheldon's ravings and the hearings, I wrote in the margins, "What's up with this?!" I asked Newt to please consider allowing me to testify when the time came. Since I knew exactly what it was like to be an isolated and confused gay teen with nowhere to turn for information or support, I thought I could provide an effective counterweight to Sheldon's lies.

The *Times* profile of Sheldon was fascinating as much for what it didn't say as what it did. Scrupulously balanced, the article was written by David Dunlap, a gay reporter who covers the gay beat. Surely, Sheldon, obsessed as he is by who's gay and who's not, knew that he was talking to a homosexual. Yet that knowledge didn't stop him from telling Dunlap that "there is no way we are going to say that homosexuality is viable" in the schools, and calling homosexuality a "perversion" and a "sin." Only in the bizarre world of American politics would such an exchange between a gay reporter and an antigay activist be unremarkable. Reading the story, I was frustrated that Dunlap didn't ask Sheldon to respond to the dark side of his programs—the harassment and violence that gay students regularly suffer—and how the minister proposed to eliminate this problem if kids weren't receiving accurate information about homosexuality.

Sheldon, whose organization is based in Orange County, had sought hearings ever since the courageous decision nearly a decade ago by the Los Angeles Board of Education to establish a gay and lesbian education project for the school district's 640,000 students. Those plans, however, had been blocked by the Democrat-controlled House. Known as One in Ten, the project teaches respect for gays and lesbians as valued members of the community. "Joined together in holding back satan [*sic*], we must protect our children and youth from this homosexual recruitment," Sheldon wrote in a fund-raising letter to Los Angeles religious leaders about the program and others like it. Asked by Dunlap for evidence of recruitment, Sheldon was dumbfounded. "Are kids crossing over?" he asked. "Not that I know of, no. I don't know of any tracking."

I'm not sure Newt was aware of the letter, but Sheldon's long history of demonizing gays and lesbians didn't deter him from working with the minister in arranging the hearings. The HRC uncovered Newt's tight relationship with Sheldon by doing a little investigative work. Cathy Woolard, HRC deputy director of public policy and a Georgia native, monitored Newt's January 1995 town meeting in Kennesaw, Georgia. In response to a question from Cathy, Newt said Sheldon had assured him that he had "serious evidence" of "things being taught that are clearly propaganda and clearly recruitment. . . . I don't believe that the taxpayers should pay for a program to teach [young students] effective methods of sadomasochistic interaction." The House would hold a one-day hearing, Newt declared to applause, "on whether or not taxpayer money is being spent to promote things that are literally grotesque."

Short on facts as usual, neither Newt nor Sheldon offered a shred of evidence that schools were teaching S&M and "grotesque" things. The only caveat Newt placed on the hearings was that they had to wait until after the first one hundred days of Congress, during which time the Republican majority would be concentrating on the Contract with America, his economics-based plan to "change the nation."

"All of the issues that are largely emotional about social policy, I think we can take a truce," he told Cathy. "I think we can focus on balancing the budget and on focusing the country, and then if we want to get back and fight over those later on, they'll still be available. We are more than busy enough without having to find new fights." Newt and his colleagues were apparently concerned that divisive social issues would distract from their government-cutting platform and that crackpots like Sheldon might cast an ugly light on the party. At the same time, however, they realized that Sheldon and other religious conservatives had served them well at the polls. As for Sheldon, it was payback time.

The only saving grace to Newt's rambling, uninformed remarks came when he acknowledged that having a lesbian sister limited the extent to which he would support Sheldon's goals. At least, I think that's what he was trying to say: "I don't want to get diverted off onto these kinds of fights. Not because they are not important on both sides. I think people here know not only my position, but some of you may well have seen my younger sister on television who is a lesbian and who went in and saw my mother and said, 'Mother, don't tell people I'm gay, I'm a lesbian. Gays are boys.' My mother said, 'Okay, dear,' and went on. [Candace] also said she wouldn't vote for me, because she's a Democrat."

Newt tried to clear up the confusion created by his remarks. "But my point is this: I think we have to have toleration, but that doesn't mean we have to back off from talking about what we believe in," he told the town meeting. "I'm very pro-family. But I'm not . . . I'm not for repression." Okay, that clears it all up. Newt's for tolerance and against repression. Sounds good. It's that pro-family thing that gets sticky. Somehow gays and lesbians pose a threat to "the family," though he just acknowledged that it didn't faze Mom in the least. Maybe I'm naive, but I'm not sure exactly what kind of threat I pose to the Gingrich family, or anyone else's family for that matter. Someday I'll confront Newt with that question directly.

Sheldon's quest for hearings stumbled for almost a year. Even in the new, right-wing–dominated House, Newt had a hard time finding a committee chairman who was willing to be associated with Sheldon and his nonsense. House Economic and Educational Opportunities Committee chairman William Goodling, a Pennsylvania Republican, announced publicly that he had no interest in presiding over such a charade.

But Sheldon knew a good fund-raising gimmick when he saw it. In his four-page solicitation, Sheldon bragged that he was doing his "very best to prevent homosexual advocacy and resulting recruitment in public schools because it truly *places our children 'at risk,'*" despite the fact that he'd admitted to Dunlap that he couldn't find any evidence to support that contention.

In the letter, Sheldon went on to praise Newt for agreeing to hold the hearings and for holding up "very well under the barrage of media pummeling concerning his lesbian sister. She has now been thrust into a national staff role with a gay and lesbian organization. Several weeks ago she held a press conference and indirectly confronted her brother concerning his response to her lifestyle. He spoke loud and clear when he said, 'I love my sister but I do not condone her lifestyle.' This gave the speaker a firsthand realization of the infiltration of the homosexual agenda within the public schools and to his credit he has not backed down despite this becoming an issue within his own family."

The letter, which sought a *"monthly donation"* to "protect our children," was filled with the usual religious-right code words. Gays and lesbians engage in "brainwashing" and have "infiltrated" the political system to "promote" their "abnormal lifestyle." Just once I wish someone like Sheldon would have the courage to acknowledge that even though he disagrees with what gay activists have to say, they play a legitimate role in American democracy and their views have a right to a fair hearing. Such an admission would go a long way toward improving the tenor of the country's political debate and lessening the anger and hostility directed at gays and lesbians. I'm not holding my breath, however. It would mean that Sheldon would have to come up with principled arguments for his positions rather than relying on well-worn, but financially lucrative, canards. Respectful rhetoric would put a damper on his fund-raising, on which he relies for his own salary and those of various family members.

The most dastardly part of the letter, though, is its postscript. For a contribution of "$50 or more," Sheldon offers to send donors *A Freedom Too Far*, a new book by the "leading reparative" therapist Charles Socarides, who has "treated over 1,000 clients who want to change from homosexual desire to heterosexual." Sheldon and other antigay conservatives advocate reparative therapy not because it works—the vast majority of reputable therapists in the country will tell you it's a joke—but because it allows them to argue that they are not mean-spirited. "We don't hate gays," they say. "We love them because we're offering them a way out of the evil gay lifestyle!"

What the postscript didn't say is that Socarides himself has a gay son, Richard, a high-level Clinton appointee. Despite his own son's obvious success and declaration of contentedness, Dr. Socarides has continued to insist that gays and lesbians are condemned to a sad, tragic life. The real sadness in the Socarides family is that a father has built a career negating his own son's existence. As hard as it is to have Newt consorting with the likes of Lou Sheldon, I can't imagine what it would be like having my own father devoting his life to defaming gays and lesbians. That Richard grew up to be such a healthy, happy adult is a tribute to his strength and courage.

In August, Sheldon finally got the go-ahead to hold the hearings. It came from an unusual suspect, Michigan Republican Pete Hoekstra, a conservative not known as a particularly antigay. The hearings, Hoekstra announced, would take place in September in the obscure Oversight and Investigations Subcommittee of the House Economic and Educational Opportunities Committee. Still, Hoekstra was forced to postpone the hearings at least three times after he came under intense criticism, and not just from gay activists. A September 22 editorial in his hometown newspaper, the *Grand Rapids Press,* called the hearings a waste of time: "For the most part, U.S. Rep. Peter Hoekstra has distinguished himself by focusing on practical solutions to substantive problems. Providing a forum for political grandstanding by antigay zealots is a marked departure from that pattern."

During the delays, Sheldon bragged that he was feeding to the committee "shocking" information about the infiltration of gay activists in the public schools. "Those hearings have been put off because of the enormous amount of information that has begun to surface concerning the funding that is beyond any comprehension we thought," he boasted. The committee, however, didn't seem overly impressed. Chastened by constituents in his own district, Hoekstra kept Sheldon at arm's length. An October 11 *States News Service* article quoted a committee aide contending, defensively, that "the committee does not work in concert with outside groups."

The hearings, which were finally set for December 5 and 6, were to feature testimony from William Bennett, the former Reagan and Bush administration official and author of the best-selling *The Book of Virtues.* In a letter to Hoekstra, I made my case for testifying by telling him of the young gay people I had met during my tour. "I know firsthand about the hate, violence, and discrimination that gay people often face in school," I wrote. "Some are lesbian or gay, while others are merely perceived to be gay by their peers. All have stories to tell that should not be left out of any sincere debate on values in our schools." Sheldon, who once called me the "black sheep" of the Gingrich family, bristled at the idea that I might testify, and not he. "What justifies her to do it?" he asked in an interview. "Just the name Gingrich?"

Hoekstra apparently agreed. In a December 1 fax, the congressman politely declined my request. The reason? By this point he was so spooked by the outcry over Sheldon that he was insisting that the hearings were not even about homosexuality, AIDS, or violence. The title of the hearings, he declared, was now "Parents, Schools and Values."

Once we received the news that I would not be permitted to testify, David Smith looked for other ways to get our message across. On the second day of the hearings, he decided we should show up at a press conference Sheldon was holding in the Capitol. Since we had no intention of an ACT-UP–style disruption of Sheldon's big moment, we stood politely outside the door and passed out literature, including testimony we had prepared for me to deliver. "Hi, my name is Candace Gingrich and this is what I would have said had I been allowed to testify," I said to everyone who walked through the door. Lou's daughter, Andrea, came over and introduced herself. Dressed in gold-sparkled pumps (RuPaul would have killed for them) and a silk blouse, she kept peeking out into the hall to see what we were up to.

In some ways, I longed for the kind of physical release of pent-up anger that an ACT-UP–type protest can bring. I was frustrated that I was utterly powerless to engage either the panel or Newt in a productive debate about gay youth and the destructiveness of Sheldon's assault on them. To clear my mind after the press conference, I walked the several miles from Congress back to HRC's downtown office. Watching the cavalcade of buses unloading tourists at the capital, I was overcome with a desire to shout, "Wake up and pay attention to what's happening in your country!" It's sometimes hard for me to summon the kind of patience needed to change the hearts and minds of a nation.

In the end, my testimony wasn't needed anyway. After nearly a year of anticipation, it's not surprising that the hearings were anticlimactic. Thanks to a stellar publicity blitz by Smith and crucial background research by Kris, we were able to get across the message that Sheldon's views were beyond the pale of respectable political discourse. It helped that HRC was assisted by a broad coalition of groups such as the National Education Association, the American Psychological Association, and the Gay, Lesbian, and Straight Teachers' Network.

At the same time, our fortunes got a boost by the surprising results of a poll conducted jointly by Democratic and Republican consulting firms, demonstrating that when it came to sex education, Sheldon was in the minority. Fifty-nine percent of parents in the survey said they were more concerned about "not providing children with enough information to protect themselves from AIDS" than about "exposing children to information about homosexuality." The respondents strongly opposed Sheldon's argument that AIDS education should be scuttled because it "presents homosexuality as acceptable."

Stung by the poll results and the revelation that Sheldon had once advocated quarantining people with AIDS, Hoekstra made sure the reverend never got near the witness stand. After nearly a year of lobbying for the hearings, Sheldon was relegated to the back of the cavernous hearing room and cruising the halls outside, dishing out antigay sound bites to every reporter within earshot. (The one interview Sheldon turned down was with me. Hoping to interview him for this book, I wrote him a polite letter requesting a meeting about his political liaison with my brother and his views on homosexuality. "I think we're too far apart to talk," he responded. So much for productive dialogue that cuts across political boundaries.)

The first day of hearings was dominated by Bennett. In his most authoritative voice, Bennett intoned that schools need to do a better job teaching "virtues." Citing the need for a civilized debate, he steered clear of Sheldon's antigay rhetoric, but it was clear what he meant by *virtues*, especially since Bennett had said three years earlier during an appearance on the conservative National Empowerment Television channel that gays were somehow a threat to the nuclear family. "When [gay activists] talk about the joys of the gay lifestyle they are lying, they know they are lying, and we know they are lying," he pronounced. "But if you speak out against it, it means you will be the subject of vilification. Ask Pat Buchanan about that, ask Bill Kristol about that. It's pretty mean." Bennett, like many conservatives who pretend to be more mainstream than Sheldon, will say one thing in the glare of the national spotlight and exactly the opposite before small, hard-core conservative audiences.

The problem with virtue is that it's relative. For Sheldon, opposition to gay rights is virtuous (not to mention profitable). For gays and lesbians and their supporters, raising money ridiculing a community of people represents the antithesis of virtue. But by any humane standard, teaching that homosexuals are a productive part of the community and should not be beaten up should be considered virtuous. We can argue over how to overcome antigay violence, but we should start from the assumption that it's wrong. For Bennett, however, such distinctions are too subtle, not to mention politically dangerous. As Jon Katz put it in the March 1996 edition of *GQ*, Bennett is the "reigning czar" to those who find it easier "to forbid graphic representation of violence, decay, poverty and social and racial disorder than to take on the real thing."

The highlight of Bennett's testimony came when Pennsylvania Democrat Chaka Fattah asked Bennett whether the safety of gay and lesbian students was not also a value that a democratic society should uphold. "The fact is many times these youths are targeted for hate violence and discrimination from other students and teachers—sometimes even their families and churches turn their backs," Fattah said. "That is a primary reason why gay and lesbian youth are more likely to commit suicide, drop out of school, or run away altogether. Any program that can provide a little comfort and understanding to these youths, and enlightenment to their peers, is sorely needed in our country."

Like a deer caught in headlights, Bennett froze. How could he avoid advocating safety and freedom from violence and maintain his antigay stance? Rather than deal with the substance of Fattah's question, Bennett mumbled something to the effect of "Of course we can't have violence, safety is important," and then changed the subject. Bennett needed to look no farther than his own book to find answers to the mistreatment of gay and lesbian youths. In *The Book of Virtues*, Bennett eloquently calls for the cultivation of a "compassionate nature" in America's children. The schools must "see that neither animosity nor prejudice stunts [the] natural growth [of compassion]. The divisive 'isms' are major obstacles," he writes, referring specifically to "racism, sexism, chauvinism, and the rest. . . . Treat *no one* with callous disregard." (Emphasis Bennett's.)

The second and final day of the hearings provided more fireworks. As Sheldon was preparing his "evidence" for the hearings, he might have spent more time looking into the background of his so-called witnesses. For instance, Sheldon presented Orange County activist Claire Connelly as an aggrieved citizen who was offended by state-funded AIDS education programs. But a little checking found that Connelly, who is openly lesbian, had been expelled from membership in the Ventura HIV Care Consortium, a coalition of AIDS service groups, for attacking the very people she was supposed to be supporting. Apparently, Connelly had begun criticizing what she called "a clique of radical gay hedonists" in rambling letters to various state and federal officials only after the group she headed, the Gay and Lesbian Resource Center, was denied an AIDS grant. Ultimately, she abandoned AIDS education in favor of an organization promoting "new age spirituality." The other Sheldon witnesses trotted out the same stereotypes about gays and lesbians that the religious right has been peddling for years. For much of the testimony, a majority of the panel's chairs were conspicuously empty.

I wish I had been provided the opportunity to impress upon the panel that when it comes to gay kids, they are playing with fire. I didn't suffer terribly growing up gay, but a lot of kids do. They are vulnerable because they have no one looking out for them. The increasing abundance of information about homosexuality means that gay kids are "realizing the truth about themselves sooner," writes Linnea Due in her 1995 book about gay youth, *Joining the Tribe.* While that's generally a positive step, it also means they face hostility—even from parents and loved ones—at ever younger, more vulnerable ages as they seek to live openly and with integrity.

In his fund-raising letter, Sheldon, quoting Socarides, had the audacity to claim that gay youths are committing suicide at alarming rates because they themselves know what they are feeling is "not normal," and not because they face an unrelentingly hostile environment. Such an attitude conveniently abdicates all responsibility for society's contributions to this suffering.

When kids are strong enough to band together and stand up for themselves, adults in the community almost invariably clamp down on them. In Salt Lake City's East High School, a small group of students formed the Gay/Straight Alliance to hold regular meetings in their homes, classrooms, and cafés to talk about their common experiences as gay and straight kids. In retaliation, the Salt Lake City Board of Education voted in February 1996—just two months after the Sheldon hearings—to ban all clubs from high school property, from the Polynesian Club to Students Against Drunk Driving. Talk about cutting off your nose to spite your face.

Thanks to 1984 federal legislation prohibiting school districts from making distinctions among extracurricular activities, the Gay/Straight Alliance may have a good legal case to make. Antigay conservatives argue that the law was drafted only to ensure that school districts can't ban Bible clubs from meeting on school property. "The act was never intended to promulgate immoral speech or activity," Utah Republican Orrin Hatch told the *New York Times.* Like Sheldon and Bennett, Hatch apparently wants to make life-and-death decisions for others. More than anything, religious conservatives know a fund-raising and activist recruitment opportunity when they see it. They are sure to take full advantage of the hundreds of such gay groups springing up in high schools across the country to engender fear and opposition—and to attract new members.

I'm no lawyer, of course, but I think a good legal case could be made that the hostile climate for gay kids in the schools violates their right to equal educational opportunity. There's a case that might do just that before the federal Court of Appeals for the Seventh Circuit in Chicago. From the seventh to eleventh grades, Jamie Nabozny was regularly assaulted by other kids for being gay. Students trapped him in the hallways and bathrooms, tormenting him. They beat, punched, kicked, and urinated on him. Mr. and Mrs. Nabozny stood by Jamie, repeatedly asking the school district to discipline their son's abusers. School officials imposed no meaningful restraints on the assailants and scoffed at Jamie, telling him he should expect such mistreatment because he was gay. "If I didn't have parents who showed they continued to love me after they found out I was gay, I don't think I would be alive today," he said.

Bobby Griffith wasn't so lucky. Even the conservatives on the Hoekstra panel were left holding back tears when his mother, Mary Griffith, testified. A former fundamentalist Christian, Mrs. Griffith, whose story is told in LeRoy Aarons's book *Prayers for Bobby*, said she has never forgiven herself for Bobby's death as a teenager in 1983, when he threw himself off a freeway overpass into the path of an oncoming truck. Shortly before his death, Bobby wrote in his diary that he couldn't bear the condemnation that he felt would inevitably come from his family, minister, and friends were he to make his sexual orientation known to them.

After Bobby's suicide, Mrs. Griffith devoted her life to alleviating the suffering of gay kids. "Our family was very ignorant, and Bobby as well," she told the committee, her voice cracking. "Our source of information was kept very narrow, and confined to one train of thought: homosexuality must be cured because it is evil. We were told it was our fault, and we believed it. . . . Bobby needed to be respected and valued by his family and his community. He needed companionship, someone to grow old with, to love and be loved by, to share the joys and sorrows of life with, to worship God with, to pray with. These are universal values. No one should be excluded from this pursuit of happiness. Everyone should have an equal opportunity to learn and live by these values. Including children like my son Bobby." Amen.

CHAPTER FIFTEEN

CRYBABY

Let us march on ballot boxes until all over America
God's children will be able to walk the earth in decency
and honor.

—MARTIN LUTHER KING JR.

The civil rights train is taking off again, and I want to help stoke its furnace—and grease its rails. For too long, the connections between various movements for human dignity have been too bumpy. I'd like to do what I can to help change that. To commemorate the Martin Luther King holiday in mid-January 1996, I traveled to Atlanta for a weekend of events at the invitation of the King Center, the foundation established in the slain civil rights leader's memory. Coming on the heels of the Sheldon hearings, during which Newt's Congress offered a national platform for intolerance, it was rewarding to take part in a gathering dedicated to a positive and inclusive vision for America.

It was also eerie to hear just how much animosity my brother generated in civil rights circles. At a stirring invocation at the famous Ebenezer Baptist Church, President Clinton set a lot of heads nodding when he paid homage to King's legacy. Since King had stood up to George Wallace and the segregationists, the president asked, what would he have said to Newt's Congress bent on destroying the vision to which he had dedicated his entire life?

But the remarks that really brought down the house were from activist Dick Gregory, who followed Clinton onstage. He alluded to Newt's temper tantrum after the president refused to speak to him—or so Newt claimed—during their return flight from Yitzhak Rabin's funeral in Jerusalem on Air Force One. "This is petty, but I think it's human," Newt had said, justifying his response—the decision to stop negotiating with the president on the budget impasse. At the time, visions of Newt's kicking Dad in the shins as a three-year-old flooded my mind. A telltale photograph of Newt at the president's table sent his approval rating into a further tailspin. Democrats gleefully displayed the November 16 edition of the *New York Daily News,* which caricatured Newt as a diapered infant under the headline "CRY BABY."

"Poor old Newt," Gregory joked. "The president made him a nigger for the day by putting him in the back of the plane. So Newt came home and shut down the government." Many of the more than three hundred congregants were in the aisles, howling and holding their stomachs in spasms of laughter.

I couldn't help laughing either, but for me the president's Wallace-Gingrich analogy was no joke. Gay activist David Mixner once called Democrat Sam Nunn the gay community's George Wallace for his role in defending the military ban on gay and lesbian service members. As a right-wing Republican, Newt is even worse than Nunn on civil rights. I couldn't picture him blocking the door to blacks trying to integrate a public school, but on the other hand, Newt had just sponsored congressional hearings for an antigay activist who would deny gay youths protection and equal access to schooling. And despite his empty calls for "tolerance," Newt had looked the other way while an epidemic of antigay attacks swept the country—just as Wallace had done when violence against African-Americans skyrocketed in the 1960s.

On the surface, it appears that Newt comes out of the tradition of angry Southern conservative politics to which Wallace once belonged. Indeed, he has repeatedly pushed many of the country's hot-button issues such as affirmative action, welfare moms, and inner-city violence—not to mention homosexuality. Yet I suspect his heart's not really in it. In his transformation from a Rockefeller Republican to a scion of the party's far right, Newt dropped his long-standing support for civil rights for a less civil approach to race. Moving to his new, overwhelmingly white Cobb County district reinforced this moral and political shift. The way I see it, he's bowed to expediency and his seemingly limitless ambition. Like Wallace, Newt's learned that it's easier to nauseate than to educate.

There's no way Newt could be overtly racist. Living in the integrated Army world, Mom and Dad never permitted expressions of prejudice. As with his attitude toward the gay movement, Newt's views on race are maddeningly complex and inconsistent. While he has called for budget cuts that would seriously hurt the disadvantaged, he also credited "the liberal wing of the Democrat Party" for ending segregation at his January 1995 swearing-in ceremony. He also reminded conservatives of the "moral imperative of coming to grips with what's happening to the poorest Americans."

Shortly after the Million-Man March in Washington, D.C., Newt urged conservatives not to dismiss Louis Farrakhan out of hand. "I don't think any white conservative anywhere in America ought to look at Louis Farrakhan and just condemn him without asking yourself: 'Where were you when the children died? Where were you when the schools failed? Where were you when they had no hope?' " While the anti-Semitic and antigay Nation of Islam leader is hardly the most appropriate black leader to champion, it took more than a little gumption for my brother to challenge white conservatives on race. Can you imagine such a feat from Pat Buchanan?

In defending himself against charges of racism—an endeavor most white conservatives don't bother to undertake—Newt says that he is trying to create a new paradigm for combating black poverty and white racism that is more effective than those proposed by the civil rights community or the federal government. "The dominant black political leadership in America has accepted a version of history and theoretical model of how life works that are both profoundly wrong," he told the *New York Times* in October 1995. "It is largely a lawyer-preacher-government model of behavior, which just doesn't work. It was absolutely necessary for organizing the effort to break legal segregation, but which then trapped the black leadership into an analysis of how you solve things (you have the government do it) and a model of how you create wealth (which is you transfer it from someone who has already created it) and a model of organization (which is a victimization-reparations-political-action model), all of which are simply wrong for this phase of African-American history."

A mouthful, but an inspired mouthful, nonetheless. Unlike most conservatives, Newt at least has come up with a provocative and original thesis regarding the nation's racial problem. There's no question that minority groups, including gays and lesbians, must be creative about the models of social change they use. In a conservative era, an entrepreneurial model is likely to be more successful than a political one. If one reads between the lines, though, Newt appears to be suggesting that the values of the black community prevent it from pulling itself up by its bootstraps. And he fails to acknowledge the devastating effect that racism plays in the lives of African-Americans.

The continuing destructive effects of racism—and other prejudices—on American society were exactly what the King rally highlighted. Coretta Scott King, who is a longtime supporter of gay rights, worked to make sure the weekend's events were inclusive. During a Monday march through downtown Atlanta, I marched at the head of the parade with Urvashi Vaid, the former head of the National Gay and Lesbian Task Force, and Patricia Ireland, the director of the National Organization for Women, who describes herself as bisexual. In 1994, Mrs. King had delivered the opening remarks at the introduction of the Employment Non-Discrimination Act in Congress. (Just one month later, a hearing on the issue broke down when opponents expressed indignation at comparisons between the plight of blacks and gays.) With the attempts by white ministers such as Lou Sheldon to drive a wedge between the gay and African-American communities, the Atlanta rally was a welcome relief and a reminder that the majority of African-Americans see the two struggles as complementary.

At a rally after the march on Auburn Street between the King Center and the Ebenezer Church, I was asked to make a short speech. After a brief introduction by actor Kris Kristofferson, who called me a "human rights activist," the huge crowd fell silent. Since many people outside the gay community at the time were unfamiliar with my name, the audience was shocked to think that Newt or some equally conservative family member might be addressing them. The *Atlanta Journal-Constitution* had mentioned my name several times in relation to the event, but it hadn't registered with everyone.

Recognizing the confusion, I went out of my way to differentiate myself from my brother. Given the choice between Dukakis and Bush in 1988, I said, my voice rising, I'd voted for the Reverend Jesse Jackson. "Not all Gingriches support tearing down civil rights," I declared. A roar went up from the crowd. I then used the opportunity to kick off the Human Rights Campaign's voter mobilization project for the '96 election, which I had been appointed to lead. From spring to fall, I would visit dozens of cities and towns on behalf of the project.

When I look back, I'm amazed at how confident I felt speaking to that huge crowd. Despite some initial jitters when I thought about the gravity of the event, I sailed through my short speech. Just one year earlier, at my first appearance for HRC in Seattle, I could barely say my name, let alone speak coherently. Somewhere in the course of my long 1995 tour, I'd realized that the cause was more important than I was, which allowed me to focus on the activism and just be myself.

"Voting was once considered a privilege, but can now be regarded as a duty, thanks to Susan B. Anthony, Dr. Martin Luther King, and countless others who fought so hard for equal access to the polls," I told the crowd. "The election will determine the political direction of the country into the next millennium." In an implicit jab at the Speaker, I said, "If and only if we organize for the challenges of the election can we turn the country away from extremism and back toward core American values of fairness and equality."

Those sentiments would become my stump speech as I traversed the country encouraging gay people to become active. Thanks to the National Voter Registration Act of 1994, which was passed by the Democratic Congress and signed by President Clinton, it's now easier than ever to register to vote. Known as the Motor Voter bill, it allows people to register to vote when they renew their driver's license. HRC hopes to capitalize on the bill to encourage more fair-minded people to go to the polls. In the '92 election, gay money and votes contributed to Clinton's margin of victory. As a nonprofit organization, HRC is officially nonpartisan. Still, it's clear that the vast majority of gay voters will end up in the Democratic camp, no matter what those pesky gay Republicans say.

It's easy to see why. The Republican primaries were an orgy of anti-gay rhetoric. At a February religious-right rally in Des Moines, which I watched on C-SPAN, every Republican presidential candidate except Sen. Dick Lugar signed a pledge to oppose same-sex marriage. Senator Dole, supposedly the most moderate and thus most electable of the candidates, sent a statement saying that the pledge didn't go far enough and asserting that marriage was for "one man and one woman." He conveniently left out the "until death do us part" phrase of the marriage vow. In Bob's case, it's been "one man and one woman" two different times.

The worst of the lousy lot were Alan Keyes and Pat Buchanan. Keyes had the audacity to proclaim that he was the only true conservative because he cared about "values, not economics." That would go over really well as a general-election slogan: "It's not the economy, stupid, it's gay marriage." I'm sure Brother Newt, who emphasized conservative economic policy in his Contract with America, would find Keyes's statement equally absurd. It was illuminating, though, to hear Keyes reel off his list of the country's supposed social ills, none of which had anything to do with gays and lesbians: high rates of teenage pregnancy, illegitimacy, divorce rates, welfare moms. He was obviously at the wrong gathering. Alan, the anti*hetero*sexuality rally is down the hall!

Buchanan, who leaves the distinct impression that he would like to drive his proverbial pitchfork through the hearts of gays and lesbians, smiled and laughed his way through his condemnation of the "so-called gay family." All the candidates who appeared at the rally made a point of showing off their happy, Hallmark-card families. Buchanan, who has no children, thank God, displayed his smiling, obsequious (at least in public) wife, Shelley.

The irony that the Buchanans failed the procreation test that antigay conservatives had set up for marriage seemed lost on the audience. I don't think they would have welcomed the idea that my gay and lesbian friends who were raising children were more deserving of marriage and the appellation *family* than their beloved—but childless—Pat and Shelley Buchanan, not to mention Bob and Liddy Dole or Newt and Marianne Gingrich.

Phil Gramm proudly introduced his Asian-American wife, Wendy, and their mixed-race children. That miscegenation laws, abolished by the liberal Supreme Court in 1967, would have prevented their marriage was another contradiction lost on the audience. Even Steve Forbes, the self-proclaimed libertarian whose own father, Malcolm, was gay, signed the pledge. As columnist Richard Cohen said in the *Washington Post,* Forbes should be "ashamed of himself" for taking a position that was contrary to the integrity of his own family.

For Newt, too, politics comes before family. During a June 2 appearance on *Meet the Press,* Newt said he would boycott my wedding to another woman. "When Candace had girlfriends with her, that doesn't offend [me]. That's her life and I don't think we want government or politics in the bedroom. But I think it's different to say what standard you set as a society, what you mean by family, and what is best for children. I wouldn't regard [Candace's wedding] as a marriage. I think a marriage is between a man and a woman." The fact that heterosexuals such as Newt, who've had multiple marriages, are the ones who're actually damaging the institution doesn't seem to bother my brother. June 2 was my thirtieth birthday. Happy Birthday to you, too, Newt! In May, Rep. Bob Barr, a Newt sidekick from Georgia who is on his third marriage, had introduced the "Defense of Marriage Act" to further discourage states from allowing same-sex marriages. Somehow, I don't think Barr had to twist Newt's arm to allow the legislation to move forward. If Newt endorses the bill, I won't have any qualms about reminding people of his personal transgressions. Instead of eyeing the White House, Newt would be better off minding his glass house. I'm hoping against hope that the specter of his own past behavior held against him will dissuade him from jumping onto the anti–gay-marriage bandwagon.

After participating in the inspiring King rally in Atlanta, what struck me about the religious political extremists' rally was its negative tone. The participants had a deep-seated need to demean others to make themselves feel whole. How else can one explain their incessant attacks on gay Americans? How else can one understand their obsessive desire to define themselves in opposition to people who are not opposed to them? Civil rights activists in Atlanta, by contrast, were working to be included fully and on equal terms in American society.

In a slick video that concluded the rally against same-sex marriage, Bill Horn, the event's organizer, said that gays and lesbians should be relegated to second-class citizenship because they fail to leave a "legacy," in the form of children. Such a view ignores the fact that gays and lesbians do in fact raise children. But even more importantly, it ignores the legacy that people—including heterosexuals who don't have children—can leave beyond their bloodlines. Those who work with the homeless or play beautiful music or educate the young make invaluable contributions to humanity. The main legacy Horn will leave, by contrast, is a long trail of hate and discrimination that others, including his own children, will be forced to clean up.

Newt had another reason to stay away from the rally. During the primary season, he'd adopted a lower profile. In the wake of the celebrated Air Force One incident, shutting down the federal government, and proposing a number of draconian cuts in popular federal programs, he'd gone from the pinnacle of power to perhaps the deepest trough of unpopularity of any politician in America. After briefly flirting with a presidential run, he quickly realized he needed to rebuild his image and concentrate on running the House.

Revolt was also brewing in the ranks. "I know [Newt] must be agonizing, but everyone remembers that he attacked the ethics of [former] Speaker [Jim] Wright, and now [his own ethical problems are] coming back to roost," freshman Republican Mark Foley of Florida told the

Washington Post. Republican Sen. Al D'Amato from New York said, "Newt Gingrich is a smart man but he misread the ['94] election entirely. People did not vote to cut education and funding for the environment. People did vote for change but not this revolution. They want lower taxes and less spending but not dirty drinking water." There was even talk that Dick Armey, the majority whip who in a radio interview had once referred to his House colleague Barney Frank as "Barney Fag," would soon mount a challenge to Newt for the Speakership.

When the papers reported that Newt broke down and cried toward the end of another long, difficult day in the office, my heart went out to him. "No one knows what my wife and kids have gone through for two and a half years of charge after charge after charge," he said. It was good to see that the Stepford Speaker was still capable of emotions.

After spending much of the last year and a half under intense scrutiny on the road, I know how the pressure and constant criticism can get to people. I spent lonely nights in austere hotel rooms wondering if I had made the right decision to leave my comfortable life in Harrisburg. As much as I cared about the cause, were all the lost sleep, hard work, and antagonism from hatemongers worth it? Ultimately, I'd discovered, the answer was yes.

Still, I couldn't help but think that Newt had contributed to his own problems. I'm no political analyst, but if I've learned one thing on the road, it's that America in the 1990s is decidedly conservative—not in the partisan sense, but in the sense of aversion to radical change of any sort. I can't fathom what Newt and his colleagues were thinking when they were talking about a conservative "revolution." Americans are in no mood for upheaval, whether it be from the left or the right. His own incendiary rhetoric, effective only for mobilizing a narrow conservative constituency, had come back to bite him in the behind.

Any constructive change, whether in gay rights or job stimulus programs, is going to move at a glacial pace, at least for the foreseeable future. Americans may have soured on the idea of cutting back on the social programs directly affecting their lives, but their antipathy to government—and the temptation to back GOP government-bashers such as Newt—still remains. Any initiative on behalf of gays and lesbians must take this fact into account. Even when sympathetic to us, voters are demanding that a painstaking case be made for the necessity of the legislation in question. Chief among their concerns is how it will affect their pocketbooks.

Despite his budget debacle, not all was lost for Newt. Looking Nixonian with a five-o'clock shadow and pasty skin, he appeared on the December '95 cover of *Time* as its Man of the Year. Dubbing him "Master of the House," the newsmagazine devoted nearly fifty pages to Newt's life and times. For Mom, who had suffered through his every setback as if they were her own, the honor almost compensated for the last six months of misery. She proudly displayed the magazine to all her friends. I, of course, worried that *Time* was glamorizing antigay bigotry.

The cover story was another example of the charmed political life of my brother. In early December, the House Ethics Committee had thrown out all but one of the Democrats' charges against him. Newt received another shot in the arm when a federal judge rejected a Federal Election Commission charge that GOPAC had made illegal campaign contributions to him and other Republican candidates. The judge's decision put a damper on the Ethics Committee's investigation of the one remaining charge. It appeared that Newt could now put the troublesome ethics questions behind him and concentrate on his legislative agenda. Despite his political troubles, the party tapped him to preside over the Republican convention in San Diego, where he and I will go head to head. In the Gingrich family, tears of frustration turned to tears of relief.

Throughout late '95, Newt's and my paths rarely crossed. Through phone calls and faxes, I continued to no avail the effort I'd begun one year earlier to reach out to him. I still thought it would be productive for us to sit down and talk, especially since I'd decided to write this book. As Mom kept reminding both of us, after more than a year of sparring with each other through the press, it would do us both good, professionally and personally, to sit down and "work things out." The public, I thought, would also benefit from seeing a family discuss its political differences at the same table with love and compassion. It would put a human face on the increasingly ugly debate over gay rights—which, apparently, is exactly what Newt hoped to avoid.

In October of '95, Newt sent me a signed copy of the *Congressional Record* of the proceedings on the 104th Congress, First Session. "To Candy," he scrawled on the cover in writing nearly as illegible as mine. "I thought you might like a historic memento. Love, Newt." Inside was a transcript of his medicaid and medicare debate with minority whip Dick Gephardt. In his remarks, Newt cited each of his sisters by name in defending his party's proposed cuts. "They love their parents and they also know that someday they are going to retire. And they wish somebody had the guts in this city to start protecting the system, so it will not collapse when the baby boomers retire," he said.

As usual, I had mixed emotions about the memento. It was sweet of him to think of me, and I certainly appreciated being included in his discussions of the family. But as a Democrat, I was unlikely to frame my brother's advocacy of brutal cuts to cherished social programs and display it on my wall. The idea that he had to cut the programs to save them didn't hold any water with me. What about making some serious cuts in the cold war–bloated military weapons budget and using the savings to shore up programs that help the poor?

In December, I faxed Newt a note wishing him and Marianne luck in making up their minds on Newt's "big decision"—whether to run for president. "I believe that you and I probably share more commonalities on how gay people should be treated in America than one would expect given the divisive 'cultural war' slant the media often projects," I said charitably, signing it "Peace, Candace." I never heard back except through his aides, who explained that he was extremely busy.

Most of our interactions continued to take place via the impersonal media. In December, I was invited to appear on NBC's hit sitcom *Friends*, where I was to play a minister who conducts a commitment ceremony for the lesbian couple on the show. (Note to Bill Horn: the same-sex couple is raising a baby boy.) Filming the show was a gas. I got to hang out with Matt LeBlanc, the heartthrob who plays Joey on the show. He asked me what it was like being a lesbian. Putting it in terms I knew he'd understand, I said, "Kinda like being a straight guy." He nodded.

My lines didn't take very long to memorize. "Nothing makes God happier than when two people, any two people, come together in love. Family and friends, we are gathered here today to join Carol and Susan in holy matrimony," I said. It was nice to see TV finally depict what has been going on in private ceremonies all across the country for more than three decades now.

After the airing of the show, which won the top rating for the week, Newt was widely quoted as saying sarcastically, "I'm glad Candace has a day job. I have another sister, Susan, who's a member of the Christian Coalition. You don't see Hollywood glorifying her, you don't see TV shows calling her up." Well, the next time the show has a lesbian wedding, I'll recommend my Christian, conservative sister Snow for the part. If Hollywood is so intent upon "glorifying" homosexuality at the expense of the Christian Coalition, why was *Friends*'s same-sex wedding one of the first on prime-time television, *ever?*

Next thing I knew, Newt, still working overtime to soften his demagogic image, appeared on *Murphy Brown.* Asked by a reporter if Newt's cameo was coincidental, I felt it was only fair to employ my own sarcasm. "You know how Newt is," I said, "always taking advantage of the things I've done. He's a theatrical opportunist, riding on my coattail." I also wondered why he hadn't declined the invitation in favor of Snow.

Though our interactions were less than productive, at least the media was not allowing my brother to forget me or the issues I was raising. At his now-famous appearance before the White House television correspondents' dinner, talk-radio host Don Imus looked directly at Newt and announced that his sister had played a "thespian on *Friends*"—about the least offensive thing he said all night. Newt chuckled. (My favorite Imus line came at the expense of Pat Buchanan: "Why does everyone think Pat's an anti-Semite? He lost a relative in the Holocaust. His uncle fell out of a guard tower.")

Hardly seeing my brother in the city we now share is a fact of life I'm still getting used to. In March, HRC helped members of Parents, Families, and Friends of Lesbians and Gays (PFLAG) lobby Congress on ENDA during their weeklong "Moms and Dads Go to Washington." Milling about with the group's members outside Congress, I spotted Newt looking down on the scene from the balcony of his office, where one year earlier he had called me a "sinner" in front of television cameras. With his bad vision, I couldn't tell if he recognized me from afar. I waved anyway. He waved back. He then disappeared into the interior of his office, back to leading the country. As far as Newt was concerned, I was, once again, out of sight, out of mind.

CHAPTER SIXTEEN

WE'VE GOT THE POWER

> However powerful a man may be, it is hard for him to make his contemporaries share feelings and ideas which run counter to the general run of their hopes and ideas.
>
> —ALEXIS DE TOCQUEVILLE,
> *Democracy in America*

It seems wherever I go, people ask me if I have mixed feelings about my brother's sagging popularity. If the Republicans lose control of the House in November and Newt loses the Speakership, they suggest, my profile as a national gay rights advocate would plummet accordingly. But neither of us is going away anytime soon. It's a mistake to underestimate the tenacity of the Gingrich siblings. No matter what happens to Newt politically, I fully intend to continue working for this noble cause in whatever way I can. I'm sure Newt feels the same way about his brand of conservatism. In any case, wishing for Newt's Republican agenda to succeed just to keep my name in the papers would be the very definition of selfishness. After all, my brother and his colleagues are at work tearing down what it's taken my community and our allies decades to construct.

In my capacity as spokeswoman for the Human Rights Campaign's 1996 voter mobilization project, I certainly wasn't pulling any punches. HRC plans to contribute to at least 150 campaigns, targeting key states and municipalities where the gay vote could turn the tide in favor of President Clinton, other Democratic candidates, and that most endangered of species, moderate Republicans. With Republicans still claiming control of Congress, the aim is to keep the presidency in

Democratic hands. We've also begun to plan what we could only dream about as recently as nine months ago: recapturing at least one congressional house for the Democrats. The Republicans' resurgent unpopularity will not alone accomplish this feat, so we've worked on building alliances with other progressive groups to get out the vote and expand our base of support.

As early as January, there were already positive signs. In Oregon, two hundred HRC members contacted thirty-four thousand voters on behalf of pro-gay Democrat Ron Wyden, who defeated Gordon Smith in a special election by less than 1 percent of the vote to capture Bob Packwood's seat. Lon Mabon, the head of the Oregon Citizens Alliance, chief sponsor of a string of antigay initiatives, entered the race for the other Senate seat, despite reports that the OCA is on the brink of financial collapse. But polls show that voters are so fed up with the group's destructive and obsessive focus on homosexuality that his candidacy will only detract further from Republican fortunes in November.

Oregon isn't the only proving ground this fall. We plan to work especially hard on behalf of Sen. Paul Wellstone in Minnesota; Dick Durbin, who is vying for retiring Paul Simon's Illinois Senate seat; and Dale McCormick, a Maine state senator who hopes to become the first openly lesbian member of the House, to mention just a few. McCormick's race has taken on special significance with Gerry Studds and Steve Gunderson having already announced their retirements. (By early '96, Gunderson had begun to hint that he might seek reelection after all.) If McCormick loses, only the stalwart Barney Frank would remain to speak on behalf of gays and lesbians. In addition, we're working with a number of groups to remove Jesse Helms from the Senate. We dubbed the gay anti-Helms campaign "Give Helms his pink slip," in honor of the senator who has devoted much of his long career to making gays third-class citizens susceptible to blatant job discrimination. Of course, some have interpreted the slogan as a reference to lingerie, in which case we just have to figure out what size he wears.

Antigay officeholders can no longer count on gays who keep a low political profile out of fear of the disclosure of their sexual orientation. HRC's voter mobilization project features a series of public service announcements. Titled "You've Got the Power," the television, print, and radio ads feature celebrities such as Amanda Bearse of *Married with Children*, Greg Louganis, and Dan Butler of *Frasier*. The ads encourage gay people and their allies to go to the polls. In sports, you sometimes hear coaches remarking on the good fortune of having too many good players to get everyone on the playing field. After decades of virtually no celebrities who are out of the closet, the movement suddenly has an embarrassment of riches. At the March Gay and Lesbian Alliance Against Defamation media awards dinner in Washington, D.C., I met Mitchell Anderson, who plays the gay music teacher on Fox's *Party of Five*. Mitchell had come out the previous week at L.A.'s GLAAD awards.

In our conversation, Mitchell said he was not sure he had done the right thing, explaining that coming out might hurt his career by making it harder for him to get acting jobs. I told him that I had had some of the same doubts, but that the experience of contributing to a cause larger than myself and the gratitude I received from the gay community make it all worthwhile. I explained "You've Got the Power" to him and asked if he would be interested in participating. A few days later, he called from Los Angeles to say he would indeed like to play a part in the project. But when I spoke to the coordinator of the public service ads at HRC, he said that he already had more actors than he could handle. Fortunately, we were later able to fit the talented and handsome Mitchell into the campaign.

My own role in the voter mobilization tour, which amounted to a sequel to my 1995 National Coming Out Day tour, consisted primarily of giving political pep talks around the country. For this project, we focused not just on the big cities, which reinforces the notion promulgated by antigay activists that all gay people either live in New York City or San Francisco or are on their way there. In Kent, Washington, for instance, I hung out at Sappho's, the city's first women's bar. In small towns like Kent, it's such a struggle for gay people to survive that voting and political organizing is often the last thing on their minds. While I was there, one of Sappho's owners registered to vote for the first time. Drinking a beer at the bar, I noticed her approach each of her staff about whether they had registered to vote yet. Now that's what I call reaching out to the grass roots! It's voters like those in Kent who will turn the election.

Gay voters, like nongay voters, are profoundly alienated from the political system. They have long felt that even the Democrat-controlled Congress had been unresponsive to the needs of their community. Still smarting from the disastrous results of the gays-in-the-military debate, and with the Employment Non-Discrimination Act still years away from serious consideration, they see little advantage in going to the polls or in working on behalf of a candidate. As unresponsive as the Democrats have been in the past, the Republican Congress is downright hostile.

President Clinton has failed to light a fire under some gay activists. Yet he's the only president ever to say the words *gay* and *lesbian* without spitting. Far too many gay voters fail to recognize the pro-gay gestures he has made. To take just a few examples, he's appointed over a hundred gays and lesbians to his administration; hosted the first White House AIDS conference; endorsed ENDA; abolished sexual orientation as a criterion for security clearances; ordered all federal agencies to prohibit gay- and AIDS-related discrimination; and appointed the first liaison to the gay community, Marsha Scott. Log Cabin Republicans, a gay group, recently issued a statement saying that Clinton's and Dole's records on gay issues are "comparable." I beg to differ. Bob Dole, after all, called homosexuality "unnatural" on MTV, spent much of the primary season sacrificing gays and lesbians on the altar of the religious right, and bungled the Log Cabin campaign donation.

The best motivation for gay voters, I'm sorry to report, is the danger posed to their interests by Newt's Republican henchmen. When you convey the absurdity of the GOP's attacks on gays, and the imperative of stopping the right, gay audiences tend to perk up. Even then, it's difficult to convey just how terrible this Congress really is, at least in part because liberal lobbyists do such a good job fending off the worst of the proposed legislation. Since the Republicans gained control of both houses in '94, there have been a bevy of antigay riders attached to various pieces of legislation. Thanks to skillful lobbyists such as HRC's Winnie Stachelberg and our coalition partners, we have for the most part been successful in thwarting the attacks.

Even if most of the amendments are unsuccessful, they put the gay movement on the defensive, leaving it unable to concentrate on its own goals. Then there are the verbal attacks: Majority Whip Dick Armey's "Barney Fag" comment, California representative Duke Cunningham talking about "homos" in the military, and Jesse Helms saying AIDS is exclusively a disease of homosexuals and drug users. I tell people that since it's unlikely we can change the attitudes of these hostile members (look at how little headway I've made with my own smarter, more open-minded brother), we must work toward changing the names on their office doors. While this may seem like a pipe dream, I've noticed during my travels that people of all stripes are fed up with the divisiveness and intolerance that characterize the right wing of the Republican Party and, increasingly, the GOP as a whole.

When I speak enthusiastically about the political process, people often ask me if I'd ever consider running for office myself. At the risk of sounding like Mario Cuomo, I usually respond that I learned long ago never to say never. To me, the thought of being in Congress is simultaneously fascinating and repellent, depending on my mood and how debased the institution is at the moment. I must admit that I sometimes fantasize about being the lesbian Pat Schroeder, the pugnacious and articulate Colorado Democrat who has announced that this will be her final term. Meeting the charismatic Dale McCormick also made me consider the possibility more seriously than I had in the past.

Around the HRC office, I joke that I'd consider running only if our media-savvy communications director David Smith would agree to serve as my press secretary. The major question is how I would translate my prominence in national gay politics to a local political base in the largely Republican Harrisburg area. Maybe I'll ask Brother Newt's advice. Somehow I can't see him offering to place GOPAC at my disposal. I'm not even sure I could count on my Republican family's vote. "Too radical," I can already hear my mom complaining of my candidacy. At least I don't think she'd use the B-word.

Most of the time, however, I'm too busy unearthing gay voters to give much thought to my future in politics. While most of my tour was dominated by the drudgery of travel and the disquieting political atmosphere, there were a few glittering moments. At South Eugene High School in Eugene, Oregon, a student group called Youth for Justice invited me to speak. I was nervous because the group had not informed the press about my appearance in advance. Talking to high school students is still risky in some parts of the country if the press gets ahold of it and religious conservatives cry bloody murder.

In early March, Elise Self, a member of the local PFLAG chapter, met me and Becky Dinwoodie, our western field organizer, at the airport in her bright red Cherokee with a cooler of fruit, sliced vegetables, and sandwich fixings, which we nibbled on as we drove to the liberal stronghold of Eugene. Elise has worked tirelessly to defeat several statewide antigay initiatives after she learned that her daughter is a lesbian. With her sense of humor and political smarts, she reminded me of a liberal version of Mom.

When we arrived on campus, we were whisked to the principal's office. My mind filled with flashbacks to my own high school days when the mere mention of the subject was verboten. I feared we were about to be informed that the meeting was canceled or that I was barred from addressing sensitive topics. Much to my surprise and joy, the principal told us that the demand for my speech was so great that they wanted to open it to the entire four-hundred-plus student body. Apparently, several teachers wanted to bring their classes to it.

Suddenly, Harrisburg in the early 1980s seemed like another planet. The principal set up the school's cafeteria for the meeting at the end of the school day. I opened my remarks by asking how many kids had come just because they had seen my appearance on *Friends*. When only one student raised her hand, I knew I was home free. The kids were so attentive that one could have heard a pin drop. I discussed coming out, the gay movement, and, employing my accidental-activist line, what people could do to get involved. During the question-and-answer period, the students asked the most altruistic questions I'd encountered during my travels. "How can we make school better for gay kids?" one asked. "How can we help friends if we think they may be struggling with their sexual orientation?" said another. "How can we help support gay rights?" Ah, the benefits of growing up in a liberal community!

I was flabbergasted. When I was in high school, kids were so insecure that all we could think of was me, me, me. But from what I could discern, the teenagers had been influences not just by their liberal parents but by years of antigay propaganda emanating from Mabon's Oregon Citizens Alliance, which is located just up the road near Salem. If adults were capable of being so cruel to gays and lesbians, the young people felt they had a responsibility to step in and protect the gay kids in their midst. They were also shaken by news of a Utah school board's move to ban all student groups from school property just to keep one small gay student group from meeting in the Salt Lake City school. If this was what the young generation was like, the gay movement had a brighter future than I'd ever dared imagine.

The students' sensitivity injected new life into my get-out-the-vote campaign. In March, I traveled to Portland, Maine, to help organize HRC members in support of Dale McCormick. As a two-term state senator, McCormick had the broad base of support necessary for a successful run, inoculating her from the charge of being a single-issue candidate, which is often hurled at budding gay public servants. Visiting the state fulfilled a lifelong dream because it had given birth to two of my passions: L.L. Bean and Stephen King.

From the instant I laid eyes on the famous catalog, I just fell in love with Bean's rugged outdoorsy look, which I first adopted during high school and embellished in college. I've gone through so many flannel shirts in my time that I make Lamar Alexander look like a high-fashion model. My love affair with L.L. Bean temporarily hit the rocks when I learned that Linda Bean Folkers, one of the Bean heirs, was heavily involved in state right-wing politics and had backed the failed 1995 antigay ballot measure.

When I inquired about the Folkers problem, I was informed by in-the-know Portland activists that it was still okay to enjoy the clothing because, other than receiving dividend checks, she has no role in the operation of the company, which is one of the largest employers in the state. In fact, the company has an antidiscrimination clause that includes sexual orientation, and Barb Wood, a lesbian former member of the Portland City Council, is now one of its executives. Even so, I can't resist a small protest against my favorite clothing manufacturer. Whenever I return a purchase to the company, I list as my reason Linda Bean Folkers's bigoted politics, as advised by activists in Maine. (The Bean situation is markedly different from the gay community's long-standing antipathy toward Coors Brewing Company. Though that company also protects gay workers from discrimination, the Coors family pours millions of dollars into the coffers of the religious right.)

McCormick looks as if she could have jumped out of the pages of a Bean catalog herself. She has one of those wonderful, weathered faces in which all the age lines are actually laugh lines—despite the scars of dozens of political battles over the years. As a young woman, she was the first female in the United States to apprentice as a carpenter, become a master craftswoman, and receive a journeyman's card. A union diehard, McCormick is so dedicated to workers' rights that she provides health care for her entire campaign staff, a practice practically unheard of in American politics.

One of the favorite cities on my tour lies down the road from Newt's Cobb County, but remains infinitely more intriguing. On St. Patrick's Day weekend, I visited Savannah, where I hoped to meet the Lady Chablis, the great drag performer immortalized in John Berendt's best-selling book *Midnight in the Garden of Good and Evil*. To canvass for new members, I sat at a table HRC set up outside Club One, a bar where Lady Chablis regularly performs. I immediately noted that at least 50 percent of Club One's patrons were heterosexual. For reasons I can't fathom, drag is a huge draw in the South. Maybe it's because Southerners love to party and they know that drag queens make for more than a few laughs, which is fine with me as long as they are laughing with, and not at, the performers. Many also don't see drag queens as gay men in dresses, but as entertainers. I'm sure that in his many years in the South, even my straitlaced brother has taken in a drag show or two, though I'd be surprised to discover he'd donned a dress and pumps himself.

Savannah is undoubtedly one of the most beautiful cities on this earth. Stately mansions overlook grand, tree-lined cobblestone streets. The Savannah River wraps the city in its shores. And as Berendt's book points out, it doesn't take long to discover the city's eccentric side. Driving down the city's main streets, one quickly realizes that the medians are planted with palm trees. What are palm trees doing in Savannah? After errant drivers took out one too many oaks, the city had palms planted because they were massive enough to absorb the shocks of tipsy motorists. Every few trees, careful observers can make out nicks in the trunks.

To my dismay, I was so busy politicking that I never got inside the club to see Lady Chablis. Fortunately, as much partying was going on in the streets as inside the club. With the exception of the obligatory preacher warning pedestrians to repent the laundry list of sins he repeatedly and loudly attributed to them, everyone was having a fabulous time. As the revelers passed the preacher, they would yell, "Whatever happened to 'Love thy neighbor'?"

On my last night in Savannah, I spoke at a small gathering for the Metropolitan Community Church of Coastal Georgia. I gave my usual pep talk about the importance of political participation. I sometimes get so inured to the enormity of my work that I forget how important it is to people who have less access to the flow of political information. When I returned home from my trip, a letter from the church's pastor, Mel Bailey, was awaiting me. "We are on the brink of making it as a church which serves the gay and lesbian community," she said, "and your presence was actually something of a little coup for us that will also give us respect among our denomination. I thank . . . you for that little moment that means so much to us as we fight to come of age."

Later, I attended a house party for a Levi's and leather club called the

Sentinels. Images of leather-clad gay men are often used by the religious right to demonize the entire gay community, most of which has little interest in the S&M pastime. In reality, the S&M community is nothing like the right's stereotype. The leather guys I met were these big, gentle teddy bears who lavished hugs and kisses on me. I was flattered when they made me their first ever honorary member of the Sentinels.

Hanging around with the group after my speech, I was particularly struck by one guy's story. The man and his partner had recently watched his daughter from a previous marriage participate in the local teen beauty pageant. The young woman had made a point of wanting them both there to share in her big moment. After she was awarded top prize, she thanked her "two daddies" from the podium for coming and for being "wonderful parents." When it comes to family, it's not what you wear, but how much you love.

PART THREE

SISTER OF THE HOUSE

CHAPTER SEVENTEEN

"WE CAN WORK IT OUT?"

The normal is the rarest thing in the world.
—SOMERSET MAUGHAM

During our brief balcony meeting with reporters in March 1995, Newt spoke the truth when he said the Gingrich family represented the American family "in all its complexity." Indeed, the family's complexity starts with Newt himself, as he has readily acknowledged: "People assume I'm some right-wing, out-of-touch Neanderthal who doesn't get it. I mean, I'm *adopted!* Both of my fathers are *adopted!* I mean, give me a break!"

Yet, just a few months earlier, Newt had this to say about family: "Over time, we want to have an explicit bias in favor of heterosexual marriage. And by the way, my mom was divorced and remarried, I'm adopted, I'm divorced and remarried. I'm not sitting here as someone who is unfamiliar with the late twentieth century. But if you look at the pathologies and weaknesses of America today, reestablishing the centrality of marriage and the role of a male and a female in that relationship is a very central issue of the next twenty years."

For the right wing, however, "reestablishing the centrality of marriage and the role of a male and a female in that relationship" translates into an unrelenting political attack on gays and lesbians—an attack Newt appears to have every intention of facilitating. No less insidious is the right's attempt to shunt women back into traditional marriage as little more than biological vessels and caretakers for their husbands. If you ask most Americans, they will tell you that what counts is love and commitment, not sex roles or family structure—as Newt's own family demonstrates.

But if complexity is a hallmark of the Gingrich family, then contradiction is Newt's middle name. I have to give Newt credit for acknowledging not just that his lesbian sister is an integral member of the Gingrich family, but also that gays and lesbians are an integral part of the American family. This rare admission, however, is the source of his undoing on the subject of gay people. As such, we deserve an equal place in every aspect of American life, from the military to marriage. This basic belief would seem to subvert Newt's "either/or" characterization of gay rights, in which the safety and security of gays and lesbians somehow pose a threat to families.

Newt, in all honesty, should know better. The Gingrich family certainly can't blame its instability on any other group of people, and no member of it would ever try to do so, what with our rather knotty family tree. After Mom divorced Newt's biological father, Newton McPherson, she married Robert Gingrich, who himself had been abandoned by his biological parents and later adopted. Mom and Dad raised Newt, Snow, Rob, and me. Newt married Jackie, his high school math teacher, while still a teenager, and the couple had two daughters. Newt then divorced Jackie and married Marianne. Early on in their marriage, the couple decided not to have children, which made sense because Newt had had a vasectomy years before. (I always chuckle when I see those NEWTER NEWT bumper stickers, because he already has been!)

My siblings and I, whatever our divergences on politics and religion, have come together on the value of love. While Rob has a "traditional" marriage to Dave, with two children, Snow waited until she was forty-eight to take her vows. I, of course, went down an entirely different path, coming out and having a long-term relationship with Ann, a short one with Jolene, then settling down with my current flame, Kris. Despite our familial differences, it's not too corny to quote the Captain and Tennille lyric "Love will keep us together."

Love has also helped us navigate our religious and political differences. My parents, for instance, are Lutherans. Mom goes to church to this day, while Dad usually stays home to work on the house or to watch the Sunday-morning political shows. The image of Mom and Dad heading their separate ways on Sunday mornings reminds me of the December 1995 cover of *Family*, a magazine published by the antigay organization Focus on the Family. The Norman Rockwell–style drawing depicts blond Mom, Bible in hand, dragging her perfect little blond kids to church while Dad, beaming, golf bag slung over his shoulder, heads off to the links. Inside, the story's writer gives moms everywhere advice on how to bring dads back into the fold. "Anyone who professes to be a Christian but who does not attend church is disregarding God's Word and thus living outside His will," the article declares.

The problem with such a view is that Christians—like families—come in all shapes and sizes. Telling Christians that if they don't go to church they are disregarding God's will is, to be blunt, a lot of baloney. If someone finds a church that gives her spiritual sustenance and joy, so much the better. But the truth is that some churches are basically cults of personality for their leaders and have little to offer in the way of moral guidance. Sensing that, many Americans have chosen to stay away from organized religion or to create their own forms of worship.

For instance, Focus on the Family, which claims several million members and a $100-million annual budget, functions primarily as a platform for the ego of its leader, James Dobson, and a fund-raising machine for his personal political agenda. The group dishes out millions of videos, books, and magazines filled with Dobson's pop psychology and armchair evangelizing—all laced with politics—but fails to provide deeper sustenance or acknowledge the complexity of moral living for its members. Gays and lesbians, of course, are among Dobson's most frequent targets, routinely denigrated as threats to country and family.

I admit that the machinations of self-serving preachers like Dobson have contributed mightily to my skepticism toward organized religion. Gay people have long seen through the facades of right-wing preachers because what they say about our community is at odds with reality. When Dobson calls gay people irresponsible hedonists, he is dead wrong. Being gay is no more about sex than being straight is. All you have to do is look at all the decent, honest, hardworking, compassionate gay people to know that Dobson and his antigay cohorts on the far right are either ignorant or, worse, deliberate liars. Gay people contribute to American society rather than detract from it. To be fair, it's not just the religious right that's unwelcoming to gays. Even more liberal, mainline denominations often shun us as well, though that's beginning to change for the better.

Former president Jimmy Carter, who describes himself as a conservative Baptist, wrote these words of wisdom about Dobson et al. in a February 1996 column: "Other Christians and the general public must not condone, even by silence, these obnoxious attitudes, increasingly promoted among a few demagogic religious and political leaders. Undisputed acceptance of a premise that originates in the religious community tends to authenticate it among those who have their own personal prejudices."

Over French toast and mimosas at Paper Moon, my favorite gay brunch spot in Harrisburg, I recently asked Mom to describe the Gingrich family's religion. She took a long, thoughtful drag on her cigarette. "Your dad and I are Lutherans, Newt's a Baptist, and you're, well, nothing," she said.

"Thanks, Mom," I joked in reply. "I really enjoy being described as 'nothing.'"

Susan puts it this way: "Newt became a Baptist when he married, Rob and I are Presbyterian, and Candace is a vegetarian."

Despite my appearance as a minister on *Friends*, I suppose there is some truth to Mom's and Susan's words. I would have to be considered agnostic—at best. In my own life, I haven't found a need for organized religion. With all the hostile messages coming at me, including from the emissaries of various faiths, it's more urgent to believe in myself. Ultimately, we all have a responsibility to remind ourselves of our ability to be compassionate, respectful, and generous. I would rather rely on the nonviolent philosophies of the more open-minded Eastern religions for my moral guidance than the fire and brimstone of the Old Testament. If Dobson and televangelist Pat Robertson, the founder of the Christian Coalition, would dedicate just a portion of the prodigious energy and telecommunications clout—to say nothing of money—that they allocate to denigrating gays and single moms instead to serving the downtrodden, we would all be a lot better off.

My own disdain for empty invocations of the Lord became clear to me one day in high school. It was an Olympic year, and as an avid athlete and disinterested student I was spending all my time in front of the television watching the Games. At one point, an American high jumper who had won the gold medal was being interviewed by a fawning reporter. The athlete said he wanted to "thank God" for his victory. Already a budding heretic, I thought to myself, "God didn't jump over the bar, you jumped over the bar. Your belief in God may have given you the confidence to jump over the bar, but God didn't actually do it."

Excessive literalness about God's will obscures personal responsibility. Despite what Robertson and Dobson claim, no one has a direct pipeline to God. That kind of rhetoric seems particularly insincere because many people who are most eager to credit God are also the most egotistical, like the right-wing political preachers. When Robertson in particular is invoking the Lord's name, all I can surmise from his arrogant tone is that he's praising himself rather than the Lord. As a young teen, I remember hanging little sayings on big blocks of paper on the wall of my room. One of them serves as my best response to the high jumper and a good credo for life: IF IT IS TO BE, IT IS UP TO ME.

Despite my antipathy for organized religion, I have immense admiration for those who stick in there and try to make their denominations and congregations more tolerant and welcoming places. They are doing the hard work of social change. As a result of years of gay activists' struggle, even some mainline denominations are beginning to sanction the ordination of openly gay pastors and same-sex commitment ceremonies. There should certainly be many more avenues for gays and lesbians who wish to remain devout.

Still, I can't get past the idea that so many religions believe they are *the* right one. How can anyone be arrogant enough to say that Christianity is the true religion and Hinduism is not, or vice versa? On a personal basis, few people would ever behave in so offensive a fashion. I don't know anyone who tells her neighbor, "I'm right and you're wrong." That would be considered not just the height of rudeness, but the pinnacle of stupidity. It doesn't take a theologian to know that as humans, we are all fallible and that a neighbor's view may be as valid as one's own.

Robertson's history of anti-Semitism is by now well-known, but he is also hostile to other non-Christian faiths. According to *Church & State* magazine, in March of 1995 Robertson took his television talk show *The 700 Club* to India, where the wealthy televangelist and his son Gordon heaped scorn on Hinduism. "They really believe this god is real?" Robertson asked incredulously, in all seriousness. "This isn't just some plaything?" Robertson went on to contend that Hinduism created the poverty and desperation that afflicts parts of India. "We can't let this kind of thing come to America," he intoned ominously. I'm sure a few greedy Christian televangelists could solve all the country's problems.

Blaming poverty in India on Hinduism is like blaming poverty in America on Christianity. And as Pat surely knows, there are already thousands of Hindus in America. Besides, who is Pat to decide who, of whatever religion, comes to America? I find that in thinking about difficult moral and ethical issues, it's helpful to put myself in another person's shoes. Doesn't Robertson realize that it would be just as easy for the Hindu Broadcasting Network to send a televangelist to America to condemn Christianity? "They really believe this god is real?" I can imagine some religious leader wondering. "This isn't just some plaything?"

My favorite description of Robertson comes from *Newsweek*'s Joe Klein, who called him an "oleaginous tele-quack." If Newt knew what I know about Robertson, he might even agree. I know our father, Robert Gingrich, does, because I asked him about it one day as we sat at the dining room table in his Dauphin home. Between well-aimed lobs toward his spittoon, my conservative, military-vet dad demolished the Christian Coalition.

"I say they have no business telling other people how to live their own lives," he said. "Don't try to put your views down someone else's throat. To me the Christian Coalition ranks right up there with the Black Muslims and other splinter groups that are so opinionated they can't stay abreast of the times. The world just ain't that simple. Not everything is in black and white. Most things are a shade of gray." In a philosophy that dates back to the founding fathers, Dad insisted that religion and politics don't mix. "I don't think religion is an antidote for every problem that comes down the pike," he said. "When I want to go to church, I will go to church."

Dad says he has never wasted any time worrying about my sexual orientation. "When I found out, I thought, 'Well, that's just Candace,'" he explained. "It was your decision and there was nothing I could do about it, even if I'd wanted to. It would have been like wishing for a million bucks. My philosophy as a father was always to try to give my children a sense of right and wrong and then turn them loose on the world. I want them to be honest, hardworking, happy people. As far as I could tell, you were all those things, so I had nothing to complain about." As for gay rights, Dad said that he is shocked that activists like Lou Sheldon devote a good deal of their time to the topic. "There's no question people like that are bigoted," he said. "If that's all he can find time to do, he's a pretty sad representative of the clergy. He could be doing a lot more positive stuff, like feeding the homeless."

Dad said he was surprised Newt, who rarely talks about religion with the family, would have anything to do with Sheldon or "the Christian Coalition people." To the extent that Newt does, Dad insisted, "I think he supports some of their positions for political reasons." In several articles about Newt's career, much is made of a story by Lee Howell, a former speechwriter for the young candidate. According to Howell, Newt told him to omit any references to the Bible because of Newt's aversion to using religion as a campaign strategy.

Even today, like the rest of the family, Newt is wary of public invocations of Christian doctrine. Yet the religious-right activists who have worked with Newt count him as one of their own. "[Newt] doesn't talk about faith much," Pat Gartland, the Georgia director of the Christian Coalition, has said. "But I played football for Bear Bryant, and he didn't say much either, but I knew he was with us."

If I were Gartland, I wouldn't be so sure. We Gingriches have a way of confounding ideological expectations. After all, my sister Snow is a member of the Christian Coalition, and she is hardly with them on every issue. Despite my lobbying attempts—I've been funneling her information regarding the more sinister side of the organization— Snow has held fast to her membership while carefully distancing herself from some of Robertson's most extreme views. Fortunately for us, Snow and I have the kind of relationship that allows us to discuss volatile issues calmly, perhaps because of the big difference in age. I did not come along until Snow was nearly eighteen.

At first Snow wanted nothing to do with the tiny addition to the family, refusing to acknowledge me until I was out of the diaper stage and safely into toddlerhood. When Mom was pregnant with me in 1965, she went back to high school to get her GED. Snow says that she was embarrassed because Mom attended the same school she did. After I became potty trained, however, Snow quickly warmed up to me.

Always a good storyteller, Snow earned her nickname by getting me to believe a doozy. She managed to convince me that she was Snow White and my sister Rob, the Wicked Witch. The Seven Dwarfs, she explained, played for the New York Jets football team. Henceforth, Susan became Snow. I let Rob off the hook, refusing to call her the Wicked Witch. In my mind, they were both wonderful sisters. I was blessed to have both Snow and Rob nearby for most of my childhood and into my young adulthood. Despite all our differences, we have remained close.

Snow has overcome a lot of adversity in her life. Before I came along, Dad didn't believe in girls' continuing their education after high school. To get her master's degree in human services, Snow, with a little help from government grants, worked her way through school. Today she is married (she kept the Gingrich name) with two horses and two cats.

Snow's take on the Christian Coalition offers insights into the views of its members. In our conversations, I sometimes think we are not so far apart after all. Snow rejects the Christian Coalition's use of the Bible to condemn homosexuality. She condemns the Christian Coalition–backed antigay campaigns in several states that seek to institutionalize discrimination against gays with inflammatory rhetoric and images. She also parts company with the group's strict antiabortion views.

"The campaigns upset me because of all the false charges about gays," she said. "Statistically gays are not child molesters, yet they make it sound like it's all they do. A male teacher is probably more likely to display inappropriate attention to a female student than a gay teacher is toward a male student. I don't understand why anyone would care about the sexual orientation of a teacher as long as they do their job. It's none of anyone's business."

Snow acknowledges that antigay bias is always wrong. But when it comes to antidiscrimination ordinances, Snow seconded Dad's libertarian stance. "I'm not in favor of any laws protecting people from discrimination," she says. "I don't believe they work. I've experienced sex discrimination at the hands not of men, but of women. I wasn't going to spend thousands of dollars in an ultimately fruitless attempt to win my rights. It's much better to work toward acceptance on the social level by convincing people of the rightness of your position." I don't agree, but it's well within the bounds of responsible debate. Snow's position is shared by many gay conservatives. As the director of a program that serves pregnant women for the State of Pennsylvania, Snow also parts company with the Christian Coalition's hard line on abortion rights. "I don't believe in abortion as a means of birth control, but there are cases when a fetus is badly damaged or the life of the mother is at risk when it is very hard to oppose it," she said.

Snow said she does agree with the Coalition on economic issues like cutting taxes, decreasing the size of government, and "people helping themselves." (Presumably she doesn't include her own government job or Rob's in her downsizing plans.) The problem is that there are many conservative organizations that promote the same economic issues but manage to steer clear of attacks on gays and lesbians.

As it turns out, Snow insisted she joined the group to moderate its views. "I feel more comfortable with Ralph Reed's vision for the organization than Pat Robertson's," she says, referring to the organization's executive director and founder/president, respectively. The flaw in Snow's logic is that the two views reinforce each other and, in fact, are mutually dependent. Snow is uncomfortable when members of the family—usually Newt and I—are quoted in the paper disagreeing with each other. I guess that when it comes to the Christian Coalition, Snow and I are going to have to agree to disagree—gently, gently.

The family member with whom I have felt the most political allegiance is actually one of Newt's two daughters, Kathy Gingrich Lubbers, the proprietor of Carolina Coffee in Greensboro, North Carolina. Shortly before the fiery 1992 Republican National Convention in Houston, Kathy broke ranks with her father and urged the GOP to reject the antiabortion platform it had embraced in 1980. "If the Republican Party is to appeal to women in general, and specifically to young women, we must throw off this stranglehold that the antichoice movement has on the apparatus of the party," she said at a news conference organized by the National Republican Coalition for Choice.

Kathy, who is now in her early thirties, said Newt supported her decision to speak out publicly. "He has never, never attempted to silence me, unlike the current action of the Republican platform committee," she told reporters. "Our family is big enough to encompass both sides of this issue, and I would only hope that our party is just as big." Reached in Georgia, where he had just bested his opponent by a mere 980 votes in the Sixth District GOP primary, Newt echoed Kathy's views. Reiterating his opposition to abortion rights, he said, "Both my family and my party are strong enough to have healthy, spirited debates, even about the most sensitive of topics."

Kathy's decision to speak out for her beliefs was admirable. Her example was crucial to me as I mustered the chutzpah to speak out as well more than two years later, when Newt became Speaker and the Republican Party turned up its antigay rhetoric to a fever pitch. But when I called Kathy at Carolina Coffee to ask her some questions for this book, she politely declined, explaining that she had recently adopted a "low profile" on politics.

While I respected her decision, I was also disappointed that she wasn't as eager to support gay causes as she was abortion rights, especially since the two are often intertwined in right-wing attacks. In our conversation, I assured her that I was mostly interested in discussing the family's ability to overcome our political differences and her personal decision to speak up about an issue she felt strongly about.

I couldn't help thinking Newt might have asked Kathy not to talk to me. Maybe she was simply deferring to her perception of his political interests. Whatever the reason, gay rights, apparently, is one debate that's too "sensitive" for some members of the family. After chasing Newt around town for the better part of a year, I was starting to think that Mom's plaintive rejoinder that the two of us could "work it out" if we just sat down together was too optimistic. Maybe our family was not as "strong" as Newt claimed or as I hoped.

CHAPTER EIGHTEEN

FAMILY MATTERS

Am I my brother's keeper?

—CAIN

And I thought *I* had it bad. Pam Walton's father, Rus Walton, thinks that "tolerance" is a liberal concept. Among the far-right fringe to which he belongs, progressive ideas are the devil's business. In her provocative 1996 film documentary *Family Values,* Pam, a lesbian activist, chronicles her tortured relationship with Rus, a fundamentalist Christian who has advocated the death penalty for "practicing" homosexuals and abortionists.

Though Rus Walton, who heads the religious-right group Plymouth Rock Foundation, is far more extreme than Newt, I saw parallels with my own predicament. "Sodomy gnaws at the vitals and rots the soul of the nation that permits it to go unchallenged," Rus Walton wrote in his book *Biblical Principles Concerning Issues of Importance to Christians.* As recently as 1989 in a PRF publication, Walton suggested that the Old Testament calls for Christians to "rid their land of the abomination" of homosexuality by executing gays and lesbians to avoid "catastrophic consequences."

Because of her father's hateful politics, which views kindness to gay children as consorting with the enemy, Pam was forced into the position of being the family member to seek some kind of reconciliation. As the video details, after more than a decade of separation, Pam, with the help of her brother and sister, set about bringing the family back together by creating a dialogue with her father. After months of hemming and hawing, he agreed to a family reunion in which he would meet Pam and Pam's lover, Ruth, at his home in Marlborough, New Hampshire.

During her visit, Pam confronted Rus, who is the author of *One Nation Under God,* which is considered a classic fundamentalist text, about his writings on the death penalty. "We took a long country drive into Vermont," she recalled in an interview. "I said, 'Dad, I need to ask you something. I need to make sure you are not some wild-eyed extremist who wants to see me dead.' He said that he doesn't agree with the death penalty, and that some of his colleagues on the religious right had gone too far. He said that the reason we hadn't connected in the past is that he always imagined that I was some hostile ACT-UP type, and he could see he was wrong about that. He said that he had never stopped loving me. I felt love for him, too."

It's one of the great injustices of the gay rights debate that gay children of fundamentalists should feel relieved when their fathers assure them that they do not want them to die. Still, the conversation was a testament to the power of love to overcome familial barriers. I long for such a moment of truth with Newt. Pam returned home to Mountain View, California, optimistic that she had lost a political foe and regained a father.

But shortly after *The Advocate* published a story about the father-daughter drama, he once again severed all contact with Pam. Rus informed Pam's brother that if he continued contact with his daughter, support for the Plymouth Rock Foundation would dry up, he would lose credibility on the religious right, and possibly face firing by the organization's board of trustees. The fact that those who preach the gospel of family values are the first to cut ties to family members for reasons of political expediency speaks volumes about their commitment to practice what they preach and the depth of the slogan in the first place. It was the lesbian daughter, after all, who cared enough to try to bring the family back together again. What kind of a person works for an organization that would consider firing a father for communicating honestly and lovingly with his own daughter? What kind of an organization would put a father in that untenable position?

These same circumstances, in less extreme form, are repeated on a daily basis across America. So much so, in fact, that it's become a uniquely American tragedy: gay kid comes out, is rejected by parents and siblings, then spends weeks, months, or even years trying to overcome fear and ignorance to return to the family's good graces, which, too often, no longer exist. I'm not suggesting that gay people are always blameless. In a few instances, they may contribute to the family's problems by overreacting to perceived slights and by lacking the patience to educate misinformed, but well-meaning family members.

During my travels, I've heard countless stories of families torn apart by a beloved relative's unexpected announcement of a long-hidden secret. Sometimes, as in Pam Walton's case, the family is never completely reunited. Other times, the conflict can serve as a catalyst for families to reexamine the biases in their relationships and recognize the love that should form the basis of family. Gays and lesbians feel so strongly about family that in gay pride parades the loudest cheers are almost invariably reserved for the contingent of marchers from Parents, Families, and Friends of Lesbians and Gays. There is nothing quite so wonderful as the realization that family members love you for who you really are, rather than for what you suspect they want you to be.

Without the bravery of those like Pam who have come out and challenged the prejudice of family members—both famous and not—I would not be where I am today. In many ways, I'm standing on the shoulders of those giants who came before me. They have made the world a far safer and more welcoming place for gays and lesbians today than it was mere decades ago. There remain, however, dozens of children of antigay politicians and religious-right leaders—including the most prominent in the country—who so far have declined to come out of the closet. As someone who has faced the fear of family rejection, I know how frightening it can be. At the same time, people should carefully weigh their obligation to their gay and lesbian brothers and sisters to disabuse us all of simplistic, homogeneous views of what family means.

Rus Walton is just the latest in a series of antigay leaders with gay children who have acknowledged their homosexuality publicly. While many have little more success in changing the behavior of their antigay relatives than I, at the very least they help gay lobbyists by publicly highlighting the hypocrisy of antigay Republicans who shun gay and lesbian family members.

One of the first gay persons who happened to be the child of a prominent conservative politician to come out was Dee Mosbacher, the daughter of former Bush-administration cabinet member Robert Mosbacher. A San Francisco psychiatrist and filmmaker, Dee helped broker an early-1992 meeting between Robert Mosbacher and gay activists, in which the activists made their case for gay rights. Even though the meeting did not lead to a more enlightened position toward gays and lesbians, it set off a vicious counterattack by religious conservatives—including Brother Newt, who sent a letter to President Bush excoriating him for allowing Mosbacher even to set foot in the same room with these dreaded gay activists. That Robert Mosbacher, who is from the comparatively moderate wing of the Republican Party, was displaying family loyalty by granting his daughter a favor seemed lost on the family values advocates, so unaware were they of the double edge to their absolutist standard.

At her San Francisco home, Dee Mosbacher displays a photograph of her and Nanette, her girlfriend of seventeen years, posing with a beaming Robert Mosbacher and President Bush. "To Nanette, Best Wishes, George," the president scrawled on the photo in black marker. The photo was taken in the relatively mild days before the 1992 Republican National Convention, during which gays and lesbians became the targets of a constant verbal siege led from the podium by Pat Buchanan and Pat Robertson. After the convention, Dee told the *Washington Post* that she felt compelled to raise the pitch of her voice. "I would like my father to understand," she said, "I would like the Bushes to understand, that it's neither expedient nor ethical to do what they are doing."

Robert Mosbacher, who served as chief fund-raiser for Bush's failed reelection campaign, publicly professed his love for Dee and his respect for her long relationship with Nanette. He and his wife often traveled to San Francisco to stay at the couple's four-story home. But like many conservative parents of gays and lesbians, he seemed blithely unaware of the conflict between the actions of his rabid political allies and the interests of his daughter. Like many moderate Republicans, he was unable or unwilling to challenge the bigotry of the religious right. "I sleep fine at night," he told the *Post.* "I haven't been worried about Dee. I know she's going to be fine."

While Dee, with her successful San Francisco practice and her open phone line to her father, may indeed "be fine," many gays and lesbians are not. The relationship between the antigay rhetoric of his political allies on the religious right and attacks, sometimes fatal, on gays and lesbians was lost on Robert Mosbacher. As Dee put it in 1992: "I really think they don't know—I hope they don't—that this affects people in the street, that people get beat up, people can get killed, teenagers can commit suicide."

At about the same time that Dee Mosbacher made her sexual orientation public, another intriguing story was shaping up in San Francisco papers. John Schlafly, the son of antigay leader Phyllis Schlafly, president of the right-wing Eagle Forum, grudgingly acknowledged his sexual orientation after reporters, acting on tips from gay people who knew him, queried him about it. At the time, John lived with Phyllis and her husband at their Alton, Illinois, home.

Questioned about the contradiction between her antigay activism and her son's homosexuality, Phyllis tried to have it both ways. "Adult children don't always do what their parents wish," she told the *San Francisco Examiner.* "He is my son, and I do love my children." Still, she was at least forced into defending herself from the charge of gay-bashing, a label many conservatives take glee in owning. While John's coming-out may not have altered her politics, she clearly felt constrained by it. Claiming that she is more concerned about abortion than gay rights, Phyllis said, "Most of what I have ever said about gays was in my battle against the Equal Rights Amendment" for women in the 1970s. "I feel and have felt that the ERA would be a tool gays could use in the courts as a hidden agenda to win same-sex marriage licenses. I oppose same-sex marriages, but I would not call that gay-bashing."

At the same time, Phyllis Schlafly refused to condemn the more obvious examples of gay-bashing at the Republican National Convention. "I just don't think you can go around with a chip on your shoulder. . . . I always say I'm the most tolerant person in the world. I encourage people to vote for George Bush for their own reasons." Of course, claiming to be "tolerant"—a dubious concept to begin with—is a far cry from actually being tolerant. In the abstract, almost everyone but the Rus Waltons of the world covet the mantle of tolerance. It's actions that count. Schlafly's comment speaks volumes about the acceptability of bigotry in the Republican Party—and the true extent to which its leaders give free rein to prejudice to influence voters' decisions.

In a view that I suspect would hit home with Newt, Schlafly said the media coverage of her son's homosexuality was a "liberal conspiracy" to hurt the political fortunes of the Eagle Forum, rather than something positive for gay rights. "I had never reached a higher profile than at the Republican convention, and the liberals wanted to embarrass me," she declared. That anyone other than Mrs. Schlafly might have legitimate political grievances did not appear to occur to her. Nor did she seem to grasp that John had a complex life of his own, with its own evident struggles.

As a forty-one-year-old lawyer living under his archconservative mother's roof, John seems to have absorbed his mother's reactionary politics. In the *Examiner* interview, he endorsed the military ban on gays and lesbians and insisted that antidiscrimination protections for gays and lesbians place an undue burden on employers. The gay movement "made a mistake years ago," he said, when it went beyond asking society for "the right to be left alone. . . . I think the country is more than willing to grant that, but I think the activists made a conscious decision to take a different road, toward what many people in the country regard as special rights or benefits."

At the same time, though, John Schlafly did have some nice things to say about the gay response to AIDS. "The gay community really has been a model for the nation, and I don't know of anything that is more worthy of being one of the thousand-points-of-light concept than that," he said, referring to then-president Bush's famous speech. Ultimately, John said, he came out to be "one small voice saying, 'Maybe there is more to it, maybe the issue is more complicated.' Yes, 'can't we just all get along?' Can't we just make a little more of an effort to understand the other side and turn down the volume a bit on the hostility?" That's one goal we all—gay and straight, liberal and conservative, Candace and Newt—should find a way to achieve.

Ty Ross and his grandfather Barry Goldwater certainly did. During the fiery 1993 gays-in-the-military debate, the country was stunned to learn that the former chairman of the Senate Armed Services Committee and sixties right-wing presidential candidate was vehemently opposed to the military ban. In a *Washington Post* commentary, Goldwater coined my favorite line about the ban: "You don't have to be straight to shoot straight." Asked if he would fly a military mission with a gay man, Goldwater answered, "Hell, yes, as long as the son of a bitch could fly."

In an interview, Goldwater declared that "the Constitution says that all men are created equal, and it doesn't say that all men are created equal except for gays. Just like everyone else who is born in this country, gays are endowed by their creator, God, with inalienable rights, and among those are life, liberty, and the pursuit of happiness. The Republican Party should stand for freedom and only freedom. Don't raise hell about the gays, the blacks, and the Mexicans. Free people have a right to do as they damn well please. To see the party that fought Communism and big government now fighting the gays, well, that's just plain dumb." Are you listening, Newt?

But Goldwater had an unspoken motive in addition to the libertarian political philosophy he espoused throughout his long career. It turned out that one of Goldwater's ten grandchildren, Ty Ross, a young interior decorator in Scottsdale, Arizona, is gay. Ross's sexual orientation put a human face on the military ban for his grandfather. "Barry would never admit it, but speaking out for gays is part of the way he shows his love and respect for his family," Ross said in an interview. "He can see how important I am to my mom and my three sisters. He doesn't really express his emotions very often, so this for me is a way for him to do what's right for me and for his family." Now that's what I call *family values.*

Mom and me in Baltimore, Maryland, 1966.

I'm about six months old here.
In a dress—not my choice.

With Mom, at Anna May's Beauty Shop in
Hummelstown, Pennsylvania.
I'm freaking out with a hair dryer bag
on my head. I'm about one.

In Fort Leavenworth, Kansas.
I'm about two. I had asked for a pony—
close enough.

Also in Fort Leavenworth, around two years old. Please note my choice of play toys.

With Mom during Easter at Fort Ord, Monterrey, California, 1971. I don't look bad in girl clothes!

Mom and me (age four) at Disneyland. Thankfully allowed to dress myself now.

At a fair in Fort Amador, Panama Canal Zone, 1972. Made the mistake of asking for a pony again.

Age nine at the Middle Paxton Elementary School. Switched at birth with Bobby Brady.

The infamous senior high school picture. At age seventeen, prior to coming out, at Central Dauphin East High School, Pennsylvania. Mother-approved hair.

David Brown, Mom, me, Rob, and Congressman Newt at the Carlisle Army War College in 1985. Note the eerie similarity among our hairstyles!

Emily visiting the "House of Cheddar" at Indiana University of Pennsylvania. I'm twenty-one; Emily is about five months.

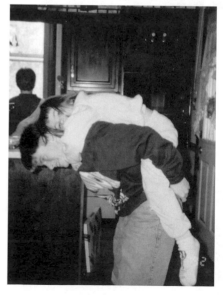

The *other* infamous picture after I came out, age twenty-two, at IUP. Mother-dissaproved hair.

Christmas at Rob's house in Camp Hill, 1993—with Susan on my back.

Me and Dad at Snow's wedding, November 5, 1994. The halo of flowers was actually my idea.

With my nieces, Susan and Emily Brown, all looking quite mischevious.

With Snow and Rob at the wedding, suitable for framing.

Me, Snow, Rob, and Connie Chung, at the taping of the *Eye to Eye* segment, December 20, 1994. As they say on Sesame Street, one of these things is doing its own thing.

January 1995. Newt's inaugaration as Speaker of the House. In the back row: David and Rob Brown, Newt and Marianne Gingrich, Jim Shurskis (Snow's husband); in the front: Mom, Susan and Emily Brown, me, and Susan (Snow) Gingrich Shurskis.

Me, Newt, Human Rights Campaign senior lobbyist Nancy Buermeyer, HRC communications director David M. Smith on Lobby Day.

In San Francisco with lesbian pioneers Del Martin and Phyllis Lyons. Short lesbians unite!

With California Rep. Sheila Kuehl, and Jane Leeves, Pere Gilpin and Dan Butler of *Frasier*. Sheila and Dan received the Dick Sargent NCOD Award for Excellence. (Photo: Ron Singleton)

With NCOD project manager Wes Combs, Dan Butler, and HRC director Elizabeth Birch on October 11, 1995, at the U.S. Capitol.

Chastity Bono and me at the Texas State Fair in Dallas for NCOD. She had a corny dog, I didn't.

With partner Kris Pratt at HRC's Washington, D.C., dinner, November 1995.

CHAPTER NINETEEN

FRIENDS OF NEWT

If you want a friend in Washington, get a dog.
—HARRY TRUMAN

Ever since he was a boy, Newt has surrounded himself with smart, intellectually unorthodox people. Though he hews to a philosophically conservative line, he is open to different points of view and incorporates bits and pieces of them into his beliefs. Deep down, he is nothing like some of these firebrand religious-right leaders who refuse to hang out with or debate anyone but their own. Maybe it's the Army brat and budding college professor in him, but at heart Newt is as restless and curious about the world as anyone I know. He loves nothing more than sitting around philosophizing about politics and the future of Western civilization. It's a trait he acquired from my father, who is an avid reader and debater in his own right, and from his many years of schooling and reading.

What makes his curiosity special is the degree to which he is driven to implement his ideas. In my continuing search for the "true Newt," I did some research into Newt's intellectual and political allies and mentors. What I learned surprised me. Almost to a tee, they disagreed with Newt's social conservatism, especially his rejection of gay rights. Among the politicians and thinkers Newt respects most, I could find none who resembled the ideologues on the religious right, such as Lou Sheldon, who are obsessed with homosexuality.

Instead, they are freethinkers who believe in justice and equality for all. Among them were Alvin Toffler, the renowned author of *Future Shock*, who sees gay people as an instrumental part of the technological future; the liberal science-fiction writer Isaac Asimov; and Peter

Drucker, the management guru who Newt says "shaped my entire life" by teaching him to "discipline, plan, think through, delegate, and trust others to build systems." I found no trace of homophobia in any of their voluminous writings. The bad apples in Newt's lot were John Wayne, the outspoken conservative actor who made sexist machismo into an onscreen virtue, and Kemal Atatürk, the Turkish president who tried to bring his country into the modern age by brutalizing political dissidents.

In his 1994 book, *Creating a New Civilization: The Politics of the Third Wave,* written with his wife, Heidi, Toffler contends that the Republican Party too often "appeals to nostalgia in [its] rhetoric about culture and values, as though one could return to the values and morality of the 1950s . . . and dreams of Ozzie and Harriet." The religious right of the party, according to the Tofflers, "blames liberals, humanists, and Democrats for the 'collapse of morality.' "

The Republican Party must start seeing minority groups, including the gay community, as essential to America's journey into the information age. "The rising activism of minorities is not the result of a sudden onset of selfishness; it is, among other things, a reflection of the needs of a new system of production which requires for its very existence a far more varied, colorful, open, and diverse society than we have ever known," the Tofflers write.

Ironically, the heretical work carries a foreword written by Newt in which he lauds the Tofflers as providing the country with the "key to viewing current disarray within the positive framework of a dynamic, exciting future." In the five-page essay, Newt never mentions the Tofflers' criticism of social conservatives. Maybe that's because Newt, who rails against gays and liberals as "counterculture McGovernicks" intent on bringing down Western civilization, fits their description of the very social conservative blocking America's evolution toward "a far more varied, colorful, open, and diverse society than we have ever known." Obviously, Newt's interpretation of his beloved Tofflers is selective.

Still, Newt defies labels. In the House, his closest friends and associates have not been the rabidly antigay Bob Dornan of California, whom Newt charitably calls an "unusual loner," or Ernest Istook of Oklahoma. Extremists hold little intellectual challenge or interest for him. Instead, he has gravitated toward social moderates like Steve Gunderson, of whom he has this to say: "I think of him as a younger brother" [that I never had]. Gunderson, Newt says, has a "sense of integrity and commitment and does what [he] believes in . . . he is a caring person who is very intensely committed to his family and his community and who really feels the anguish of problems of rural health and rural education and rural income."

Based on Newt's recommendation, I decided to get to know Steve and his boyfriend, Rob Morris, by inviting them out to dinner. In some ways, Steve holds the key to understanding Newt's views about the gay community. A House veteran from western Wisconsin's dairy lands, Gunderson has known Newt since 1980, when Steve arrived in Congress at the young age of twenty-nine. In 1983, Steve met Rob—whom I can only describe as wonderfully eccentric—at a Dupont Circle gay bar named Badlands. The two soon began their life together.

Steve has worked closely with Newt, serving as his chief deputy until the Republican National Convention in Houston in 1992— shortly after which he quit the leadership post to protest the incendiary antigay tone that dominated the convention, frightened much of the nation, and helped elect Clinton. Despite his friendship with Newt, Steve is one of those Rockefeller Republicans the Speaker so often assails.

"I have described our relationship as a brother-brother relationship," Steve told me over pasta at an Italian restaurant in the heavily gay Dupont Circle neighborhood in Washington. "We do not interact as often as we used to, what with the party's turn to the right. And that's partly because when my colleagues go up to him all the time and say the sky is falling, he writes them off immediately. He knows that I only come to him when I am very serious, very adamant about something. I always get a response. Despite our philosophical differences, we trust each other."

Steve came up with one of the best explanations I've heard of Newt's contradictions. "Newt is an intellectual visionary with a right-wing political base," he said. "You have to understand the dichotomy of that scenario to understand the complexity of the man. The frustrating thing is that one day he says something I deeply appreciate and then follows it within the week with something that completely blows my mind. Left to his own devices, I have no doubt where he would come down."

In a town where it is only a small exaggeration to say that sexual identity has become as important as party affiliation, Steve's protracted coming-out was a circus. In 1991, maverick AIDS activist Michael Petrelis, an aggressive proponent of outing, threw a soft drink in Gunderson's face at a Washington-area gay bar, apparently because the congressman refused to make his sexual orientation public.

The far right has been no easier on Steve. In March 1994, Dornan, who is known both affectionately and derisively as B-1 Bob, angrily accused Gunderson of having a "revolving door on his closet" during a debate on an education bill. "He's in, he's out, he's in, he's out," a red-faced Dornan screamed at Gunderson as his shocked colleagues looked on. (Under the threat of official censure, Dornan withdrew the remarks, and they were stricken from the *Congressional Record*.)

Dornan's intemperate comments highlighted both the personal and political hypocrisy of antigay crusading by so-called conservatives. His tantrum came amid debate on a bill sponsored by Mel Hancock of Missouri that would have denied funding to public school districts that supposedly "encourage or support" homosexuality as a "positive alternative lifestyle." Gunderson had given an eloquent speech defending the gay youths whose prospects would have been damaged had the bill become law.

Thanks to smart work by Rep. Jolene Unsoeld—who was later swept out of office in the '94 GOP riptide—the odious bill was eviscerated. Hancock's legislation was introduced as an amendment to a White House education-funding bill, passing 301–120, with Newt, of course, among the majority. But later that same day the House voted 224–194 to pass an Unsoeld amendment prohibiting the federal government from interfering with local school curricula, effectively nullifying Hancock's version. Once again those in Congress who most vociferously opposed federal intervention in local matters were most outspoken in supporting the federal government's intrusion into how local school districts deal with homosexuality. (Nothing causes antigay activists to lose their philosophical bearings quite like attempts to help gay youths or efforts to civilize the discussion of gay issues in schools.)

Gunderson has paid a personal price for such forays into gay advocacy. At the time of Dornan's much-publicized attack, Gunderson's father was in the hospital for heart bypass surgery. As he watched Dornan on a local news broadcast, Gunderson's father told Steve's sister, who was by his hospital bed, "Why is this man attacking Steve? Just because my son is different doesn't make him a bad person."

The reason "this man" was attacking Steve has nothing to do with Steve and everything to do with the far right's need to use homosexuality as a wedge issue to raise money and win votes. Dornan, who later announced his candidacy for the presidency, was merely trying to flaunt his right-wing credentials in a field that coveted the badge of *ultraconservative.* In all honesty, gay activists sometimes use people like Steve to further their own cause, and Petrelis goes way too far for my liking. But at least they have a good cause, unlike Dornan, Hancock, and their fellow demagogues.

Newt watched the entire sideshow with dismay. "I remember calling Steve—he was attacked by Dornan as he was leaving to fly home to his father, who goes into this process of anesthesia that they can't get him out of—and I called him at the hospital early on [be]cause Dornan had talked to the newspapers," Newt recalled in an interview. "And so here's a guy who is this open, compassionate person, with his mom just coming out of the hospital, trying to wrestle with his party and himself and his reelection all in a very open way, and whose basic response to that is to come home."

Nice sentiments, to be sure, but they make me wonder why Newt didn't speak out publicly on Steve's behalf and condemn Dornan for his ugly antics. The obvious reason is that Newt can't afford to alienate the right wing of his party, which holds Dornan in high regard, and because Newt's afraid that in speaking out for his friend Steve, he would somehow be advocating for the entire gay community.

After describing his admiration of Gunderson's version of family values in the interview, Newt launched into another attack on gays, employing the canards of the religious right. "This is not a guy of Greenwich Village and the bathhouses of San Francisco," he said. "This is a guy who is Midwestern and has his own totally personal vision of his sexuality. Deep commitment, long, caring relationships, I suspect deeply offended at the idea of six guys in one night." Newt then went on to bestow his highest honor on Steve: "And in that sense he is an example of what a 1990s Norman Rockwell would paint . . . a very human, caring person."

The implicit message is that Steve Gunderson is one of the few "good homosexuals" while the rest of us—who he seems to think mostly reside in New York City and San Francisco—are "bad homosexuals," nothing but promiscuous hedonists lacking in family values. While no one can question Steve's rock-solid values, I might remind Newt that Steve did meet Rob at Badlands, one of those gay establishments that Newt would condemn for its wild side. His characterizing Gunderson as an exception to the rule allows Newt to ignore the widespread discrimination that gays and lesbians routinely face and the fact that the vast majority of us don't reside in major metropolitan areas.

No wonder Steve's coming-out was so painful. After the '92 Republican National Convention, with Rob's gentle prodding, Steve began making tentative steps toward identifying himself as the only openly gay GOP member of Congress. During the 1993 congressional debate over the Pentagon ban on gay and lesbian service personnel, Gunderson compared the ban to activists' attempts to force him into the open. "I have experienced what it feels like to have my life—who I am, what I am, and what I have accomplished—reduced to a single irrelevant factor," he said in a speech on the House floor.

Shortly before the debate over the Hancock amendment—and the Dornan attack—Steve had addressed a Baltimore fund-raiser for the Human Rights Campaign Fund. In the speech, he talked about sharing a beach house at Rehoboth Beach, Delaware, a popular gay resort, with Rob and "our two dogs." Steve told attendees that he and Rob "have been touched by AIDS in the last year. Two of our closest friends died from AIDS, and while for Rob and I this was the first personal loss from this tragic disease, it makes its impact no less painful for us." He went on to articulate what has become one of his major themes when addressing gay topics: reaching out to heterosexual Americans. "Unless a son or brother is gay, a daughter or sister is lesbian, most families will not encounter challenges to their traditional values."

Steve believes that Newt, like many Americans, is what he calls "homo-ignorant," meaning that he is not personally hostile to gays and lesbians. He simply does not understand us or our lives. Though Steve acknowledged that Newt's voting record on gay issues is abysmal and that Newt has made scores of antigay statements over the years, he insisted Newt's stance has more to do with the far-right constituency Newt feels he must mollify than with his own convictions. As Newt consolidates his power in the party, Steve said, he will be in a better position to reach out to gays and lesbians in a positive way or at least to discourage the antigay attacks coming from his own party.

"This is just one part of the intellect that this guy has not delved into," Steve told me. "Newt just doesn't understand gay issues. Rather than challenging him directly, the better strategy with Newt is to figure out how we can reach a similar point in the future. It's more productive. I don't spend a lot of time trying to get any of my politician colleagues to agree with me, because politicians are never wrong. Trying to get them to admit they are wrong is a valiant exercise in futility."

Pointing to a recent political battle, Steve said that gay and AIDS issues are a low priority for most members of Congress. In January 1996, Dornan and Senate Republican whip Trent Lott of Mississippi proposed an amendment to the Department of Defense authorization bill requiring the Pentagon to discharge all HIV-positive service members. Even though the Pentagon opposed the policy, Clinton signed the bill because refusing to do so might have resulted in another government shutdown, a funding cutoff of his Bosnia effort, and a pay raise for military personnel. With gay activists' encouragement, Clinton directed the Department of Justice not to defend the constitutionality of the measure against legal challenges.

Dornan told the *New York Times* he proposed the amendment, which would have led to the discharge of over one thousand service members, because in the midst of military personnel cuts he could not "tolerate a politically protected class while we're letting go healthy men and women who have not used drugs, infected prostitutes, or engaged in unsafe homosexual sex." In a subsequent letter to the *New York Times*, Dornan later blamed the HIV-infected soldiers for their own illness, regardless of the circumstances of their infection.

Newt didn't behave much better than B-1 Bob. Asked about a letter from Magic Johnson imploring him to reconsider the Dornan amendment, Newt, at his most condescending, said that the HIV-positive basketball star doesn't understand "the nature of being in the military and the danger of being in combat and what happens in a field hospital if you have people bleeding, people wounded, and you don't have a clue who has HIV." I'm afraid it's Newt who doesn't "have a clue" when it comes to the Department of Defense's HIV policy. Contrary to his statement, HIV-positive service members are assigned exclusively to noncombat duties. At least Dornan actually served in the military. Newt, who took a 4-F for poor eyesight, once said that women shouldn't serve in combat because of "infections" they could pick up in fox holes. Not having served, he's prone to laughably ill-informed notions about military life.

"I'll bet not five percent of my colleagues understand the HIV amendment," Steve said. "Not out of intention, just out of pure oversight." He cited another classic example of Republican "oversight." At a meeting of the Tuesday Lunch Bunch, a group of moderate Republicans, Newt "filled us in about the continuing resolution to keep the government open. He said he would fund programs slated for elimination at seventy-five percent and prohibit any new grants from the

Department of Labor or Health and Human Services. I nearly jumped out of my seat. 'Time out, that's Ryan White grants you're talking about. You're talking about wiping out Ryan White.' Newt responded, 'I didn't know that.' I said, 'You have to get to Representative [Robert] Livingston right away to make sure the grants happen.' That's a classic example of what's happening on the Hill. It's literally an oversight. It was the first time it really sunk in for me how important it was having someone on the inside like me who can monitor their behavior." Frankly, what Steve views as "oversight," I see as negligence. Maybe that's what makes me a Democrat and Steve a Republican. The incident underscored how much we will miss Steve if he leaves Congress this year.

Steve and I do agree on at least one thing about Newt: he's the consummate politician. "I'm a member of the Congress of the United States, and I could not discuss with you on an intelligent basis the telecommunications bill," Steve said. "I have no reason to know it. My schedule, my priorities, preclude me from having the time to understand it fully. Similarly, Newt's agenda is about raising money and, right now, keeping the government operating. The gay issue is way down on his list of priorities. And when he does delve into it, he gets nothing but grief. When he appointed me to head up D.C. school reform, the religious right beat him up. For them, appointing a gay person is the equivalent of betrayal. It legitimized an orientation they are doing everything in their power to fight. Newt has to pick and choose his fights. How much time can he spend trying to please his sister Candace Gingrich and his friend Steve Gunderson?"

In Newt's position, it's far easier to characterize gays, and not his antigay constituency, as threats to "Western civilization." I reminded Steve that I'm not asking Newt to please me. It's one thing to argue, as Newt does, that we don't need a federal bill protecting gays and lesbians from discrimination. But it's entirely another to say we're incapable of being families or that we are using the schools to recruit.

For someone in Newt's position not to understand the real concerns of groups over which he wields power is simply irresponsible. It says something about the priority this country places on the lives of gays and lesbians that the Speaker of the House thinks that the enactment of gay rights legislation would mean that men will suddenly start arriving at work in a dress. By virtue of our relationship to Newt, Steve and I have a special responsibility. As hard as Newt works to avoid a conversation about gay issues with me, Steve and I are two of the very few people who can get to him in the midst of his impossibly busy schedule. "Occasionally I will pull him aside when I can get a few moments from him or write him a very personal letter," Steve said. "But you have to be strategic about it. I've watched your brother break down from physical and mental exhaustion. I certainly could not handle his schedule."

Steve said the Sheldon hearings on youth and values, overseen by Rep. Pete Hoekstra of Michigan, were yet another example of homo-ignorance. "Hoekstra's decision to hold the hearings was clearly ignorant," he said. "As the hearings approached, he called me up and said, 'Steve, I'm in an unbelievable mess and I don't know how to get out of it. Everyone thinks I have an agenda, and I can't convince either side that I'm fair.' That's after Newt had said to him, 'I'm trusting you to be fair, honest, and not an embarrassment to the party.' So I sat down with Hoekstra. To his credit, his staff sought me out. I explained that fairness does not mean that you let the Democrats have their say at the hearings. It will only be fair if you have Republicans speaking out on our side of the issue, or taking a more neutral stance. That's what ended up happening. Bill Bennett helped out by making it clear to them that he was not going to discuss homosexuality. 'If you want to talk about values,' he told them, 'I'm all for that, but don't come to me asking me to attack gays.'"

In the end, Steve said, the Sheldon hearings were good for the gay movement. "Newt asked me early on what I thought about the hearings—and here's where I disagree with many gay activists—I said we should have the hearings and conduct them as openly as possible. The truth will set us free. I'm absolutely convinced that there is no more and probably much less recruitment by gays than there is by heterosexuals. Moreover, there is a growing consensus that there should be no federal role in determining local school curricula. Once again, that's the kind of argument that is more likely to appeal to Newt. He loves the intellectual engagement. He wants to be challenged. He won't listen if you simply blast him. He loves to sit down and have these kind of discussions over a few drinks."

The man Steve calls his "best political counselor" is less inclined to cut Newt and his right-wing colleagues slack. After reading the 1994 *Washington Blade* interview in which Newt equated homosexuality and alcoholism, Rob says he became so enraged he called Steve at his parents' home in Wisconsin. It was sometime after midnight, and everyone was asleep. Bleary-eyed, Steve came to the phone. "I'd had a few drinks and I yelled at him, 'I'm drunk and queer and they are not related.' Steve didn't know what I was babbling about so I explained the story to him. It just drives me crazy when people make generalizations about homosexuals that I know don't apply to me or the gay people I know." Rob insisted that Steve confront Newt about the story once he got home. He did, but I'm not sure it made any difference.

In the Steve-Rob debate, I lean toward Rob's position. I agree with Steve that Newt is often just ignorant about homosexuality. But as Rob points out, there is a cynical side to Newt. Like politicians on both sides of the fence, he is willing to sacrifice people and causes close to him for political expediency. At the same time, I try to give people in general, and family members in particular, the benefit of the doubt. I don't put Newt in the Dornan-Helms category of those who seem to hate gratuitously, for the pure sake of hating.

Because of his intellectual bent, Newt has some room to grow on the issue. My early 1995 meeting with him is a case in point. With Roberta and me by his side before the cameras, he said he loved me and talked about the "American family in all its complexity." The very next day, he was quoted saying that it should not be against the law to fire someone if they come in to work as a transvestite. Again with the red herrings! Transvestism is not an orientation. That's not at all what we're talking about when we seek to outlaw workplace discrimination on the basis of sexual orientation.

Ignorance or malice? I will never know the answer for sure. It's probably better to concentrate instead on making it politically painful to cast antigay votes and to undertake antigay crusades. "Look at my colleagues, both Republican and Democratic, who live and die on pro-choice votes, but will make no similar commitment on the gay issue," Steve pointed out. "We in the gay community have a tendency to focus on known enemies. The ambivalence of people who should be our brothers and sisters is killing us. There is just no danger attached to taking antigay positions."

The only way we are going to create that kind of pressure is to educate aggressively. Rob has an explanation for the homo-ignorance of many Americans that I know to be true from my own travels. "I remember Jesse Helms saying once that he had never met anyone gay," Rob said. "But I've seen him shake Steve's hand, so I know that's a lie. Years ago, I was talking to my parents, who live in Columbus, Georgia.

It wasn't that they didn't love me and want me to be happy, it was that they had a hard time incorporating the fact of my being gay into their own lives. So I had to delve back into my childhood for examples of gay people they might have known. I said, 'Remember this friend of yours who was married to so-and-so? Did you know he hung out at the gay bar on Saturday nights?' As they went back through their lives and realized the people they knew who were gay, their feelings about homosexuality changed dramatically. They realized that they had actually been surrounded by closeted gay people all their lives. I just happened to be the first openly gay person they knew."

Steve said that families face almost as much stigma identifying themselves as having a gay child as do the children themselves for being gay. "My sister, who lives in Madison, Wisconsin, told me that she had been asked to conduct a Bible study class on antigay verses in the Bible," he said. "She said that she had clearly been asked because of having a well-known gay brother. 'What do I say?' she asked me. For her, this was a traumatic experience."

Steve said that once Americans work through difficult coming-out experiences on a widespread basis, they will begin to reject antigay messages. "I was at a radio station in my district for an interview recently," he said. "After it was finished, the news director, totally unsolicited, came up to me and said that he appreciated my coming-out. 'When I listen to people talk about agriculture, health care, and other issues important to the district, they always add, "I don't care what people say about Steve, all I know is that he works hard for us," ' he said, meaning that it was okay with them that they know I'm gay. It's a testament to the fine people back home." Steve, however, displayed an uncharacteristic bit of anger in discussing the shenanigans of the far right in his district. "We went through the most vicious personal campaign that we have ever gone through in 1994," he said. "The opposition's intent was to destroy me, not elect their own candidate. And they got money from all over the country to do just that."

I asked him about the wealthy national religious-right groups that funnel money into local antigay campaigns. The Christian Coalition, for instance, has donated at least $60,000 to Lon Mabon's Oregon Citizens Alliance. Steve responded that "Ralph Reed has said to my face that when he brings up the values agenda, he never gay-bashes."

This was too much for Rob, who quickly interjected, "Yeah, he has too many people under him to do it for him."

Indeed, the Coalition regularly mails antigay fund-raising appeals that bear Reed's or Robertson's signature. Robertson's *700 Club* is a veritable orgy of antigay pronouncements. If Reed is less vitriolic in his rhetoric, it's only because he knows that polls have consistently shown that most Americans don't want to see gay people discriminated against, especially in employment. So Damien, as I like to call the baby-faced Reed because he resembles the Devil child in the movie *The Omen*, does most of his gay-bashing in private, particularly when his organization is in need of cash.

Chuckling at Rob's retort, Steve said he agreed that the burden should be on Reed: "I've told him that until you are willing to stand up and repudiate these kinds of antigay efforts, it's very hard to accept that you are not a gay-basher."

We discussed the most effective way to approach dedicated antigay activists such as Lou Sheldon and Gary Bauer, head of the Family Research Council, a religious-right group allied with James Dobson's Focus on the Family. Steve said that Sheldon has always been "very civil" to him. "Sheldon and his daughter Andrea came to me last year when they knew articles about my sexual orientation were about to come out, and they made a point of saying that it didn't matter to them that I was gay. They said they would work with me just the same. During the Hoekstra hearings, Sheldon came by my office to compliment me for what he saw as my fair approach to the hearings. My chief of staff didn't even want to let him come into the office. But I wanted to talk with him."

Rob interjected, "What I read in the papers is very different from the way you describe Sheldon." For several years now, Rob has kept a voluminous file on the preachings of Sheldon and other religious-right leaders. "I know I'm going into my Martha Mitchell mode here," Rob said, referring to the Watergate figure long rumored to be the famous Deep Throat, "but I'd just love to confront him about some of the things I've got in my file. What I'm worried about is that by being charming, Sheldon might allow Steve and others to forget what he is really about. He's just sucking up to Steve. If someone is friendly to you, you're drawn to them, but if someone is ugly, you move against them. If you think, 'He doesn't discriminate against me, he must be okay,' that's just wrong. You have to go beyond that to find a pattern in his words and actions."

Steve said that some religious-right leaders are not even willing to "suck up" to him. For instance, he said, "when Newt put me in charge of D.C. school reform, Gary Bauer publicly said he would have nothing to do with me or the cause. He made a philosophical debate into a personal vendetta, which Sheldon didn't. I'm not saying he wouldn't, but he didn't."

Turning to Rob, Steve said, "The easiest thing for me to do is to declare war on the religious right. But that would make it impossible for me to change anything and makes me an irrelevant moderate in the Republican Party."

Rob would have none of it: "I understand that taking a less combative approach is usually better. However, I always understand that there is a point in time when you are part of a community that has footprints all over it from someone and you have to say, 'Time out! Enough is enough! I'm just not that naive.' "

"Just because someone is ugly politically doesn't mean you have to be personally ugly," Steve replied.

"I'm not saying that you say, 'Your mother wears army boots.' I'm just advocating calling Sheldon and Bauer and all the others on the carpet and saying, 'This is the truth,' " Rob said. "What about this. What if I gave you eighty articles from my clips and you went to Lou and said, 'Lou, I have this friend, and this friend keeps saying to me, "Steve, Lou's a schmuck," and I keep saying, "You just need to know him." But I started flipping through the file myself, and I'm starting to see what my friend means. What do you have to say for yourself?' "

That's a question I'd like to ask my brother. My relationship with Newt parallels Gunderson's conflicted relationship with Sheldon. Like Rob, I sometimes want to confront Newt with my hefty file of his greatest antigay hits and demand restitution. At other times, I feel it's best to take Steve's more conciliatory approach, hoping that Newt will come to a more humane position over time. My strategy will ultimately rest on Newt's willingness to, as Mom says, "work things out" with me and to wrestle with his own antigay demons and those in his party. That is, after all, how families overcome their differences and how justice is served.

CHAPTER TWENTY

TO REVISE AMERICA

You have to blow down the old order in order to create
the new order.

—Newt Gingrich

M y brother Newt's views on our society are an open book. In 1995,
the Speaker of the House negotiated a $4.5-million advance from
HarperCollins for his text *To Renew America,* in which the former college professor argues for a six-point platform he believes is necessary to
"leave our children with an America that is prosperous, free, and safe."

In the uproar over the size of the contract and the fact that the
House was scheduled to take up legislation affecting conservative
media magnate Rupert Murdoch, who owns HarperCollins, Newt
agreed to accept instead a token one-dollar advance on the substantial
royalties the book was expected to earn. To his credit, Newt donated all
the profits from the books sold on his subsequent tour to Earning by
Learning, a nonprofit organization he founded to reward poor children
for reading, and Habitat for Humanity, which builds homes for low-
income people.

But lost in the furor was the content of the tome, which had disappointing sales in part because it reads like an undergraduate term paper
in political science. *To Renew America* displays the author's characteristic mix of creativity, conservative bombast, and disregard for society's less fortunate. While Newt already has considerable teaching
experience under his belt, I hope someday, from my own academic
position as a feminist scholar, to grade his work, or at least request a
rewrite. For now, I'd like to suggest a few modest changes to, improve-
ments on, and outright refutations of his political philosophy.

Excerpts from Newt's book are italicized and followed by my own analysis—and a generous helping of suggested revisions:

1. We must reassert and renew American civilization. From the arrival of English-speaking colonists in 1607 until 1965, there was one continuous civilization built around a set of commonly accepted legal and political principles. From the Jamestown colony and the Pilgrims, through de Tocqueville's Democracy in America, *up to the Norman Rockwell paintings of the 1940s and 1950s, there was a clear sense of what it was to be an American. Since 1965, there has been a calculated effort by cultural elites to discredit this civilization and replace it with a culture of irresponsibility that is incompatible with American freedoms as we know them.*

We must acknowledge the mistakes and appreciate the diversity of American civilization. Upon his arrival in the Bahama Islands, Christopher Columbus wrote of the natives, the Arawaks, "With fifty men we could subjugate them all and make them do whatever we want." America's European colonists treated Native Americans with equal contempt, attacking them as savages and banishing them westward and to reservations. Only twenty years after their settlement in Jamestown, America's early white settlers began the enslavement of black Africans that would dominate many of the colonies and much of the young nation's economy for over two centuries. Later, Asian immigrants were forced to survive on slave wages as they labored to construct a transcontinental railroad. As recently as World War II, Japanese-Americans were rounded up and shipped to internment camps.

The system of constitutional democracy the settlers brought to America would be the envy of the world. But even the Constitution owes its formulation in part to the Iroquois Confederation, whose system of self-governance our founding fathers studied and borrowed from liberally. And we must remember that the history of America is as much the history of repression as it is of freedom. To create an America that's true to its promise, it's essential that we have an accurate picture of our history. We have to expand upon the good and work to end the bad. Romanticizing the past will lead to only more repression and violence against women as well as gays and other vulnerable minorities.

A prolific reader, Newt could benefit from Howard Zinn's *A People's History of the United States.* In discussing the founding of the nation, Zinn writes: "Even allowing for the imperfection of myths, it is enough to make us question, for that time and ours, the excuse of progress in the annihilation of races, and the telling of history from the standpoint of the conquerors and leaders of Western civilization."

Diversity, however emptied of meaning by uncritical repetition, looms as a very large issue—on both the cultural and political horizons. I read in the paper recently that whites will soon officially make up less than 50 percent of the country's population. Worldwide, we represent an even smaller minority. As the Tofflers say, the conservative movement in this country has to come to grips with pluralism. It's dangerous to think exclusively in Eurocentric terms when such terms don't mesh with reality.

Thomas Jefferson lobbied to keep the word *tolerance* out of the Constitution because it implies that individuals and minority groups exist only at the behest of the majority. He wanted to make sure that all men (with the inexcusable exception of blacks and women) were indivisible from the majority. I'd like Newt to take this principle seriously and work to make sure that all Americans are treated equally under the law.

It's also telling that he invokes the artist Norman Rockwell. Those paintings he's so fond of actually reflect the artist's struggle to expand the boundaries of acceptable popular art in the forties and fifties. My favorite is the image of the African-American schoolgirl under siege from bigots on her way into a soon-to-be-desegregated Little Rock school. Behind every proverbial white picket fence in a Rockwell painting is a real family struggling to overcome the devastating effects of the Depression—its ravages seen in the thin faces of some characters—and the abuse of power that Americans were only beginning to confront.

Jonathan Katz's *Gay American History* documents the tortured history of American gays and lesbians since the nation's birth. In Newt's beloved Virginia Colony in 1625, Richard Cornish, a ship's master, was hanged for allegedly making a pass at another man, a penalty even Newt, who has called for the execution of convicted drug dealers, might find extreme. When they were not being harassed, beaten, or executed, gays and lesbians lived peacefully in both small and large communities and played a crucial role in the eclectic social movements of the eighteenth and nineteenth centuries.

It's characteristic of demagogues ranging from Joseph McCarthy to Lou Sheldon to fail to define their terms. Who are these "cultural elites" to whom Newt refers and why have they worked to "discredit this civilization"? Why date their campaign to 1965, the year the Civil Rights

Act took effect? The mid-1960s were also when welfare, medicaid, and medicare were adopted. How could helping others be wrong? And with his six-figure salary, book advances, and access to power, Newt is the personification of what C. Wright Mills called the "power elite," if not the "cultural elite." The Speaker speaks for ordinary Americans about as well as Ross Perot speaks for the poor, Pat Buchanan for Jews, and Pat Robertson for gays.

Truth be told, when referring to the "cultural elite," Newt is actually referring to Americans like me who happen to disagree with him. Yet instead of granting them the sincerity of their beliefs and values, Newt turns them into archenemies of American civilization. Democracy requires that we refrain from impugning the motives of our opponents and allow them the respect they deserve.

2. We must accelerate America's entry into the Third Wave Information Age. The scientific and technological changes going on around us are far more significant and unprecedented than we have recognized.

We must not leave people behind in our rush to capitalize on the information revolution. To me, surfing is still something one does in the water, but I do understand the potential for technology like the World Wide Web to be harnessed to expedite social change and improve democracy. If Newt insists that "technological changes" are the key to the future of civilization, I'll take him at his word.

But it concerns me that the vast majority of people in this country do not have access to the technology that he touts. Last year, Newt suggested that giving laptop computers to every inner-city child would alleviate poverty by creating new opportunities for the kids. As his liberal critics were quick to point out, computers are of little value in the face of poverty, run-down schools, and a total lack of health care.

As Newt surely knows, Mom has owned a VCR for almost a decade now and still hasn't the foggiest idea how to program it. Many people who can afford these technological toys don't know how to use them, let alone master a complicated (and often expensive) process like gaining access to the Internet. The real challenge for Congress should be in figuring out ways to teach people to use the innovations in addition to the technology we already have, and to retrain workers who have lost jobs in declining industries.

In one of my favorite episodes of *Roseanne*, the comedian applies for an administrative position at a meat plant after working for years on the assembly line at a plastics factory. She gets the job, but when the secretary asks whether she uses IBM or Mac, she says she's never had an IBM, but that Big Macs are one of her favorite meals. When the secretary figures out she's not joking, Roseanne loses out on the job.

If it does not reinforce economic bias, the information age has the potential to improve democracy by making knowledge more readily available to ever larger numbers of people. Harkening back to his days defending the publication of nude photographs in the Tulane University paper, in June of '95 libertarian Newt criticized a Republican bill to ban "obscenity" on the Internet. The bill is "clearly a violation of free speech, and it's a violation of the rights of adults to communicate with each other," he said. But after the Christian Coalition and the Family Research Council expressed disappointment over his remarks, Newt quietly dropped his criticism of the bill. By the end of the year, social conservative Newt had caved in to the right wing of the party and endorsed a modified version. Why should he care anyway? As Speaker, he has instantaneous access to cutting-edge technology and up-to-date information.

The already disadvantaged lose out when institutions limit access to data, sometimes applying biased standards in their screening. Open access to the Net is especially important to gay and lesbian youths, who use it to meet others like themselves and evade the opprobrium of adults and young gay-bashers alike. In many cases, reaching out for support on-line can be the difference between life and death for these vulnerable youths. I wonder if Newt ever felt as if he were the only one enduring a particular feeling, the only one facing scorn just for being himself. If so, he might be a little more empathetic toward gay youth and less likely to put his imprimatur on censorship.

Lest Newt accuse me of Luddite tendencies, I should point out that under the leadership of Elizabeth Birch, the Human Rights Campaign has dived headfirst into the information age. HRC now has a Web site and is working on joint projects with Planet Out and Digital Queers, Silicon Valley groups of gays and lesbians in the computer industry. E-mail now goes out to members of Congress from thousands of gay voters with the touch of a keypad. Elizabeth, who served as worldwide legal counsel for Apple Computers, knows that the computer industry, which represents the future of the American economy, is squarely in the corner of gays and lesbians. High-tech companies from IBM to Microsoft have adopted antidiscrimination protections and domestic partnership benefits for their employees because they understand the importance of attracting a diverse and highly qualified workforce.

Elizabeth likes to say that the Web has the potential to overcome the obstacles in gay organizing posed by the closet. Now anyone with access to a computer and one of those pesky modems can get up-to-date news about the state of gay politics and disseminate information without anyone in a position of power over their lives using it against them. If Newt really understood the "Third Wave Information Age," he'd have no choice but to trade in his contact lenses for lavender-tinted glasses.

3. We must rethink all the things that inhibit our ability to compete: regulation, litigation, taxation, education, welfare, the structure of our government bureaucracies. We want our labor to add the highest values so that we can be the most productive and effective competitor on earth.

An economist Newt is not. Then again, neither am I. But I do know that it is neither effective nor ethical to subjugate workers' rights to the false god of international competition. It doesn't take a rocket scientist to realize that by raising the living standards of workers, through strengthening unions and raising the minimum wage, Americans would have more money to buy American products, thereby boosting the economy. We need a return to classic Keynesian economics, which advises that surplus value produced by the economy should be reinvested in the country's disintegrating infrastructure and in human capital.

Regulation—particularly with regard to discriminatory personnel practices—does not "inhibit," but rather helps society as a whole to flourish. Just as guidelines on pollution keep companies from poisoning their surroundings, so protections against bias prevent the disintegration of communities into two- and three-tier caste systems. Workplaces should foster an appreciation of diversity, not just a fixation with the latest technology. As President Clinton has said, we can't afford to waste the contribution of a single person.

We can't have workers, uneducated about human difference, refusing to cooperate with one another. We need models of cooperative productivity. Whites need to be able to work with blacks, straights with gays, and vice versa. At UPS, we had to overcome our differences to get packages out on time. From kindergarten on, education needs to stress the "gorgeous mosaic" of American life, as former New York City mayor David Dinkins eloquently put it. Economic leadership is important, but we also need the moral leadership to help us into an age free of prejudice and discrimination. As good a leader as Newt is, this is one area where he gets poor marks.

4. We must replace the welfare state with an opportunity society. No civilization can survive for long with twelve-year-olds having babies, fifteen-year-olds killing one another, seventeen-year-olds dying of AIDS, and eighteen-year-olds getting diplomas they can't read. Americans have lost faith that government can improve the lot of the poor and want their children reeducated in core American values.

If Newt really supports an "opportunity society," he should put his money where his mouth is. By any standard, gay Americans don't have the same opportunities as nongay Americans. How else can one explain why there are so few openly gay corporate executives, professional athletes, construction workers, or, for that matter, members of Congress? Because of antiquated marriage laws, gays and lesbians lack equal access to credit, tax breaks, and hospital visitation rights. What could be more damaging to what he calls an "opportunity society" than judging people by whom they love rather than by how much they can—and do—contribute?

As for the string of exaggerated social pathologies Newt cites, sad as they are, teenagers have been killing one another and having babies since long before the relatively recent advent of welfare. While "the dole" may encourage indolence in a few cases, it provides a safety net in a hundred times that many. A wholesale attack on the "welfare state" is hardly the answer. Whether Newt likes it or not, many Americans simply could not get by without government aid or relief, including his own constituents, who receive more federal money per capita than those in any other congressional district in the entire country. And while Newt spends his time attacking welfare, he is silent on the handouts that fill the coffers of corporate America, upon which he and his party are mightily dependent.

Underlying Newt's critique of welfare is the assumption that it somehow contributes to irresponsibility. But it's not clear how government activism inhibits individual responsibility. After all, it's not just teenage moms on welfare who may be irresponsible; it's the men who impregnate them, many having long fled by the date of birth. A 1995 study by the highly regarded Alan Guttmacher Institute concluded that 50 percent of babies born to girls age seventeen and under have fathers twenty and older. But because of biases in the enforcement of statutory rape laws and loopholes in child support payment laws, most of these men get off scot-free. If Newt wants to promote responsibility, let's talk about the fact that one-third of women report being raped sometime in their lives; let's talk about incest; let's talk about violent gay-bashing.

No one would think of blaming these problems on welfare. After all, if Newt really thought the law could change behavior, he wouldn't support repeal of the assault weapons ban. Seventeen-year-olds aren't getting AIDS because of big government. They are contracting the deadly virus because congressional conservatives, under the sway of right-wing pressure groups, are squeamish about giving young people access the information they need to protect themselves and save their lives.

5. America is too big, too diverse, and too free to be run by bureaucrats sitting in office buildings in one city. We simply must shift power and responsibility back to state governments, local governments, nonprofit institutions, and—most important of all—individual citizens.

This is great dinner conversation, but who's picking up the tab? Devolution costs money. It's true that the more people have a direct say in their lives, the better they feel about their country and democracy. Too often Americans have felt alienated from their political system because so much power is concentrated in the hands of the federal government, too frequently seen as a far-off, aloof entity. But the solution is not as simple as Newt suggests. We can't simply "shift power" back to already overburdened local governments without expecting them either to raise taxes, neglect their most vulnerable citizens, or impose discriminatory policies.

Throughout this century, the federal government has assumed power in direct proportion to the inability of local governments to provide for their residents in a fair and equitable manner. Conservatives who give lip service to local control far too often fail to countenance the dislocation it could cause—or the higher tax burden that localities and states would be forced to impose to pick up the slack in services and oversight, for which most citizens clamor.

AIDS is one issue that strikes at the Achilles' heels of Newt's devolutionaries. As it stands, the federal government establishes the benefits that people with the disease receive for medical care and housing, as well as disability payments. Were these responsibilities turned over to states and municipalities, divisive funding battles would erupt, and many local budgets would be unable to fill the void. Even more people than those already suffering homelessness would be forced onto the streets. States, according to the political climate of the day, would set benefit levels according to the popularity of the constituency involved. In liberal Massachusetts, benefits might be adequate; in Georgia, conservative voters might seek to punish people with AIDS by lowering their benefits.

Ultimately, states would create a confusing and discriminatory patchwork of laws and social spending similar to the gay rights landscape. Since the federal government fails to include sexual orientation in civil rights laws, gay people are subject to firing in all but nine states and the District of Columbia, which prohibit antigay discrimination. If America is to live up to the promise of its founding, people shouldn't have to pick and choose where they live according to the protections, both political and economic, that the law affords them.

6. We must be honest about the cost of government programs and balance the federal budget. No civilization can survive if parents and grandparents cheat their children by leaving them crushed with debt. We have a moral obligation to balance the budget now.

Yes, we have a "moral obligation" to be fiscally responsible. But we also have a moral obligation to keep the water clean, preserve the earth, educate the population, train workers, and provide health care and a living wage to everyone. If the cuts we impose are too severe, debt is not all we will be leaving our children. We will also leave them a legacy of decaying cities, bigotry, and disease.

Frankly, Americans don't trust the Republicans with the budget. It's easy to see why. It was during the Reagan administration, when conservatives tried to have their cake—huge defense spending—and eat it, too—tax cuts—that the deficit really took off. Democrats have proven to be the responsible budget cutters. Under Clinton, the deficit has steadily declined without the radical and irresponsible cuts Newt has promoted.

Anyway, the Republicans are more interested in targeting the president's pet projects than in balancing the budget. How else can one explain that AmeriCorps, Clinton's community jobs program for young people, was the first project targeted for the ax in 1995? One would think that a program that got young people off the streets and encouraged them to seek higher education would be a favorite among conservatives. But as James Carville has said, "the right-wingers just can't think that Bill Clinton created a winner."

My girlfriend Kris once commented that leaders who fancy themselves historians are the most dangerous. They think that they have learned from the mistakes of the past and are incapable of making their own. If Newt is such a great student of Western civilization, how can he fail to see the parallels in antiquated policies now regarded as wrongheaded, if not morally corrupt, and current inequalities? One good example is the similarity between the ban on interracial marriage and that on same-sex marriage. If he is such a great historian, how can he fail to see the resemblance between Jim Crow segregation laws and antigay initiatives in several states? If he is such a historian, why can't he see that if a group of people are systematically demonized and scapegoated in the political arena, they are vulnerable to violence and discrimination? In *Portrait of the Artist as a Young Man*, Stephen Dedalus says that "history is a nightmare from which I am trying to awake." Newt seems determined to make sure we slumber on—our hearts and minds awash in monstrous images.

CHAPTER TWENTY-ONE

NO PLACE LIKE HOME

A woman is like a teabag—only in hot water do you
realize how strong she is.

—Nancy Reagan

If my brother had shown a little more courage when the whole thing
started, I might never have set foot in Cobb County, Georgia. But
then again, that may be expecting too much, even from family. He's
hardly responsible for how all events shake out in his district, which
encompasses a large chunk of the county, lying just west of Atlanta
across the Chattahoochee River. Thus, he can't be held accountable for
the firestorm over homosexuality that broke out there three years ago
and has smoldered ever since. But he did throw in a little fuel.

In August 1993—the tail end of the protracted national gays-in-the-
military debate—the Cobb County Commission adopted a resolution
describing homosexuality as "incompatible to the standards to which
this community subscribes." The resolution was sparked both by the
military debate and the performance of two gay-themed plays at Theater in the Square, an innocuous red-brick building overlooking a quiet
park. Proprietors of the theater had received a small grant from the
county. After approving the antigay measure, the commissioners canceled all county arts funds. Adding insult to injury, the commission
voted shortly thereafter to spend the $110,000 earmarked for the arts
on police dogs and video cameras for patrol cars.

The chairman of the Cobb County Commission, Billy Byrne, said
he was offended that city money was used to back the "shocking" plays
M. Butterfly and *Lips Together, Teeth Apart*, which don't actually have
any gay characters in them, only sympathy for them. Referring to the

military ban, Byrne said, "Unfortunately, we have elected a president who has raised the issue of alternative lifestyles to a national debate. It will have a trickle-down effect on every local and state government." Byrne and other commissioners were sending the message that Cobb County was not Atlanta, where officials had recently approved a domestic partnership policy for same-sex partners of city employees and extended an invitation to organizers of the 1998 Gay Games, a large Olympic-style competition for gay and lesbian athletes.

While the intense debate raged in metro Atlanta, reaching the pages of the *New York Times* and the *Washington Post*, I had no clue that it was even transpiring. I had distanced myself so much from my brother's politics that at age twenty-seven, still working the night shift for UPS in Harrisburg, I was unaware of the resolution or of Newt's tacit support for it. When Olympics Out of Cobb and the Cobb Citizens Coalition, two predominantly gay groups, banded together to protest the resolution by pressing organizers of the 1996 Olympic Games in Atlanta to move volleyball events out of Cobb County, I was still asleep at the wheel.

Maybe I could have helped the gay activists counteract the damage inflicted by my brother, who accused them of "emotional blackmail" for threatening Olympic protests. Cobb County is a "dramatically freer and more decent place than some of the countries that participate in the Olympics," he said. His statement, ignoring the fact that many gays and lesbians do not feel safe living in a county that has condemned their very existence, clearly left a lot of room for education.

But as would become apparent in the protracted battle over the resolution, the activists hardly needed my help. Mobilizing from scratch, they announced plans for a massive gay demonstration that would bring the Summer Olympics to a grinding halt, whereupon the Olympic Committee agreed not to hold any events in Cobb County. Olympic diving champion Greg Louganis pitched in by delivering an impassioned speech at an Olympic Committee awards banquet. "I'm concerned about some of the athletes who are scheduled to participate in the volleyball preliminaries at the 1996 Olympics in Atlanta," Louganis said. "In addition to the normal pressure of competition, gay athletes will have the added pressure of knowing they are not welcome in Cobb County."

Meanwhile, another daughter of a conservative politician took a stand. Shannon Byrne, the daughter of Billy Byrne, held a press confer-

ence to announce both that she was a lesbian and that she was profoundly saddened by her father's role in the whole saga. "I'm sorry for
what my dad has done," she said. "My dad and the commissioners have
absolutely no right to condemn us. The resolution serves no positive
purpose. It sends a message of intolerance. I am not a threat. I am a
peaceful, loving, productive member of society." For the first time,
Commissioner Byrne was placed on the defensive. "I'm not going to
damn her because of it, but the gay lifestyle as a lifestyle, I cannot, will
not, and do not condone," he said, adding, almost as an afterthought,
that he loved his daughter.

Two years later, I finally had a chance to add my voice to the chorus
of protest against the resolution during my National Coming Out Day
tour for the Human Rights Campaign. At a July '95 dinner in Atlanta,
I presented awards to Shannon Byrne and Olympics Out of Cobb for
their work combating the antigay resolution. They had told America
that there was a steep price to be paid for antigay bigotry. Describing
Shannon as one of my "heroes," I credited her with making my own
public coming-out easier.

Shannon and I, it turned out, were not the only relatives of antigay
politicians at the dinner that night. After I finished my talk, I was
approached by a handsome young man in a military crew cut. My jaw
almost fell to the floor when he introduced himself as Darell Gingrich,
a distant cousin. A newfound Gingrich relative—and a gay one at that.
As Darell explained it, his father, Thomas Gingrich of Fort Lauderdale,
Florida, is a cousin of one of my father's nine brothers. But since
Robert had been adopted, there is no blood relationship between us.
The bond is distant enough that when that side of the Gingrich family
held a big family reunion in Michigan last year, Mom and Dad did not
attend. I, of course, was thrilled to welcome Darell into my family.

Darell and I talked for as long as time would allow and since then we
have kept in touch by phone. At twenty-seven, after a long, painful
struggle, he had come to terms with his homosexuality, moving into an
Atlanta apartment with the "man of his dreams," thirty-two-year-old
Trace Ussery, a social worker who had studied to become a Baptist
minister. Darell is now studying electrical engineering at the Southern
College of Technology in Atlanta.

Darell's coming-out story is far more representative of what gay and
lesbian people generally go through than my own relatively painless
process. Under pressure from his parents to "change," Darell under-

went two years of "reparative therapy" in a futile attempt to become heterosexual. Administered by Sought Out, an offshoot of the fundamentalist-Christian organization Exodus, which is based in San Rafael, California, the therapy asks subjects to starve themselves of love and affection by devoting themselves to God. Somehow, as if by miracle, they are supposed to miraculously discover attraction to the opposite sex. Yeah, as Roseanne would say, and the air is chocolate.

"I spent two years asking the Good Lord to do away with my homosexuality," Darell explained. "I gave it my all, but it never left me. Not even for a second. The only conclusion I could come to was that God loves all gay men and women. The Bible is the word of God, yes, but men put things into it that God didn't intend. The biblical condemnation of homosexuality is one of those things."

Sought Out—the program in which Darell participated—is located in Virginia Beach, Virginia, where Darell served as an aviator's electrician's mate at Oceana Naval Air Station. Darell had long dreamed of being a pilot like his friend Tracy Thorne, who was a top gun in an aggressor squadron based there. But since Darell lacked the requisite degree, he settled on electronic work. (Thorne would go on to achieve fame for a high-profile legal challenge to the military ban on openly gay service members. He made his bold announcement on *Nightline* in the middle of the 1992 presidential campaign.) Living in the midst of two institutions dedicated to the elimination of homosexuality made for a tortuous period in Darell's life. The forbidding presence of Pat Robertson's antigay empire, based in Virginia Beach, loomed large in the background.

Darell is a veritable saint. Despite being forced through this gruesome process, he bore no grudges, even toward Katherine Allen, the force behind Sought Out. "She was a beautiful person who really meant well," he said. "She really believed that Exodus was her calling from God. I give her a lot of credit for her strength, which made my life easier at times. Ultimately, I think the program was wrong for me. But who am I to say that it's not right for everyone? The main thing is that it helped me understand who I am more fully. If I hadn't experienced what it's like to deny my sexual orientation, I might not have felt so good about my community and who I am today."

My own opinion of such organizations is far less charitable. To me, the groups, as well as the antigay therapists, take advantage of social prejudice to prey on gay people when they are at their most vulnerable.

It's simply another form of psychological abuse. Instead of showing respect for gays and lesbians by encouraging them to come to terms with who they are, the antigay groups work to eviscerate the essence of their beings. The "ex-gays" I've met are mere shadows of their former selves, spending more time repressing their sexual orientation than in loving another human being or contributing to their community. It's important to remember that virtually all the social science research into sexual orientation indicates that, whatever its source may be, it's as immutable as gender or race. While you can change your sexual behavior, you can't alter your sexual orientation.

Having made his Exodus exodus, Darell severed his ties to the equally repressive and antigay military. "When I signed up at nineteen, I really needed the structure and discipline the military brought to my life," he explained. "Eventually, I decided I wanted to go to school and live my own life. I had led a gay life in the military, but I knew that as I gained rank, it would have been harder. People would start saying, 'Why don't you bring your girlfriend or wife to functions?' and I would have been forced to lie. The military is still immature when it comes to gays. There are plenty of gays and lesbians already in the military and always have been. They keep the clause in place because they don't want to deal with that fact."

When I told David Smith of HRC about my meeting with Darell, he envisioned another Gingrich taking on Newt and the Pentagon. As he was still in the reserves, Darell was forced to decline David's invitation to assume a higher profile in activism. "Several years ago I was asked to sit down with Newt and talk to him about the gays-in-the-military issue," he said. "I didn't feel comfortable then being thought of as a 'militant' homosexual because I was going through so much personal stuff. I feel much more comfortable now."

Darell said that now that he's left the Reserves, he's happy to add his name to mine in registering a family complaint against Newt's antigay positions, especially regarding the military. "Someone has to break through those good-old-boy Southern values that teach people to look down at gay people even if they don't know them," he said. "If I sat down with Newt today, I'd say, 'Wake up, Newt, you're not giving us gay people a chance to show you what we have to offer the country. Please give us a chance.' "

By their opposition to President Clinton's attempt to lift the military ban on gay and lesbian service personnel, Newt and his far-right colleagues made sure Darell's plea would never come true. The proposal, which Clinton first made on the campaign trail and repeated to rally support among gay voters, was immediately opposed by right-wingers in Congress and by top Pentagon officials, including Colin Powell, the chairman of the Joint Chiefs of Staff. As the ban debate escalated, military leaders fretted over the supposed "invasion of privacy" that heterosexual members might face. They worried about recruits with antigay religious beliefs. They gnashed their teeth about "morale" problems that might beset the ranks if gays and lesbians in the service were allowed to disclose their sexual orientation in the same ways that heterosexuals take for granted.

I had been immersed in military life long enough to know just how ridiculous the ban supporters' line of reasoning really was. As Darell and activists have so often repeated, gays and lesbians have always served in the military, with varying degrees of openness. Getting rid of the ban would simply eliminate the tyrannical military witch-hunts, in which Pentagon officials waste millions in taxpayer dollars to investigate the private lives of enlistees. Each year, after turning up "evidence" of their homosexuality, the Department of Defense expels hundreds of hardworking, loyal enlistees. Since the ban was imposed in 1942, shortly before the Red Scare took hold of America, it has damaged the lives of tens of thousands.

It's always dangerous to take politics, especially gay politics, personally. It can lead to ulcers. But it was hard not to take offense at the incendiary defense of the ban. From the floor of the House to the stratosphere of talk radio, we were called everything from perverts to traitors. "Without the ban, America's young service men and women will be forced by law to share barracks and showers with homosexuals," announced the Family Research Council's Gary Bauer. Horrors! Showers with the homos! "Military families with children could face living next to openly homosexual couples in base 'family' housing and would have to compete with homosexuals for already overburdened medical services." The implication is that we are disease-ridden pedophiles who should be glad we're not automatically subject to more brutal forms of bigotry.

Newt did not go nearly so far in defaming gay and lesbian service members. But he didn't douse the flames either. Mostly, he stayed in the background while lobbyists and fellow members of Congress attacked. After the compromise among the president, Congress, and the Pentagon was hammered out, Newt had the temerity to announce that it went too easy on homosexuals and that he intended to codify a far more restrictive version. (To the dismay of the far right, he later abandoned that effort.)

Why, I thought as the debate raged, should I and other loyal Americans be denied the opportunity to serve just because it makes a few people uncomfortable? Isn't it obvious that recruits should be judged on merit, not on who they happen to love? It should go without saying that one can judge people only as individuals, not as members of whatever group(s) to which they might belong. I felt that, had I chosen to enlist, I would have been a damn good member of the service. I've always scored well on entrance examinations, and as a pretty decent athlete, I'd have more than measured up to the physical rigors of military training. Newt, who took a 4-F to avoid the draft, could not make the same claim.

With Dad's encouragement, I did put some thought into enlisting. At Indiana University of Pennsylvania, I briefly enrolled in ROTC. I quickly realized, however, that the values taught in the courses conflicted with my emerging pacifist philosophy. Living in the midst of military culture for the first eight years of my life was more than enough. Even though I was still in the closet at the time, I realized the military would only add to the difficulty of my coming-out process, on which I was beginning to embark. The psychological toll would have been far too damaging to withstand.

Dad and I had never spoken about it, but I'd long had a feeling that he had brushed up against the ban during his Army days. I resolved to ask him about it—not an easy conversation, given how reserved Dad can be. I knew that a number of prominent retired and active-duty military officials who opposed the ban refused to do so publicly because peer pressure was so great. For instance, the nation watched with fascination as Marine colonel Fred Peck testified before the Senate Armed Services Committee during hearings on the military ban that his own son Scott was gay. Even though he said he loved Scott, Colonel Peck said he would be loath to see him in the military for fear that he would be physically attacked. Of course, the obvious response is that rather than giving in to these threats, Colonel Peck and other high-ranking officers should have discouraged the *attackers*, not the victims.

To my surprise, Dad was eager to talk. During his long career, he knew there were many gay people in the ranks, but he had never allowed himself to become friendly with them. "The Women's Army Corps was full of [lesbians], and they did a great job, as far as I could tell," Dad said. "There is no doubt in my mind that I served with people who were gay, but at the time in the fifties, everyone was covert. Few could come out of the closet."

As an officer, it was Dad's duty to report homosexuals if he had personal knowledge of their sexual orientation. He said he had played a minor role in the court-martial of several homosexual soldiers who were reported to his office while he was stationed in Germany. "At the time we had no choice," he said. "There were a bunch of guys who turned an off-base bar into a gay bar. At the time, we had no scruples about discharging people who were gay. You followed procedures and they were gone. There was no distinction between gays and alcoholics. You just got rid of them without really thinking about the human beings involved." Dad, I realized, had inadvertently supplied the source of Newt's antiquated equation of homosexuality and alcoholism.

Dad told the story with obvious sadness. Yet he refused to take a stand on the military ban. "I just don't know enough about it," he said. "I've never been in a position of working directly with gay people. If I did and they did a hell of a good job, then it would be no problem. It's hard to tell if lifting the ban would be good or bad for the military."

I was disappointed that Dad, unlike former senator Barry Goldwater, refused to issue a ringing denunciation of the ban right there at the dining room table. It would have meant a lot to me. But then again, he didn't really have to. Though he may not have sorted out the issue in his mind, it was obvious where his sympathy lay, given the glint in his eye when he looked back at me smiling slyly.

CHAPTER TWENTY-TWO

THE POLITICAL ANIMAL

Sometimes, I feel discriminated against,
but it does not make me angry.
It merely astonishes me.
How can anyone deny
themselves the pleasure
of my company?

    —ZORA NEALE HURSTON,
     "How It Feels to Be Colored Me"

After trying to arrange a meeting with my brother for close to two years, I finally took the Newt by the horns. My sister Rob called to say that she and her husband, Dave, were bringing my nieces Emily and Susan into town to view the April 5 taping of a special segment of CNN's *Larry King Live* in which Newt would serve as guest host. The topic of the show was national zoological month, and the girls were looking forward to playing with the exotic animals that would be appearing with Newt. Their visit seemed an ideal opportunity to see him again. And, heck, I'm not *that* afraid of elephants.

In fact, I didn't even have to barge in. Aware that I'm an inveterate animal lover, and with the girls as eager as ever to see their aunt Dandy, Rob invited me to tag along. Of course, I really wanted to see the family, but I had ulterior motives. I saw this as my final chance to ask Newt to sit down with me for an on-the-record conversation about gay issues through which we might come to a better understanding of each other. I wanted to speak to him about everything from AIDS to the federal Employment Non-Discrimination Act. Most importantly, I hoped to figure out who or what were Newt's sources of information on homosexuality and to find a way of funneling him more honest and accurate data.

The political backdrop to the meeting was the furious debate over a House bill that required the Department of Defense to discharge all HIV-positive service members. The stakes were high. If it were to become law, the legislation would have meant that more than a thousand loyal military men and women, not all of them gay or lesbian, would have lost their livelihoods and health insurance. Newt had initially voiced his support, erroneously arguing that the presence of HIV-positive soldiers endangered the health of troops in the battlefield. In fact, HIV-positive service members are already barred from combat duty and deployed only in the United States.

Newt's harsh comments seemed to contradict his recent public relations campaign—which included the *Larry King Live* appearance—to portray himself as the "kinder, gentler" Speaker after his standing among voters had plummeted to a record low. According to an April poll, Newt's approval rating fell to 22 percent, earning him the appellation "the most unpopular politician in America" by the *Wall Street Journal*. Things were so bad that *USA Today* reported that aides to Republican presidential nominee Bob Dole were "worried that Gingrich will be the dominant face of the GOP when he chairs the Republican National Convention in August. They are floating the idea that he should share the gavel with deputies better able to project diversity, toleration, and moderation." Then again, Newt's red-meat AIDS rhetoric was consistent with his long-standing willingness to use gays and lesbians and people with AIDS as scapegoats in his efforts to shore up his base among religious conservatives.

Perhaps to counteract the harsh image his position betrayed, Newt accepted an invitation to address a group of corporate executives who are heavily involved in AIDS philanthropy. Sponsored by the Whitman-Walker Clinic, a Washington, D.C., AIDS service group, and the National Association of People with AIDS, the March 27 appearance was to be one of Newt's first major AIDS speeches. When I learned about the speech, I blanched. "Shouldn't Newt learn something about AIDS before he gives a speech about it?" I asked Kris. (The speech was anticlimactic. Newt droned on in a series of platitudes, failing to address the HIV military ban. To his credit, he did promise to pass Ryan White AIDS funding legislation which had repeatedly been jeopardized by his right-wing compatriots.)

HIV and the military was the most pressing of the many topics I hoped to discuss with Newt, but first I had to secure the meeting. Unsure how Newt would feel about seeing his lesbian activist sister, I called his assistant Ann to see if it would be doable. She reassured me that Newt would be happy to see me, and we made arrangements to meet in the Speaker's office in the late afternoon before the show, which began at 9 P.M. By this time, I felt as if I knew Newt's trusted aides Ann and Rachel better than I knew my own brother. (I understand that it's their job to run interference for Newt by being nice to everyone, but I sometimes wondered if, as working women, they were secretly sympathetic to liberal causes like my own.)

The last time I'd laid eyes on Newt was about two weeks earlier, when, standing on the balcony of the Speaker's office, he'd waved to me as I walked toward the Capitol with members of the group Parents, Families, and Friends of Lesbians and Gays. We'd missed a chance to see each other four months earlier at the family Christmas dinner at Rob and Dave's house in Camp Hill. Mom, who's convinced our differences are more semantic than real, had planned to lock us both in the den with a bottle of good wine so we could "talk it over." But Newt and Marianne had chosen instead to spend Christmas with Marianne's family. In some ways, I was relieved. The last thing I wanted was for political tension to ruin everyone's holiday.

For the entire week leading up to the meeting, I had an uncharacteristic case of nerves. My excitement at seeing Rob, Dave, and my nieces was tempered by the thought of confronting Newt. The night before in my apartment, Kris comforted me by assuring me that I was as much family as Rob, and that I had the right—indeed the responsibility—to raise my heartfelt concerns with my brother. I got through the day by repeatedly reminding myself that I'd made arrangements to fly to Charlotte the day after the meeting to be with Kris at an HRC event. No matter what happened with Newt, I'd soon be back at work pursuing my mission in life and feeling the pulse of change.

The Capitol police only worsened my anxiety. Arriving shortly after Rob, I was met at the entrance by a gruff security guard who made it clear that he wanted nothing to do with me. He made me stand awkwardly at the desk for what felt like an eternity before he bothered to come over and ask me my purpose. When I told him I was the Speaker's sister, he looked skeptical.

"Do you have an appointment?" he asked.

"No, but he's expecting me, sir," I responded, annoyed. "Do I need an appointment to see my brother?" I preferred to think of the meeting as a family visit rather than some kind of official meeting. I'd dressed in a conservative blouse, cable-knit sweater, and barn coat, but I could tell that all the guard noticed was the short cut of my hair, which had *dyke* written all over it.

Finally, the guard called up to the Speaker's office and Newt's secretary instructed him to allow me in. Grudgingly, he handed me a pass and waved me in the direction of Newt's office. Maybe my nervousness was making me hypersensitive, but Rob later heightened my suspicion when she let me know the guard had treated her and Dave and the girls with the utmost courtesy.

The Speaker's chamber is awe-inspiring. With its arched ceiling, ornate chandeliers, wood paneling, velvet drapes, and plush red carpeting, it looks like something out of a Merchant-Ivory film. The room, which is painted an elegant shade of green, is filled with the artifacts of my brother's hobbies. In one corner sits a giant dinosaur fossil and a large piece of petrified wood encased in glass. In another case stands a football, also in glass, signed by the great Penn State football coach Joe Paterno, one of Newt's heroes. I did a double take when I noticed a huge framed print of Martin Luther King, who would surely turn in his grave knowing that he was being honored on Newt's wall. Somewhat more appropriate are huge oil paintings of Teddy Roosevelt and Thomas Jefferson.

Upon arriving, I was greeted by Ann and Rachel, who told me that Newt was tied up in meetings and pointed me in the direction of Rob, Dave, and the girls. It was Rob's forty-sixth birthday, and I gave her a snazzy Human Rights Campaign mock turtleneck, which she loved. Sitting at the end of an elegant velvet sofa that filled one side of the waiting room, I chatted with Rob and Dave while the girls went off to make colored cards for Rob. As we talked, I could hear Newt's booming voice emanating from an adjacent conference room. I imagined, incorrectly as it turned out, that he was discussing the repeal of the HIV military ban. Every now and then, small groups of tourists were led through by a guide. I felt like the fossils and petrified wood on display, my vulnerabilities exposed to the world.

At around five o'clock we were informed that Newt was unavailable for at least two more hours, so we fetched Emily and Susan and strolled to Bullfeathers, a Capitol Hill restaurant that is one of Newt and Marianne's favorite haunts. It was located just a few blocks from his office and his home, a modest apartment in the Presbyterian Building on Maryland Avenue. Coincidentally, I had once addressed a meeting of the Interfaith Impact, an interdenominational group that has its offices on the first floor of the same building. On several occasions, staff members of the liberal organization, which supports gay rights, had their access blocked by anti-Newt protesters who surrounded the building. They found themselves explaining that they disagreed with Newt's policies as much as the protesters.

In a comfortable booth at the old-fashioned tavern, I ordered a stout and tried to get my mind off politics for a short while. Susan and Emily, a great diversion, carried on as usual. Nine-year-old Emily practiced standing on her toes, and for a moment I thought she had grown taller than I, which, admittedly, is not a very challenging proposition. I'd like to put off the inevitable day when I become the shortest in the family. Rob and Dave, who was suffering from bronchitis, were in good spirits, excited about seeing Newt and his nieces in the midst of animals. They suffered none of the ideological angst that I was experiencing.

After a light supper, we returned to Newt's office, where the Speaker was finishing off his final interview for the day. We were joined by Newt's half brother, Randy McPherson, his wife, and their two adorable kids. (Mom had declined to join the family gathering out of a long-standing antipathy for the McPherson side of the family, who she feels reclaimed Newt after he became famous.) As Dave and I made small talk, Newt came out of his inner office to greet us. Everyone stopped. It was impossible not to notice how his presence dominated the room. Next to my brother's physical stature and charisma, everyone else—especially I—seemed insignificant. In that sense, his phenomenal political rise from obscurity to Speaker seemed like no accident at all.

Newt grabbed me around the shoulder, squeezed my head to his torso, and issued his usual warm, folksy greeting, "How ya doin'?" Exhausted by another long day in the Republican trenches, he was polite but distant. I felt for him. Even after his Friday was supposedly done, Newt dutifully, and without complaint, signed copies of *To Renew America* for several colleagues and posed with stuffed animals that kids in a classroom somewhere in America had created and shipped to him.

Newt sweetly told me he had heard I was "doing a lot of traveling these days," and we chatted about the vagaries of life on the road. He said something about scheduling my visits to cities I enjoy for warm weather. I agreed, having been in Phoenix in July, that when it was 108 degrees, such planning was "a very good idea." He told me he'd been in Phoenix for his book tour last summer, and it had been scorching hot then, too.

In a nearby room, Newt's staff had set up a small surprise party for Rob. The room had been festooned with brightly colored balloons and the girls' "Happy Birthday, Mom" paintings. A luscious chocolate cake with candles was laid out on a table. After Rob was ushered into the room, we broke into a rousing rendition of "Happy Birthday," led by Newt's booming but slightly off-key baritone. We devoured the cake, while Randy made obsequious toasts to Newt and said annoying things like, "You've really scored some victories lately, Newt." I rolled my eyes but managed to hold my tongue, a necessary survival skill for the only Democrat in a room filled with doting Republicans.

The event provided me a rare glimpse into Newt's frantic life. As much as I wanted to buttonhole him for our long-awaited discussion, I realized that one is never alone with the Speaker of the House. Even in the midst of a family gathering, he was surrounded by eight or nine staffers, reporters, Secret Service agents, and various hangers-on. Literally every minute of his day is accounted for. I felt a sense of awe at the physical, mental, and emotional stamina that Newt must possess to accomplish what he does. Even with the strength I'd built up from lifting boxes at UPS, playing countless rugby matches, and endless flights across the country, I knew I wouldn't be up to the task. I value my long evenings lounging with Kris in front of an Orioles or Braves game on the television, sometimes with a six-pack of cold beer, or dining out with friends. Leisure time is too important to give up—even for politics.

I also felt a profound sense of guilt and more than a little hurt that I was just one in a long line of people who wanted a part of him. On one hand, feeling like an imposition, I wanted to flee. On the other, I was angry that he made members of his own family feel as if they were just another burden on his schedule. With a little more empathy, it would have been simple for him to put me at ease. Yet his daily grind probably impinges on his ability to stay attuned to such subtleties.

When we'd finished the cake, we headed off to the CNN studio for the taping of *Larry King Live*. Newt thrilled Emily and Susan by letting them ride with him in his van with the bulletproof, darkened windows, followed closely by the Secret Service car. Yet the girls seemed more impressed by the animals that awaited them at the studio than by the glamour of limos and dark-suited Secret Service men. (I didn't notice any Service *women*.)

The huge CNN studio was filled with exotic animals of every kind. The kids of politicians and producers milled around, playing with them. I wished I had brought my cat Mingus, who would have loved getting some of the attention from the children. There was the purring baby cougar that had made headlines a few months earlier when he nipped Newt on the chin during a stunt on the House floor. There were bullfrogs, a legless lizard, and a giant hissing cockroach from Africa that climbed up Newt's necktie as he sat at Larry King's desk. There was a cute little donkey (sneaked in by some knavish Democrat, no doubt), an adorable Australian wallaby, which is a small kangaroo, a little newt, and one big, powerful Newt. Feeling vulnerable to the sting of my big brother's ire, I wanted to curl up in a little ball with my quills sticking out like the porcupine that Newt was treating gingerly, afraid of being pricked.

I met Jack Hanna, the zookeeper from Columbus, Ohio, who through his frequent appearances on the Letterman show has become the Marlin Perkins of late-night television. He was charming and handsome in a rugged outdoorsy way, but I secretly wished that he would use his fame to push harder for animal rights and challenge Newt's abysmal record on the environment. It was appalling that Newt was presenting himself as a softhearted animal lover and environmentalist when GOP policies risked destroying animal habitats around the world, not to mention clean air and drinking water.

Whoever on Newt's staff thought up the idea of having Newt appear surrounded by animals should be given a promotion and a raise. Newt came across at his warmest, most genuine, and most articulate since he had been elevated to the Speakership in November 1994. Like Snow, Newt has always been great with animals. They have a humanizing effect on his relentless energy and ambition. (Newt is, after all, the consummate "political animal.") He played with and petted the cougar on the desk and said all the right things about how we have to treat animals and their habitats with love and respect. Gone was the fire-breathing ideologue, replaced by a free spirit whose only care in the world was the well-being of fuzzy little creatures. For a moment, I thought I glimpsed the soul of a conservationist under the skin of a right-wing Republican.

The only blemish on Newt's performance was his failure to resist the temptation to tout repeatedly the accomplishments of the 104th Congress. "Blah, blah, blah," I thought whenever he referred to the Republicans. Newt's guests included the resolutely apolitical president of the ASPCA and Betty White, a star of the pro-gay sitcom *Golden Girls*, who spoke via satellite from Los Angeles. I was a little annoyed that Betty, a liberal, was being so easy on Newt. I had met her one year earlier while doing an interview for Fox morning news in L.A. After I walked off the set, in the solicitous tone for which her character, Rose, was known, she shook my hand and looked me in the eye. "It's a shame you can't be more articulate, dear," she said with a wink and a widening grin.

I didn't question Newt's love for animals, and anyone who loves animals can't be all bad. I remembered Mom's stories about how ten-year-old Newt had initiated a campaign to build a public zoo in Harrisburg so other kids could share his fondness of creatures great and small. At the same time, however, I fantasized about getting Emily to ask Newt why he supported gutting the Endangered Species Act if he liked animals so much. There was something hypocritical about going on TV to proclaim your respect for the natural world while supporting legislation that would do the opposite. "What about the spotted owl," I wanted to shout. "One issue at a time," I had to remind myself, "one issue at a time."

A few days later, during an appearance on *The Tonight Show with Jay Leno*, Newt didn't fare as well. Once again posing with animals, an adorable piglet squealed when Newt held it awkwardly to his bosom. To the great amusement of the studio audience, Jay was able to quiet the animal by holding and stroking it gently. Later, referring to a tiny salamander that has bright-colored skin to warn other animals of the venom it secretes if bitten, Newt said, "It's better to be protected than to die." That, I thought, could apply equally well to humans facing discrimination and violence.

After *Larry King Live*, Newt prepared to head off to the airport, where he was scheduled to catch a plane to Atlanta. Congress was out of session the following week, and he planned to take a few days off. He hugged me and Rob, said good-bye to the girls and the McPhersons, and headed out the door surrounded by an entourage of aides and Secret Service agents. Newt knew full well that I wanted a chance to speak to him, but he was allowing the circumstances to make it impossible. Clearly, he just wanted his lesbian sister and the whole gay rights issue to go away.

My heart pumping like a jackhammer, I realized this was my last chance to nail him down for a conversation. I followed him out of the door and into the lobby, where he boarded the elevator. At six feet one and more than two hundred pounds, Newt towered over me by almost a foot. Again, I felt an urge to flee. It was hard to maintain my composure in the presence of the person third in line for the presidency, especially when he was letting me know that he didn't want anything to do with what I had come to represent to him over the last couple of years—trouble.

Without fully contemplating the enormity of what I was doing, I placed my foot in the elevator door, looked Newt in the eye, and declared, "Newt, we have to talk." Shifting uncomfortably, he looked away. "Is there anything I can do to make you feel better about talking to me?" I asked. "Is there any question I can answer so you can understand why I'm doing what I'm doing? I don't think we should communicate solely through the press."

"Well, Candace," he replied, still refusing to look me in the eye. "On a professional level, I don't think—"

Laying it on thick, I cut him off. "Newt, this is not about politics. This is about how family allows a diverse group of people to love each other, despite their differences. This is about our relationship."

At that, Newt softened a bit. He promised to talk to his staff about my request and that maybe we could at least arrange a "phone conversation." For a split second, at least, I think he recognized that he could not treat me as just another person who wanted to lobby him on some obscure issue he cared nothing about. We needed some time alone to work out our problems and talk about the book I was in the midst of writing. As much as he wanted to walk away from the quicksand of gay rights, "family values" somehow enticed him forward.

Exhilarated that I'd finally worked up the courage to challenge him, I felt a wave of relief sweep over me. I was grateful that Kris had given me the courage to confront him by reminding me that I was no longer just some docile, closeted kid afraid of speaking her mind. I had just as much right to advocate my position as Newt did his. "Have a safe flight," I said with a smile and a wave. As the doors slammed shut, for a moment I thought I saw my brother in the elevator, and not the Speaker of the House.

I returned to the greenroom to find that Emily and Susan had gone to the bathroom for the eight hundredth time that evening. When they returned, they said they wanted to see Mingus, so Dave drove us to my cozy one-bedroom apartment in Dupont Circle, which I'd meticulously cleaned in expectation of just such a spur-of-the-moment visit. Once inside my apartment, I repeated the conversation I'd had with Newt to a sympathetic Rob so I wouldn't feel that I was completely nuts. My nieces ran happily around the room playing with the cat, whom they hadn't seen in a year. After they left at around 11 P.M., I climbed under the covers of my bed. Exhausted, I fell asleep dreaming of furry creatures and reconciliation with my brother. Finally, I hoped, I was one step closer to creating the grounds for a genuine dialogue with the Speaker of the House. For me and Newt, the bed seemed to have been made. But as Robert Frost said, I still had miles to go before I could sleep.

After returning Monday morning from a satisfying weekend of activism in Charlotte, I faxed a list of sample questions to Newt so he would have a sense of what I wanted to talk to him about. Playing journalist, I tried to make the topics fair yet as challenging as possible. They ranged from the innocuous—"What values did you learn growing up from Mom and Dad?"—to the more demanding—"Are you aware of how antigay rhetoric and legislation affect me, not to mention millions of other gays and lesbians?"

Two weeks later, my heart sank when I received a message from Newt's deputy press secretary, Lauren Sims, informing me that Newt had finally decided to decline my request for an interview. She said that Newt, who was extremely busy preparing for a new round of budget negotiations and the fall election, had not bothered to provide a reason. In the past, she said, Newt had felt that anything he said on the topic would be distorted by the media. I guess my brother must consider me part of the liberal conspiracy out to ruin him politically, which he's always going on about.

Shortly after the call from Lauren, in what the *Washington Post* described as a "rare Hill victory for gay rights activists," the Senate voted unanimously to reject the military ban on HIV-positive service members. Rep. Bob Dornan, the measure's sponsor, denounced his GOP colleagues for "caving in" to gay rights activists, saying the vote doomed Dole's presidential bid. President Clinton, Dornan said, is a "pro-homosexual, draft-dodging, pathological liar." At HRC, however, it was a chance to savor one small triumph over the forces of hatred and bigotry that Dornan and—sad as it is to say—my big brother have come to personify to gay and lesbian Americans.

EPILOGUE

A fter my ill-fated elevator encounter with Newt, the next time I saw him was a happier occasion: Mom and Dad's fiftieth wedding anniversary celebration in October 1996. Everyone was in good spirits, with a hundred of my parents' closest friends and family attending. Because they had eloped, Robert and Kathleen had never had a proper ceremony, which made the whole event extra-special.

At the banquet table, I sat next to Snow and Dad. On the other side were the grandchildren and spouses, including Kris. Snow very graciously asked me how I would like Kris introduced in her remarks. For a politically conscious lesbian like me, this is not a simple question. Within the gay community, the debate over "partner," "lover," or "girlfriend" has been raging for years. After some thought, I chose partner.

All four of us kids got a chance to pay tribute to Mom and Dad from the lectern. Newt made a point of mentioning the virtue of diversity. The Gingrich family, he said, accommodates everything from conservative politics to my work for the Human Rights Campaign, a gay rights group that he mistakenly labeled "the Coalition." At another point in the evening, he leaned over to Kris and said, "I'm glad you're here. It seems really special." Kris took this to be a positive commentary on our relationship. I'm not so sure. Always the cynic, I think Newt was probably referring to the occasion, not the relationship.

After Newt finished his mercifully brief remarks, I told the story of interviewing Dad for this book: Sitting at his dining-room table as he meticulously filled his spittoon with tobacco juice, I asked him what he thought of Mom's infamous comment in a gay magazine that she wished I was "natural." Smirking, he said, "I might as well wish for a million dollars." As a parent, he explained, the only thing you can hope for is that your child is happy. As far as he could tell, all his children— gay and straight—were happy. That's what made him happy. Everyone chuckled at the anecdote because Dad's sense of humor and pragmatism rang true.

As fate would have it, though, the family happiness would be short-lived. About two years ago, Dad experienced an episode of labored breathing, which doctors quickly identified as emphysema. Prescribed treatment was bed rest and oxygen. It wasn't that surprising, really, since Dad had smoked for years. Still, he cut back to two cigarettes per day and felt pretty well until last summer and fall, when he began to lose weight again at an alarming rate. The day after the party, which was physically exhausting for him, he felt too weak to get out of bed. A CAT scan later in the week revealed an inoperable tumor on his lung. The doctors thought that radiation could extend his life, with predictions ranging from six months to two years.

Dad began treatment as an outpatient. But it soon became clear that he was not strong enough to fight off the side effects of radiation, which include nausea, vomiting, weight loss, and weakness. He faced a future of lying on his back with an oxygen tank at his side. That was no way for a vigorous man, who prided himself on his physical strength and self-reliance, to spend his last days on this earth. After fifty years as a provider, one of the hardest things for him was depending on other people for his sustenance. He just hated that.

I began commuting weekly from Washington, D.C., to be at his bedside at the Polyclinic Hospital in Harrisburg. I also spent time with Mom, who of course was still smoking, though at least not in his hospital room. Suffering has a way of causing denial. Mom seemed to be under the illusion that it was just a matter of time before Dad was home again and life was back to normal. She kept asking, "Why is he doing this to us?" as if we were the ones who were suffering. His condition told the rest of us otherwise. He wasn't eating, but taking his liquids intravenously. In fact, the doctor, noticing further weight loss, warned us to prepare for "closure," a euphemism for death. Just before the November 5 election, I spent several hours talking quietly with him. I felt close to him, and I think he had a pleasant time, but it wasn't one of those cathartic moments you see in movies like *Terms of Endearment*. I didn't apologize for throwing rocks at cars as a teenage tomboy. We both understood what was taking place. Nothing needed to be said.

In the week before the election, I went home again for a couple of days. Mom visited Dad during the day, so Snow, Rob, and I decided we would start all-night vigils. We wanted to be sure Dad would never have to be alone, not even for a minute. By this time, he was only occasionally lucid. He was on a morphine drip, which could be triggered with a button. Every fifteen minutes or so we would push it, just to make sure he didn't suffer any more than was absolutely unavoidable. He slept most of the time, waking up to look around, squeeze my hand or engage in small talk. The other family members got a brief lift—bittersweet for me—when the Republicans retained control of the House with surprising ease.

Dad's days generally passed peacefully, without much pain or disruption. I was astounded how even in such dire straits, the life of the family assumed a sort of balance. But that changed one day early in the course of his hospitalization. I couldn't help blaming myself for what happened, even though it wasn't my fault at all. Mom and I paid Dad an afternoon visit. He had been sharing a small room with an elderly African-American minister, whose ailment was less serious than Dad's. Rob said the minister had spent a lot of time praying with his family. Dad, who had never been one for public displays of faith, joked about how the man's son had sought him as a partner in prayer.

During my visit, the preacher's son, whose name I never learned, struck up a conversation with me. Pointing to the radiation marks on Dad's chest, he asked, pleasantly enough, if Dad was preparing for surgery. I explained his condition, and we chatted amiably for a few minutes. Then he abruptly changed the subject.

"Are you the Speaker's sister?" he asked.

As soon as I could answer in the affirmative, he shot back, "Are you going to renounce your lesbianism?" Maybe he said "homosexuality."

"This is not the time or place for that conversation," I responded, my heart sinking.

With evangelistic fervor, he refused to leave me alone, even though we were standing directly in front of my father's bed, contemplating his death. Mom witnessed the whole thing.

"Please, sir, leave me alone," I said, at which point he picked up a Bible and started praying loudly, waking Dad from a deep slumber.

Shaking with anger, I excused myself and left the room. I hadn't felt so powerless in years. Even the vituperative anti-gay preacher Lou Sheldon would have been more polite. (Well, I take that back: maybe not.) It wasn't right to argue with him, but it pained me that he got away with such an astonishing display of rudeness. Politics aside, I was dumbfounded that someone would actually proselytize around a deathbed.

Back in the room, the preacher's son gone, I apologized to Dad. He was gentle, saying that the minister's prayers always ended up sounding like mini-sermons. Mom agreed that it was an appalling display. I felt good that Mom and Dad stuck up for me, but I couldn't quite shake my anger. When the minister (and his son) were released shortly thereafter, Dad, thank God, had his own room for the duration.

Dad's health took a turn for the worse November 16. As I drove between Hartford, Connecticut, and Northampton, Massachusetts, where I was to deliver a speech, I received an electronic page. Since the number contained the hospital's area code, I had a gut feeling that the news was not good. When I reached the hospital by phone, my brother-in-law, David Brown, informed me that Dad was faring poorly, gasping for breath the minute he was taken off oxygen. Dad told the doctors that he didn't want any heroics. He wanted morphine and to be left alone to die. That was it. The entire staff, which was very gracious, respected the family's wishes.

On Sunday evening, on my way back to the District to pick up clothing, I stopped at the hospital with Kris for a visit. Dad was hallucinating, insisting that his slippers, which he wasn't even wearing, were going to fall off the end of the bed. I retrieved them for him, and he relaxed a bit. When it was time to depart, Kris said, "See you later, Colonel." Then Dad grabbed my hand and smiled good-bye. I didn't realize it at the time, but that would be my last exchange with him. When I came back the next day and rejoined our nightly vigils, he was unconscious pretty much the whole time.

On Tuesday night, I drove to Bethlehem for a speaking engagement at Lehigh University. When I arrived on campus, the buildings were dark. The nice lesbian campus cop explained that my engagement was actually the next night. Apparently, the stress was making me hallucinate as well. I stayed at my old friend Bob's place that night, the night my father died. Dad's final, ironic act was to wait until November 20, Mom's birthday, to die. The next day, Newt was renominated as Speaker.

On Saturday morning we had a family service at Tref's Funeral Home in Hummelstown. Thanks to Newt's influence, an honor guard from Virginia conducted a Saturday military service later in the day, which was held at Fort Indiantown Gap, where Dad had asked to be buried. It was a glorious service, with great pageantry and a twenty-one-gun salute. When we pulled into the cemetery, the entire drive was lined with crisp American flags. The precision of the ceremony, from the hearse to the viewing stand to flag folding, was breathtaking. The sergeant read a long list of Dad's military honors and presented the flag to Mom. Pastor Nancy from Mom's Zion Lutheran Church said a few words.

The whole thing made me feel proud of Dad and my family. Representatives Gekas and Goodling showed up to pay their respects. We all received certificates from the president acknowledging Dad's military service. Snow read a passage from Gore Vidal's *Lincoln* about steel wrapped in velvet, which accurately captured Dad. Newt got up to say what an enormous influence Dad had been on his life. When he declared that the kind of central Pennsylvania conservatism that Dad espoused was partly about "tolerating diversity," I squeezed Kris's hand. I hate the word "tolerance" because of its implication of condescension. My gut reaction was that Robert Gingrich was not the kind of conservative Newt is—he lacked the bile. He didn't see diversity as something you tolerate, he saw it as a fact of life. Newt said that Dad had lived his motto of "duty, family, and country" by adopting Newt as a little boy when Newt McPherson had abused and abandoned Mom.

The most memorable night was the Friday after the viewing, when a small group of family and friends retreated to the Warwick Hotel in Hummelstown, an old family haunt. We sat around a thick old wooden table—Mom, Newt, and Marianne; Newt's daughter Jackie Sue and her boyfriend, Jimmy; a friend of Newt's from Georgia named David; and Kris, Snow, Rob, her husband David Brown, and their girls. Kris and I were drinking beer; Newt, bourbon straight. Suffice it to say, none of us was feeling pain.

Someone brought up cigars, and Newt sweetly suggested he would make sure Kris and Dave Brown got some of his best. He had some good ones at home, he explained, and he'd be happy to share them, if they didn't mind Rush Limbaugh cigars. Kris responded that she didn't care whose cigars they were, if they were as good as Newt said. Newt remarked that because of the temporariness of life, it's important to keep your extended family happy. He repeated several times that he and Marianne and Kris and I would have to get together for a double date for Guinness at the Dubliner on Capitol Hill, where he would later celebrate his nail-biter reelection as Speaker. With Newt as instigator and cheerleader, Kris, Jimmy, and Newt's friend David had a hot-wing-eating contest. By that time, I was pretty far gone, but I'm proud to say Kris won. For a night at least, all our political differences dissolved into thin air. There's nothing like death to bring a family together.

Candace Gingrich
Washington, D.C.
February 1997

ACKNOWLEDGMENTS

Activism is not an individual pursuit. This book would not have been possible without all the hardworking and talented gay and lesbian advocates who paved the road for me to step forward.

My formidable editor Lisa Drew at Scribner and her stellar assistant, Marysue Rucci, brilliantly shepherded the project from the beginning, when they recognized the value of the book's message, to the very end, when their editorial direction improved the final product beyond measure. My agent George Greenfield believed in me and had the foresight to direct me to Lisa.

For the historical chapters, I relied heavily on several excellent documents. Judith Warner and Max Berley's *Newt Gingrich: Speaker to America* was invaluable to my understanding of Newt's formative years in politics. Connie Bruck's profile of Newt in "The Politics of Perception," published in the October 9, 1995, edition of *The New Yorker,* is a masterful example of political journalism. Dick Williams's *Newt! Leader of the Second American Revolution,* while uncritical, was also helpful. Newt's book *To Renew America* was grist for my mill. The definitive biography of Newt and the Gingrich family has yet to be written. In the meantime, I hope *The Accidental Activist* will shed some light on the subject.

David M. Smith, the Human Rights Campaign's communications director and my mentor and friend, has taught me an enormous amount about gay politics and the media, much of which found its way into the book. Elizabeth Birch, HRC's executive director, saw in me an accidental activist who wasn't just accidental. Elizabeth is one of those extraordinary women who's become a role model both in the corporate and political worlds. HRC's dedicated staff welcomed me into their family and showed me firsthand that activism is a labor of love.

My family members who allowed me to interview them—Roberta,

Snow, Mom, Dad, and my cousin Darell—generously shared their recollections and insights into the Gingrich family. Through them, I've learned that the love of family can transcend differences. My nieces, Emily and Susan, gave and continue to give me hope for the future. Through his political accomplishments, my brother Newt unwittingly unleashed my own.

My friend Bob offered years of friendship. She and Trish provided much-needed access to their Perry County hideaway. My Harrisburg friends who chose to remain nameless, at least for now, have never allowed me to forget where I came from. The women (and the occasional enlightened men) of Cheddar, Pez, and R-1136 provided me a legacy of fearlessness and support during my "formative" college years from which I continue to draw.

Kris Pratt's unconditional love and understanding during times of duress helped me realize of what I'm really capable. She has helped me overcome my lingering insecurities about my legitimacy as an activist and a book author. She's also a formidable lobbyist in her own right who has an insider's grasp on the nuances of life on the Hill. With any luck, some of her prowess will rub off on me.

Hans Johnson, whose editing ability and encyclopedic knowledge of politics in America are unparalleled, literally improved every page of this book. Finally, I met Chris Bull in February 1995, when he interviewed me for an article in *The Advocate*. In a kind and playful way, Chris and Hans helped me understand my unique ability to get an important message across through the media. From the formulation of the proposal to the manuscript, Chris's insight, curiosity, and writing skills focused my thoughts and made him invaluable to the completion of this project. From sarcasm to the Orioles to WHFS, we shared more than a commitment to this book. Our writing partnership was not just a marriage of convenience—it became a friendship.

INDEX